Sacrificial Logics

Thinking Gender

Edited by Linda Nicholson

Also published in the series

SACRIFICIAL LOGICS

Feminist
Theory
and the
Critique
of Identity

Allison Weir

1996

Routledge • New York and London

Published in 1996 by
Routledge
29 West 35th Street
New York, NY 10001

Published in Great Britain by
Routledge
11 New Fetter Lane
London EC4P 4EE

Library of Congress Cataloging-in-Publication Data

Weir, Allison.
    Sacrificial logics: feminist theory and the critique of identity / Allison Weir.
        p. cm.—(Thinking gender)
    Includes bibliographical references and index.
    ISBN 0-415-90862-0 (cloth).—ISBN 0-415-90863-9 (pbk.)
    1. Feminist theory.   2. Women—Identity.   3. Women—Psychology
4. Gender Identity.   5. Group identity.—I. Title.—II. Series.
HQ1190.W46 1995
305.42'01—dc20   95-8033
                                                                      CIP

For my mother and father,

and in memory of my grandmothers,
Elizabeth Speirs Weir and Vina Gray Allison

Contents

Preface

This book emerges out of a problem. As a graduate student immersed in critiques of the identity of the individual in contemporary feminist, poststructuralist, Hegelian-Marxist, psychoanalytic, and early Frankfurt School critical theories and as a teacher in women's studies courses, I was trying to reconcile the project of subversion of identity with a strong sense of the importance of individual agency and collective solidarities. This was a very practical problem. At a pro-choice rally, a friend and I found ourselves asking what it meant to be fighting for a women's right to choose when the concepts of women, rights, and choice were, for us, highly problematic. Maybe we were just thinking too much. But it seemed to me that the problem lay not in a disjunction between theory and practice but in a certain clumsiness in some of our theories.

My attempt to work through the problem led to a critical analysis of the ways in which identity is theorized in contemporary feminism. In particular, I am criticizing a tendency to understand identity as a force of domination: a tendency to understand the identity of the self as a repression of connection, or of internal difference; social identity as a repression of women's difference; women's identity as a repression of differences among women; linguistic identity as a repression of nonidentity. My aim has been to find a way out of the paradox of identity: to find a way to affirm individual agency and collective solidarity without thereby affirming domination and exclusion.

If a tone of frustration enters into my authorial voice, it's because the political stakes are so high—and because I identify so strongly with the authors/texts I'm discussing, and to whom this book is addressed.

I owe a great intellectual debt to my colleagues and teachers in the Graduate Programme in Social and Political Thought at York University in Toronto, who created a unique community of radical thought and practice that sustained me through the late 1980s. In particular, I want to thank all of the members of the Bad Sisters reading group in all of its incarnations over the years, and especially Patricia Elliot, Lorraine Markotic, Kathleen Robertson, Kim Sawchuk, Carol Moore, and Helen Fielding, for the pleasures of intellectual rigour and subversive solidarity. Christian Lenhardt, my dissertation supervisor, provided invaluable encouragement and support for this project, and for me. I am very grateful to him and to the other members of my advisory committee, Mariana Valverde and Karen Anderson, and to Greg Nielsen and Barbara Godard, for their advice and criticism on earlier versions of this book. Mary Grayhurst provided administrative expertise, as well as friendship.

Many of the ideas in this book were worked out during research periods at the University of Frankfurt, which provided another exciting community of intellectual and political discourse. I particularly thank the students in my seminars on feminist theory in the Philosophy Department and the Institute for English and American Studies, members of Jürgen Habermas's and Herta Nagl-Docekal's research colloquia in the Philosophy Department, and members of the Institute for English and American Studies, particularly Gisela Engel.

Earlier drafts of some chapters were presented at the colloquia in Philosophy and the Social Sciences at Dubrovnik and Prague, and at meetings of the Society for Phenomenology and Existential Philosophy (SPEP), the Canadian Women's Studies Association, and the Canadian Society for Women in Philosophy (CSWIP). I am grateful for comments and criticisms from participants in these meetings. Financial assistance in the form of Ontario Graduate Scholarships and Social Sciences and Humanities Research Council of Canada Doctoral and Postdoctoral Fellowships is gratefully acknowledged.

I want to thank a number of individuals who, as teachers and advisors, have provided inspiration and help over the years: John Bolton, Gad Horowitz, Pat Mills, Kathryn Morgan, Mary O'Brien, Ruth Pierson, Kaja Silverman, Johanna Stuckey, Nancy Mandell, Nancy Fraser, Jürgen Habermas, Axel Honneth. I owe a very special debt of gratitude to Linda Nicholson, a wonderful advisor, colleague, and friend.

My thanks to Maureen MacGrogan for her generous humour and intelligence, and to Alison Shonkwiler and Kim Herald for their patient and persistent editorial assistance.

Special thanks go to Barbara Crow for her constant enthusiasm and solidarity, and to Audrey Walzer and Lori Spring for sharing their insights and their lives with me. I thank my parents, Ellie Weir Sloan and Walter Weir, for their love and encouragement, and for the examples of integrity, resistance to convention, and commitment to ideals that are the roots of this project. Finally, I thank Nikolas Kompridis for his love and care, conversation and provocation—and much more.

Introduction

Some of the most important questions in contemporary feminist theory concern the meaning and significance of identity, and the relationships between identity and difference. The way we ask these questions, and the answers we come up with, are defining the terms and setting the directions of feminist theory and feminist politics.

At the center of contemporary debates is the issue of individual identity: do feminists want to advocate the identity and autonomy of the individual as a normative ideal, or is the identity of the individual a specifically masculine or phallogocentric white western capitalist ideal which represses the fragmentation and multiplicity of the self, or which represses the connectedness of human beings? Is it possible to affirm some sort of self-identity which does *not* repress the differences within the self, or the connectedness of the self to others, and to do so without making false claims to authority and authorship?

These questions of individual identity are related to questions of women's identity and of gender identity: what does it mean to "be" a woman, or a man? What does it mean to be identified as a woman, to identify oneself as a woman, to identify with women, and to identify a category of women? Is there any way of affirming any kind of women's identity without repressing the differences of race, class, culture, sexual orientation, and so on, which divide women, without reinscribing the oppressive institutions through which gender identity has been constituted, and without denying the wide historical and cultural variation of what the concept of woman means? Do we

1

really want, after all, to affirm any kind of women's identity? If not, what can serve as the basis of feminist solidarity?

The same sorts of questions have to be confronted in our attempts to affirm and to problematize other collective identities: lesbian and gay identities, black identity, native and ethnic identities. . . . To what extent does self-identity depend on a collective identity, and how does this work in modern societies where identities are multiple and often conflicting? Do collective struggles depend on the affirmation of collective identities? Without some sense of collective identity, what resources can we draw on for social and political solidarity?

Finally, is there a basis for some kind of universal social identity based on such ideals as universal humanity, equality and freedom, rights and obligations, and is it possible to affirm such ideals without repressing particular differences?

All of these questions of individual and collective identity open up questions of the identity of human meaning and language: what does it mean to have shared understandings, shared or identical meanings? *Can* we have shared understandings, or is meaning always fragmented by particular perspectives? To what extent are our meanings and our language the effects of systems and institutions of power? How open are our languages to the expression of difference? And to what extent are we able to participate in the development of new meanings, and in making meanings change?

In this book, my focus is on the question of the identity of the self, and on the ways in which self-identity and its relation to nonidentity, difference, and connection have been formulated in the work of contemporary feminist theorists. But the analysis of self-identity inevitably takes us through issues of collective identity (in particular, women's identity), social identity, and the identity of meaning in language.

All of the debates around these questions emerge out of what might be regarded as a tradition of affirmation, problematization, and critique of identity that runs from Hegel to queer theory. For feminist theory, the questions and problems around identity issues have been tremendously productive.

Too often, however, the very important critique of repressive identity has led to a reductive equation of identity with repression. Thus, the questions around identity are closed off with the invocation of a simple formula: any identity is necessarily repressive of difference, of nonidentity, or of connection. Identity is the product of a sacrificial logic, a logic of domination. Thus, it is too often assumed: 1) that any concept of self-identity necessarily represses the fragmentation or multiplicity of the self, or the connectedness or relationality of the self to others; 2) that any claim to a universal social identity or equality among men and women entails a repression of women's difference; 3) that any claim to women's difference, or an identity of women, entails a repression of differences among women. Too often, then, there has been a tendency to understand identity as always and only the product of a repression or domination. Thus, feminist theory has become caught in a series of impasses, produced by a failure to theorize nonoppositional, nondominating relationships between identity and difference.

The reliance on a repressive or sacrificial model of identity is certainly not specific to feminist theory. But the role of this model in feminist theory has its own specific history.

Feminism is a modern political movement, based on modern ideals of universal equality, collective identities, and the rights and freedoms of individuals. Feminism, then, is based on the assumption that women as a group must be *included* in a universal collective identity of humankind, which is understood as a collective of autonomous individuals, each with their unique identities yet united by a universal claim to equal rights. But equally central to feminism (and to modernity) has been a range of *critiques* of the liberal values of equality, autonomy, and universality. These critiques rest on a critique of the ideals of universal and individual identity in liberal theory, and of the ways in which these have been formulated in modern culture. These critiques have been made on two levels.

First, feminists have argued that the historical formulation of these ideals has too often been tied up with the repression of women's difference, or with the construction of Woman as the excluded Other. At this point, it can be argued that the ideals need to be separated from the particular ways in which they've been caught up with repressions of difference, with a logic of sacrifice and exclusion.

The second and more totalizing critique is the critique of the very logic of identity as a sacrificial logic, which is founded upon the exclusion of women, of "the feminine," of otherness, of difference.

The tendency within feminism to collapse these two arguments together can be traced back to Simone de Beauvoir's *The Second Sex*. De Beauvoir argued, quite radically, that men have typically defined the universal identity of "man," and of "mankind," in ways which by definition exclude women. The concept of "man," de Beauvoir argued, represents both the positive and the neutral, the absolute human type, whereas woman is defined as negative, relative, and lacking. Woman, she said, is always the Other.

But de Beauvoir herself, drawing on Alexandre Kojève's reading of Hegel and on Lévi-Strauss's structuralist theory of human culture, argues that individual and collective identities are always and necessarily defined through an opposition to, and an attempt to negate, or exclude, an other. Following Lévi-Strauss, de Beauvoir asserts that the passage from nature to culture entails the development of an understanding of reality in terms of fundamental oppositions. And following a particular Kojèvian reading of Hegel, she asserts that "we find in consciousness itself a fundamental hostility towards every other consciousness; the subject can be posed only in being opposed—he sets himself up as the essential as opposed to the other, the inessential, the object."[1] With Kojève, de Beauvoir locates "the other" not only in other subjects but in one's own body: thus, one's identity as a subject is established only through the constant (and constantly failing) attempt to negate the otherness of other subjects, and of one's own body. In this way, de Beauvoir accepts that identity is necessarily a product of a subject-object opposition, of a negation and exclusion of the object by the subject; and therefore, women will be able to affirm their collective and individual identities only through opposing themselves to an object/other.

Contemporary feminists have taken the critique of the logic of identity a step further, through what might be seen as an immanent critique of de Beauvoir. If men's definitions of universal and individual identity rest, as de Beauvoir argues, on an exclusion of women or of "the feminine," then it is incoherent to call for an inclusion of women within those definitions. Instead, what is required is a critique of the sacrificial logic of opposition and exclusion which is fundamental to these definitions of identity.

Nancy Chodorow argues that the ideal of the separate self-identity and autonomy of the individual is in fact based on a masculine denial of connection to the mother. Carol Gilligan argues that the assertion of this ideal as a universal value—as the basis of a human universal identity—amounts to a denial of women's difference. Luce Irigaray makes very similar arguments, but she situates them within the context of French poststructuralist theory, moving from the structuralist claim that culture is a function of binary oppositions (the claim accepted by de Beauvoir) to the poststructuralist claim that this binary structure is not "natural" but is a function of power, and that the apparent complementarity of the binary structure conceals an identitarian logic. Irigaray brings together the specifically feminist critique of masculine identity as a sacrifice of the relation to the mother, and to women, with the poststructuralist notion that identity is always a function of a sacrificial logic, a logic of exclusion of nonidentity, or of *différance*—a repression of otherness by the logic of the Same. For Irigaray, the logic of identity is a phallocentric logic, and what is sacrificed is feminine nonidentity.

Like Chodorow and Gilligan, Irigaray tends to posit women's difference—women's connectedness, or nonidentity—as a source of resistance to the sacrificial logic of identity. Increasingly, however, many feminists have argued that the appeal to "women's difference" is itself based on a claim to identity—to an identity of women—and thus simply repeats the sacrificial logic of identity on another level. The claim to a "women's identity" is essentialist: it posits a defining characteristic or essence of women, whether this is seen to emerge out of nature (for example, Irigaray tends to ground feminine nonidentity in the experience of female anatomy), or whether it is believed to result from a social experience which is transhistorical and universal (for example, Chodorow argues that the feminine sense of self as connected is a product of the virtually universal social institution of women's mothering). Moreover, the claim to a "women's identity" represses the reality and value of differences among women, by appealing to a normative ideal of femininity (for example, Gilligan's argument rests on the assumption, based on empirical findings, that women are more caring, empathic, and relational than men, but these findings probably reflect the conformity of her subjects, most of whom have been white, middle-class Americans, to a normative ideal for white middle- and upper-class women in modern western culture). This latter argument—that the assumption of women's identity has often been predicated on a *false* claim to universality which in fact *represses* differences among women—can be traced back to Sojourner Truth but has only become influential with the foregrounding of issues of race, class, and sexual orientation in contemporary feminism.

The contemporary critique of the claim to a women's identity has led to a deeper critique of gender identity: feminist theorists drawing on Lacan and Foucault have argued that gender identity, like self-identity, is constituted through social symbolic systems or institutions of power. Monique Wittig and contemporary queer theorists argue that gender identities are products of the institution of compulsory heterosexuality.

Judith Butler draws on all of these theorists to criticize not only claims to feminine essentialism or normative ideals of femininity, and not only the constitution of gender identity through institutions of power, but any notion of a "category of women," on the grounds that to invoke "women" as a category is to invoke an identity, and every identity is based on a logic of exclusion, or sacrifice. For Butler, all identity categories are expressions of the metaphysics of substance which is entrenched in language. More precisely, any identity is the product of a system or logic of power/language which generates identities as functions of binary oppositions and seeks to conceal its own workings by making those identities appear natural. Butler's central argument, then, is that any identity is always a product of a logic of exclusion or of sacrifice.

With this argument, Judith Butler carries to its logical conclusion a tradition of feminist thought which stretches back to de Beauvoir: the assumption that individual and collective identity are always and inevitably based on a logic of opposition to and exclusion of the Other.

I want to argue that this tradition represents a failure to take the critique of de Beauvoir far enough. For de Beauvoir's fundamental assumption—that identity is necessarily based on a subject-object opposition which entails the exclusion of the other by the self/same—is not questioned but simply accepted.

Once this fundamental assumption is recognized, the debates within feminism emerge in a different light. In particular, it becomes necessary to reframe the opposition, on the issue of individual identity, between relational (cultural, maternal) theorists like Chodorow and Gilligan, on the one hand, and postmodernist and poststructuralist theorists, on the other.

Relational feminists argue that the concept of the independent, autonomous self represses the empirical reality of our embeddedness in and dependence upon relationships, and that the normative ideal of the separate self betrays a masculine denial or repression of the original relationship with and dependence upon the mother.

Poststructuralist feminists argue that the concept of self-identity is a fiction which covers up the systems of language and power which constitute us. Those on the side of Derrida argue that the ideal of the identity of the self must be subverted in favor of an affirmation of nonidentity and multiplicity. Those on the side of Freud and Lacan argue that self-identity is a product of a fundamental repression, but that that repression, rather than being rejected or subverted, must be stoically accepted as the foundation of an identity which is fundamentally divided.

As different as these positions are, they are united by the common assumption, unchanged since de Beauvoir, that identity is *necessarily* a product of the repression of difference, the domination of the other, and the negation of nonidentity. Thus, self-identity is reduced to an instance of the repression or negation of "the other" (and "the other" can refer variously to other selves, to the unconscious, to the body, to nature, and to otherness as an abstract category).

In this book, I attempt to trace the ways in which the acceptance of this assumption has consistently worked to mire our theories in spurious paradoxes and to constrain the possibility of reformulating and reconstructing relatively nonrepressive, nonsacrificial identities. I want to argue that rather than simply rejecting identity in the name of difference, or accepting it as something oppressive but inevitable, we need to develop alternative theories of universality and of individual identity which do not exclude but include difference and otherness. This requires that we make distinctions among different forms of identity, and among different forms of repression and exclusion. For, while the development of a self in any society probably does require some sort of repression, and while any identity can be seen as an exclusion (and therefore, a surreptitious inclusion) of what it is not, the view that repression and exclusion are the essences of individuation and identity obscures some crucial questions: Is the exclusion of others from my sense of self an act of domination? Is every distinction a form of violence? Do we want to equate this violence with lynching, wife battering, and gay bashing, and with the subtle systems of oppression which make such acts possible? The equation of identity with a logic of sacrifice leads us to a simplistic, and destructive, equation of capacities for individual autonomy and for collective solidarity with repression, and hence with domination.

To get out of this equation, we need to distinguish between repressive, sacrificial forms of identity and other possible forms. This makes it possible to shift from a sacrificial model to a model of self-identity as a capacity for participation in a social world. So long as we accept the sacrificial logic as *the* logic of identity, we will be unable to move beyond a conception of society as an other which is always and only violent. I develop this argument in the chapters that follow.

In Chapter One, I analyze the Kojèvian reading of Hegel which is the foundation of Simone de Beauvoir's conception of the self. Following Kojève's preoccupation with Hegel's master-slave struggle as the basis of subjectivity, de Beauvoir assumes that the struggle for domination between self and other is essential to the establishment of self-identity. Feminist theorists since de Beauvoir have been very critical of this assumption. However, both poststructuralist feminist theories which draw on Derridean deconstructions of identity and relational feminist theories that attempt to reconstruct the self as a function of connection are ultimately based on the same assumption. I develop this argument through analyses of Jacques Derrida's and Jessica Benjamin's critiques of Hegel and Freud. According to Derrida, both Hegel and Freud betray their own very powerful critiques of repressive identity by ultimately reinstating it. Derrida's interpretations of Hegel and Freud are based on a reduction of self-identity to an instance of mastery or repression. But against this repressive identity, Derrida can only posit a negativity—a "negation of what is"—which sounds very much like de Beauvoir's and Kojève's. Similarly, Jessica Benjamin criticizes Hegel and Freud on the grounds that they are unable to transcend a conception of the subject as an isolated, autonomous individual who develops through aggressive selfishness—through negation of the other. But Benjamin herself is unable to move beyond this conception, for she too sees self-identity as a function of fundamental opposition to, and negation of, the other—as one pole of a fundamental duality between self-assertion and mutual recognition.

In Chapter Two, I analyze the relational feminist critique of autonomy, focussing on the work of Nancy Chodorow. Many feminist critics of de Beauvoir argue that in accepting the model of the independent ego established through opposition to and domination of an other, de Beauvoir is simply accepting and valorizing an ideal of masculine self-identity that can be upheld only through the subordination of woman as other. The critique of the subject-object model of self-identity as a model which upholds male dominance is central to much of contemporary feminist theory. And feminist psychoanalytic theorists have argued that there is an integral connection between the concept of self-identity as negation of the other and the model of self-development through opposition to, or negation of dependence on, the mother.

However, this often results in a repudiation of the separate self as a product of violence. As a case in point, Nancy Chodorow argues that the fact that boys develop self-identity through separation from their mothers is sufficient to account for male dominance. Self-identity, or autonomy, is all too easily equated with violence and domination and opposed to a feminine form of self-development through connection or identification.

I argue that Chodorow's argument, far from being a critique of de Beauvoir's oppositional conception of the self, is based on an acceptance of this conception as an accurate description of male self-development and as an adequate account of the development of a separate, autonomous self.

In Chapter Three, I take up Jessica Benjamin's attempt to get out of the model of self-identity as repression by developing an intersubjective model of the development of self-identity. Central to Benjamin's argument is the critique, drawn from Jürgen Habermas, of Theodor Adorno's continued dependence upon a Hegelian subject-object model of self-identity. For Adorno, the development of the self entails a tragic paradox: Adorno is convinced that individuation, or the development of a rational autonomous self, is necessary for the capacity for rational critique of society, but he assumes, following Freud, that individuation is a product of repression, of the internalization of paternal authority. With Habermas, Benjamin argues that Adorno's tragic paradox is the product of an insistence upon a transcendental opposition between subject and object, which blinds him to the possibility of an intersubjective theory of subjectivity. But Benjamin argues that Habermas, like Adorno, is too preoccupied with the establishment of a rational autonomous self, and she turns to Chodorow to develop a critique of the preoccupation with separation in Hegel, Freud, and Adorno, and to develop a theory of intersubjective recognition based on affective connection. I argue that because Benjamin accepts Chodorow's equation of separation, and hence of rational autonomy, with domination, she is unable to transcend the paradox of the self; she ends up oscillating between simply trying to evade it and arguing that we must accept it.

In Chapter Four, I discuss the critique of identity as phallogocentrism in the work of Luce Irigaray. Irigaray accepts Derrida's argument that identity is fundamentally repressive, and, like Derrida, argues for the subversion of identity on the grounds that the logic of identity is a phallogocentric logic, structured in terms of a binary opposition of presence and absence. However, Irigaray tends to locate the origin of the logic of identity in the experience of the masculine body and, like Chodorow, in the masculine repression of connection to the mother. Irigaray's valorization of nonidentity becomes an affirmation of and identification with feminine multiplicity—with woman as the unrecognized other, the embodiment of différance. Irigaray has been sharply criticized for her essentialist position—her claim for a feminine essence (however "nonidentical" that essence may be). I argue that the controversy over Irigaray's essentialism has distracted attention from the more fundamental problem: her acceptance that the identity of the self is necessarily repressive of otherness, and must be subverted through a relentless identification with nonidentity.

Judith Butler's position is more consistent than Irigaray's, in that she rejects both self-identity and women's identity on the grounds that any identity is repressive of nonidentity and difference. Butler extends the Nietzschean (Derridean, Irigarayan) critique of the "metaphysics of substance" into a nominalist critique of naming, arguing that names such as "women" repress the fluidity of difference. In Chapter Five, I argue that this critique amounts to a conception of language, and of the social, as forms of (inevitable) domination. Thus, Butler is able to criticize the use of the "category of women" as the basis of feminist identity politics without attending to the problem of feminist solidarity, and without addressing issues of identification, moral and ethical identity, and existential identity. I argue that Butler's critique of the repressive constitution of gender identities would be strengthened by a differentiation among different types and different logics of identity.

In Chapter Six, I take up Jacqueline Rose's defense of individual and collective identities, and the identity of meaning in language, on the grounds that these identities are indispensable to social and political struggles. Against Irigaray and Butler, Rose argues, following Jacques Lacan, that self-identity, achieved through an internalization of the symbolic order, is necessary for social participation. However, following Lacan's structuralist theory of language, Rose too accepts the model of self-identity as repression. Self-identity is achieved only through an acceptance of lack, only through the internalization of the repressive law of the father. But whereas Irigaray, following Derrida, wants to repudiate and evade identity, Rose, following Lacan, advocates a stoical acceptance of the fundamental lack (or repression) which underlies identity. This is because, I argue, she fails to differentiate between repressive and emancipatory forms of language, self-identity, and women's identity. Thus, she ends up with a rather tragic model of the subject, caught in an identity with the law which must be accepted and resisted but can never be escaped.

In Chapter Seven, I argue that Julia Kristeva goes beyond the tragic stoic model with a theory of the possibility of a reconciliation of identity and nonidentity in the subject. Kristeva's theory is typically read as either a critique of identity in the name of negativity or a reiteration of the Lacanian tragic model of identity. While I believe that both of these assessments have some validity, I argue that the strength of Kristeva's work lies in her ability to theorize dialectical forms of identity—in particular, of the identity of the self, and of what she refers to as the "sociosymbolic order"—which are not closed and repressive but are open to reflection, to question, and to change. Thus, in Kristeva's work, the identity of the self is understood not only as a product of repression or domination but as a capacity for participation in a social world, a capacity which ideally entails the recognition, acceptance, and expression of nonidentity.

This model of self-identity is predicated on a model of language as a dialectical interaction between socio-symbolic structure and the "heterogeneous" practice of subjects—a practice which is always social and which always includes psychosomatic dimensions. Against the model of language as a fixed phallogocentric structure impermeable to practice, Kristeva develops a model of language as a dialectical interaction between system and practice: language is seen as a product of social practices and therefore as open to change through social practices. Similarly, language, like all human products, is constrained by human (historical, social) psychosomatic needs. This conception of language opens the way to an understanding of self-identity as a capacity for social interaction, mediated through language—that is, as a capacity for full participation in a social world, which entails a capacity for the realization and expression of the self through social symbolic interactions.

Against Derrida, then, Kristeva argues that the identity of the self is best understood not as an instance of the law of identity but rather as a capacity for coherent expression of nonidentity. The internalization of linguistic and social systems does not necessarily lock the subject into a conformity or identity with a phallogocentric regime; rather, internalization is a prerequisite for full participation as an individuated self in a social world. Thus, while Kristeva does insist that self-development requires an internalization of socio-symbolic structures, she argues that this internalization can facilitate rather than repress change, for it can foster the expression rather than only the repression of the "nonidentity," the heterogeneity, of subjects.

At the same time, against relational theorists who equate the separation of the self with domination, Kristeva argues that the *separateness* of the self is not necessarily a product of repression of relationship to the mother, but can be a product of a recognition and acceptance of the otherness of the other—a recognition and acceptance which is essential to any true relationship. If the separation of the self is a form of violence, she argues, it is a form of violence which is not reducible to but, on the contrary, is fundamentally opposed to domination. Kristeva calls for an acceptance of the violence which underlies separation, but she also provides a theory of the development of self-identity as a pleasurable process.

In short, I argue that while relational and poststructuralist feminists too often share with de Beauvoir a tendency to equate the separateness or identity of the self with domination—whether as a constant struggle to negate and transcend immanence, as a repression of connection to the mother, or as a repression of nonidentity through conformity to a phallogocentric identitarian regime—Kristeva allows for the possibility of differentiating between dominating and nondominating identity. Ideally, Kristeva argues, any affirmation of identity requires an acceptance of internal difference, of nonidentity. Ideally, the identity of the self is based on the acceptance of the nonidentity of others, and of the nonidentity within oneself.

In a brief conclusion to this volume, I begin to move in a different direction, toward a theory of existential or ethical self-identity, understood as the capacity to experience oneself and one's relationships with others, with the world, and with oneself as meaningful. This requires, I argue, a theory of the identity of the self allowing for both identity of meaning in language and identification with others, such that the individual can be understood as a participant in a social world of contested meanings.

1

Self-Identity as Domination

*The Misrecognition of Hegel in de Beauvoir,
Derrida, and Jessica Benjamin*

> Thus humanity is male and man defines woman not in herself
> but as relative to him; she is not regarded as an autonomous
> being.... She is defined and differentiated with reference to man
> and not he with reference to her; she is the incidental, the
> inessential as opposed to the essential. He is the Subject, he is
> the Absolute—she is the Other.
>
> —Simone de Beauvoir
> *The Second Sex*

With her analysis, in *The Second Sex*, of the social, historical, cultural,
and psychological construction of Woman as Other, Simone de
Beauvoir provides one of the most important foundations of contemporary feminist theory.[1] De Beauvoir analyzes the relationship
between man and woman in terms of a subject-object or self-other
model, according to which man's subjectivity—his self-assertion as a
free, autonomous, and independent being—is established only through
opposition to, and thus dependent upon, woman's absolute and eternal Otherness.

De Beauvoir's brilliance lies in her insight into the structure of male-
female relations in terms of the subject-object model. Her analysis,
however, is limited by an assumption that this model describes a uni-

versal and transhistorical situation (in fact, the concept of the individual, and the concept of the self which is defined through opposition to an other, is specifically modern) and by her acceptance of this model as definitive of the development of human subjectivity. For de Beauvoir, self-identity can be developed only through opposition to an object/other. Thus, the imbalance in the male-female relationship can be remedied only by women's assumption of the position of subject, against an other/object.

For de Beauvoir, the essential opposition between self and other, and the struggle for domination between self and other, are fundamental facts of human existence.

> The category of the Other is as primordial as consciousness itself. In the most primitive societies, in the most ancient mythologies, one finds the expression of a duality—that of the Self and the Other. . . . Otherness is a fundamental category of human thought.[2]

De Beauvoir supports this statement with a quotation from Lévi-Strauss:

> Passage from the state of Nature to the state of Culture is marked by man's ability to view biological relations as a series of contrasts; duality, alternation, opposition, and symmetry, whether under definite or vague forms, constitute not so much phenomena to be explained as fundamental and immediately given data of social reality.[3]

In something of a departure for an existentialist phenomenologist, de Beauvoir accepts Lévi-Strauss's account of the fundamental structures of human society, but she turns to Hegel, read through Kojève, for an understanding of these structures in terms of a philosophy of consciousness.[4]

> Things become clear . . . if, following Hegel, we find in consciousness itself a fundamental hostility towards every other consciousness; the subject can be posed only in being opposed—he sets himself up as the essential, as opposed to the other, the inessential, the object.[5]

De Beauvoir provides no textual reference and no indication as to where Hegel develops this position, but she is clearly referring to the story of the master-slave struggle in the *Phenomenology of Spirit*. According to de Beauvoir's account of it, human society is constituted simultaneously with the process of individuation, which is achieved through opposition: one defines oneself as a self through opposing oneself to others. But the others whom one confronts are defining themselves in the same way, against oneself. Thus, human society is fundamentally antagonistic, composed of "fundamentally hostile," competitive individuals who define themselves against each other, who demand recognition from each other, and who are forced to recognize each other's sovereign selfhood.

But de Beauvoir argues that the forced reciprocity which constitutes human society is absent from the relationship between man and woman. Women have not taken part in this process. Women do not engage, with men, in the struggle for sovereign subjectivity. Throughout history, women have been assigned—and have, for the most part, accepted—the position of Other.

Thus, de Beauvoir accepts a definition of human subjectivity which excludes women—and thereby repeats the very problem she has identified and criticized: "Thus humanity is male and man defines woman ... as relative to him" [16]. At this point it seems not to occur to de Beauvoir that a definition of human subjectivity which does not include women might require some revision.

De Beauvoir attempts to explain woman's position as Other in a number of different ways. One source of the problem is man's lapse into "bad faith": man attempts to evade the arduous and unending struggle with other men by assigning to women the place of eternal Other.

> [B]y making Woman the eternal Other he dreams of quiet in disquiet and of an opaque plenitude that nevertheless would be endowed with consciousness. This dream incarnated is precisely woman; she is the wished-for intermediary between nature, the stranger to man, and the fellow being who is too closely identical. She opposes him with neither the hostile silence of nature nor the hard requirement of a reciprocal relation; through a unique privilege she is a conscious being and yet it seems possible to possess

her in the flesh. Thanks to her, there is a means for escaping that implacable dialectic of master and slave which has its source in the reciprocity that exists between free beings. [172]

This doesn't explain, of course, why women have accepted this position. This acceptance is partly attributable to woman's "bad faith": women have been all too willing to leave the constant struggle for sovereignty to men, and to fall prey to the temptation "to forgo liberty and become a thing" [21].

But there are also structural, material explanations. De Beauvoir recognizes that the assumption of individual identity depends upon the establishment of a community identity.

> If woman seems to be the inessential which never becomes the essential, it is because she herself fails to bring about this change. Proletarians say "We"; Negroes also. Regarding themselves as subjects, they transform the bourgeois, the whites, into "others." But women do not say "We." ... They do not authentically assume a subjective attitude. [19]

Thus, de Beauvoir recognizes that the capacity to say "I" depends upon the capacity to say "We." But, once again, opposition to the "others" is required. Women have been unable to say "We" because "women lack concrete means for organizing themselves into a unity which can stand face to face with the correlative unit" [19]. The fundamental problem is that women "live dispersed among the males" [19]. (The fact that men live dispersed among the females, and yet have managed to regard themselves as subjects, would seem to call this argument into question.) Ultimately, de Beauvoir locates the source of the problem in women's collective failure to transcend brute nature. "The division of the sexes is a biological fact, not an event in human history. Male and female stand opposed within a primordial *Mitsein,* and woman has not broken it" [19]. Thus, for de Beauvoir, the opposition between man and woman is not a historical development, not a product of human meaning systems, but a biological, primordial fact. Men have transcended mere nature insofar as they have asserted themselves as subjects, but they have done so only by preserving women's status/position as mere object; men have lacked the will to go further, to transcend this simple opposition through engaging with women in a genuine struggle, a life-and-death battle which could result in victory for both opponents: in true mutual recognition between women and men as subjects. For this, woman is ultimately to blame: woman has not broken the primordial *Mitsein,* for she has failed to assert herself as subject, to confront man on the battlefield of recognition.

If we are to understand de Beauvoir's conception of subject-development as a transition from a state of primordial opposition to a state of warfare, we need to go back to her reading of Hegel. We need to return to her assumption that "things become clear . . . if, following Hegel, we find in consciousness itself a fundamental hostility towards every other consciousness; the subject can be posed only in being opposed—he sets himself up as the essential, as opposed to the other, the inessential, the object" [17].

De Beauvoir bases her understanding of the master-slave struggle, and its significance for the development of human subjectivity, on Alexandre Kojève's interpretation of Hegel's *Phenomenology* as a history of negativity, embodied in human violence. For Kojève, Hegel's philosophy is summed up in the idea that negativity is the motor of history. With his concept of negativity, Hegel provides a way to understand human history as a history of conflict and struggle, in which human freedom is repeatedly enacted through the *negation of what is.* For action is free only insofar as it is a "negation of the given. . . . Freedom = Negativity = Action = History."[6]

For Kojève, the master-slave story is the key to the *Phenomenology.* As Vincent Descombes points out, it is this story which, through the conjunction of the concepts of labor and war, generates, for Kojève, "the paradoxical notion of a fruitful negation," the idea of the "productive power of negation" as the essence of freedom.[7] In Kojève's reading, the idea of productive negativity becomes definitive of consciousness. And this definition of consciousness is taken up by Sartre and de Beauvoir, for whom the self is constituted in and through conflict and contradiction.

This concept of the self as pure negativity is dependent upon Kojève's construction of what he calls a "dualist ontology."[8] According to Kojève, this dualist ontology allows us to distinguish between the being of nature, which is self-identical and determinate, and thus merely "positive," and the being of human history, which is defined by negativity. Kojève argues that a truly faithful reading of Hegel requires the rejection of Hegel's philosophy of nature. Hegel's concept of a dialectic of nature is, according to Kojève, an "error" which springs from Hegel's "('Schellingian') imagination" [217]. A reading faithful to the spirit of Hegel must draw from the places in the *Phenomenology* where Hegel "underlines the *essential* difference between Man and Animal, between History and Nature. . . . Nature is dominated by Identity alone, whereas History implies Negativity and is consequently dialectical" [216–17]. For "Hegel expressly says that Negativity is the specifically dialectical constituent element. Identity is not at all dialectical, and if Totality is dialectical, it is only because it implies Negativity" [216]. Kojève adds that "By accepting that only the human being is *dialectical* in the Hegelian sense of the term, one can say that Hegel's Dialectic is an *existential* dialectic in the modern sense of the word" [219]. Thus, Kojève's "dualist ontology" is the basis of the existentialist definition of human subjectivity in terms of "transcendence" (freedom, defined as action which negates what is), which must be posited in opposition to "immanence" (mere existence, the determinate being of the object).

But, for all the talk of dialectics, Kojève's dualist ontology results in a peculiarly static relation between subject and object. Following Kojève, de Beauvoir understands the relation between subject and object as a fixed opposition: the subject is defined by negativity, and the object by mere positivity. (In other words, the subject is defined by freedom of self-enactment and the object by determinate being.) And there is never any movement from this original position. According to de Beauvoir, the subject originally "sets himself up as the essential, as opposed to the other, the inessential, the object" [17]. Now, the subject is forced to recognize that others are in fact subjects who perceive him as object. But, as de Beauvoir describes it, this merely requires him to reassert his own subjectivity through transcendence of his own immanence. The free recognition of others as free beings is, de Beauvoir argues, man's highest achievement, "and through that achievement he is to be found in his true nature. But this true nature is that of a struggle unceasingly begun, unceasingly abolished; it requires man to outdo himself at every moment.

We might put it in other words and say that man attains an authentically moral attitude when he renounces *mere being* to assume his position as an existent...." [172]. In her discussion of the struggle between subjects, de Beauvoir has slipped very quickly back into the struggle between "man and himself"—between the subject and his own natural determinate being. And if we examine de Beauvoir's conception of the relationship between subject and object *within* the subject, we find that there is in fact no movement from the original position, wherein the subject is the "essential" and the object the "inessential." This relationship is not a dialectical relationship but is rather constituted by an act of simple, abstract negation. The subject is constituted by the attempt to negate his objectivity. But of course this attempt cannot in fact be successful, for the successful negation of one's own objectivity would be death. So the subject is doomed to a life of unending, unsuccessful struggle against the "mere being," the body, which resists all efforts at transcendence. And the struggle between subjects takes exactly the same form: the other is forever an obstacle to my own transcendence but, as the obstacle, becomes the instrument—for my transcendence can be established only through the other's resistance. What we have, then, is a plurality of selves struggling with themselves to achieve transcendence by recognizing others as free subjects, and this always requires the ongoing, and necessarily unsuccessful, struggle to negate our own and each other's objectivity.

This is de Beauvoir's model of subject development, and Sartre's, and Kojève's. But it is not Hegel's. First of all, the master-slave story must be understood in the context of Hegel's critique of the Enlightenment conception of the subject as an atomistic individual. Thus, the struggle for recognition represents only one stage in the historical development of human "self-consciousness": it is not meant to be taken as a description of the eternal, transhistorical condition of human existence. Rather, it is one stage which is doomed to failure, and hence to change. For Hegel, the ultimate aim of the dialectic of self-consciousness is the recognition of the object/other as, in Charles Taylor's words, an "expression" of universal *Geist,* or Spirit. "What is aimed at is integral expression, a consummation where the external reality which embodies us and on which we depend is fully expressive of us and contains nothing alien."[9] The master-slave story demonstrates the inadequacy of the Enlightenment conception of ourselves as individual, finite subjects, isolated consciousnesses, who exist in opposition to the world, to other subjects, to our own bodies. The struggle between the two subjects who become master and slave is one step toward the recognition that self and other, subject and object, are in fact not opposed but united, integrally related. This entails, on one hand, the recognition that the other is a subject, like myself. But it also entails the recognition that the body is not mere inessential nature, mere objectivity which exists in simple opposition to the freedom of subjectivity, and which the subject must therefore transcend in order to achieve free subjecthood. For Hegel, it is not the body but the opposition between the individual and his/her body—not the object but the opposition between subject and object— which must be transcended. The subject must come to recognize his/her body not as something incidental and arbitrary, external to oneself, and not as the mere nature which frustrates our aspirations to freedom, but as the essential appearance or expression of our consciousness, without which we would not be. Embodiment must be seen as self-expression, self-completion, rather than self-negation. And thus self-consciousness requires not the simple, abstract negation of the body which renders it permanently other, but the dialectical negation which negates its otherness.

For Hegel, the two selves engage in the "struggle to the death" in an attempt to prove that they are above mere attachment to life. For each self, at this stage of simple self-certainty, the "presentation of itself ... as the pure abstraction of self-consciousness consists in showing itself as the pure negation of its objective mode, or in showing that it is not attached to any specific *existence*, ... that it is not attached to life."[10] But this is just one stage—one necessary stage—of human experience. "In this experience, self-consciousness learns that life is as essential to it as pure self-consciousness."[11]

For now, the two opposed extremes—pure self-consciousness and pure attachment to life—are divided between the two consciousnesses of master and slave. But the slave comes to recognize his own subjectivity (self-consciousness) through recognizing the subjectivity of the master, and through his ability, in his work, to transform objects such that they reflect himself as universal, as a conscious, thinking being. "He recognizes in the power to transform things the power of thought, the power to remake things according to concepts, and thus universal models."[12] Eventually, the division between master and slave comes to be repeated within the slave's consciousness: in Hegel's discussion of "Stoicism, Scepticism and the Unhappy Consciousness," the slave has emerged from his embeddedness in his own particularity, and has come to recognize the universality of thought. "We are in the presence of self-consciousness in a new shape, a consciousness which, as the infinitude of consciousness or as its own pure movement, is aware of itself as essential being, a being which *thinks* or is a free self-consciousness.... In thinking, I *am free*."[13] But this new consciousness is still unable to recognize any concrete relationship between the freedom of thought and human reality. At first this consciousness corresponds to the stage of stoic philosophy, characterized by an indifference to and withdrawal from "mere life": "its aim is to be free, and to maintain that lifeless indifference which steadfastly withdraws from the bustle of existence ... into the simple essentiality of thought" [121]. But, as Hegel points out, "Freedom in thought has only *pure thought* as its truth, a truth lacking the fullness of life. Hence freedom in thought, too, is only the Notion of freedom, not the living reality of freedom itself" [122]. Out of stoicism develops scepticism: "*Scepticism* is the realization of that of which Stoicism was only the Notion, and is the actual experience of what the freedom of thought is" [123]. Thus, the indifference of the stoic is turned into the active negation of the sceptic: "a negative attitude towards otherness, to desire and work" [123]. Finally, the self must acknowledge that it is not pure thought but is "a single and separate, contingent and, in fact, animal life, and a *lost* self-consciousness" [125]. However, at the same time, "it also, on the contrary, converts itself again into a consciousness that is universal and self-identical; for it is the negativity of all singularity and all difference" [125]. Thus we have arrived at the stage of the Unhappy Consciousness: the "consciousness of self as a dual-natured, merely contradictory being" [126]. The Unhappy Consciousness has come to accept that the other—mere being, which is changeable and contingent—is within the self. But he is unable to reconcile this other with "the Unchangeable"—with his ideal of self-identity. Thus, he experiences the self as "unessential being" on the one hand and as "essential Being" on the other [127]. He sees these two sides as entirely alien and contradictory, and thus sees his own self as a being fundamentally divided between an ideal of self-identity, of the self as immutable consciousness, pure thought, and an embodied state which is subject to its environment, to the vagaries of internal and external reality, which contradicts that identity.

It seems to me that de Beauvoir is stuck at this stage of the Unhappy Consciousness. For de Beauvoir, the self is still and always engaged in a constant, unending struggle for transcendence over "mere inessential being" or immanence. For her, the essential, or universal, and the inessential, or particular, are fundamentally incompatible. We are trapped in an endless contradiction between the identity of the self, defined by negativity, and the identity of mere being, or positivity. The identity of the self is defined by one's ability to be entirely self-determined, to determine oneself according to one's own concept, and thus to negate absolutely any determination or influence from "outside"—to negate, that is, one's immediate identity with nature, with otherness. But we can never escape our "mere being"; thus, the struggle for transcendence is the eternal condition of humanity. For de Beauvoir, the self strives always for an impossible identity, which is defined through constant negativity, a constant struggle for mastery over an otherness which cannot be mastered.

As important as de Beauvoir's analysis of the subject-object/male self–female other relationship has been for contemporary feminism, so has the critique of de Beauvoir's assumption that women must become subjects by adopting the subject-object model—that is, that we must develop self-identity through negation of an object/other. Many feminist critics of de Beauvoir argue that in accepting the model of the independent ego established through opposition to and domination of an other, de Beauvoir is simply accepting and valorizing an ideal of masculine self-identity, which can be upheld only through the subordination of woman as other. De Beauvoir's opposition of transcendence and immanence, her repudiation of the body as "mere being," is based on the same logic of domination and subordination, the same logic of negation of the other, which underlies the subordination of women. Thus, feminists must reject this model as a universal ideal, because its dependence upon the domination of woman-as-other is not incidental but essential to it.[14]

The critique of the subject-object model of self-identity as a model which upholds male dominance is central to much of contemporary feminist theory. And feminist psychoanalytic theorists have argued that there is an integral connection between the concept of self-identity as negation of the other and the model of self-development through separation from, or negation of dependence on, the mother.[15]

These criticisms have been important. But I want to argue that the feminist critique of de Beauvoir has not been taken far enough. For de Beauvoir's fundamental assumption—that self-identity is necessarily based on a subject-object opposition, on a logic of negation of the other—tends not to be questioned but is too often simply accepted. Thus, rather than reformulating identity—rather than developing alternative theories of individual identity, and of autonomy—there is a tendency to simply reject identity and autonomy in the name of either intersubjective connection, or irreducible nonidentity.

In the next two sections, I shall show how this same assumption operates in two otherwise very different perspectives: in the deconstructive theory of Jacques Derrida, and in the intersubjective theory of Jessica Benjamin. I take these perspectives as representative of two dominant streams of feminist theory: Derrida's theory is the basis of feminist deconstructive critiques of identity, and Benjamin's is representative of what I am calling "relational feminism"—of theories which reject individual autonomy in the name of intersubjective connection. These two positions are commonly considered to be diametrically opposed: relational feminists uphold a humanist ideal of intersubjective connection and wholeness; deconstructivists reject such ideals as manifestations of an identitarian logic which represses fragmentation, multiplicity, and difference. Both, however, share in common the view that self-identity is based, necessarily, on a repression or negation of the other.

As I shall show, both Derrida and Benjamin share de Beauvoir's understanding of self-identity as negation of the other, and both base their positions in a Kojèvian reading of Hegel. Both end up affirming a "dualist ontology." Thus both, like de Beauvoir, regress behind Hegel in their analyses of self-identity.

The Deconstruction of Identity: Jacques Derrida

For Jacques Derrida, the concept of the identity of the self, like that of any other identity, is founded upon the denial or repression of difference. "The subject" is an instance of mastery, of narrative closure, of the freezing of a process of difference/différance. The attempt to affirm the presence of identity against absence, or nonidentity, is one instance of the oppositional and repressive logic of western metaphysics. This logic, which Derrida identifies as the logic of all western philosophy, is based on pairs of terms in hierarchical opposition— mind and body, identity and nonidentity, subject and object, presence and absence, male and female. Within the structure of opposition, one term is valorized through the repression or denial of its dependence on the other. This repressive logic is exemplified by the traditional understanding of philosophy as a search for absolute truth. In fact, this search is always undermined by its dependence on its medium: writing. Thus, the history of metaphysics is a history of "the repression of language as writing"—that is, "the belief that language can ultimately be transcended in a direct apprehension" of truth.[16]

Derrida argues that this oppositional structure, this logic of repression, is the basis of all domination. And the aim of deconstruction is to expose this structure of repression in philosophical texts—to uncover the "latent" text which the "manifest" text attempts to deny. As this description suggests, Derrida's argument is indebted to Freudian theory, and his critique of oppositional structures and their production of domination owes much to Hegel. Derrida acknowledges the debts, but argues, through deconstructive critiques of their texts, that both Freud and Hegel betray their own insights and end up following in the tradition of western philosophy by reaffirming the logic of repression.

Derrida is not interested in Kojève's "anthropological" reading of Hegel. He focusses on Hegel's logic, arguing that Hegel's insight into the logic of negativity provides a critique of the oppositional logic of western metaphysics. However, Hegel betrays his own insight, with his affirmation of the ultimate resolution of the movement of negativity into absolute identity. Thus, Hegel's theory is both the critique and the fulfilment of western metaphysics.

But Derrida's celebration of negativity as the negation of what is, now construed not as freedom but as transgression, owes more to Kojève than Derrida would want to acknowledge.[17] And as I shall argue, Derrida's construal of identity as domination—as the Law of the Father which must be constantly transgressed—renders his "critique" of the subject-object model of identity only an abstract negation, and thereby traps him in the very structure of opposition he denounces.

Derrida draws from Hegel the argument that nonidentity, or difference, must be understood as neither simply in opposition to, nor simply identical with, identity, but rather must be understood in terms of a logic of negativity.

> For if one appropriately conceives the *horizon* of dialectics—outside a conventional Hegelianism—one understands, perhaps, that dialectics is the indefinite movement of finitude, of the unity of life and death, of difference, of original repetition, that is, of the origin of tragedy as the absence of a simple origin.[18]

This idea is expressed somewhat more clearly by Hegel himself:

> The disparity which exists in consciousness between the "I" [the subject] and the substance which is its object is the distinction between them, the *negative* in general. This can be regarded as the *defect* of both, though it is their soul, or that which moves them. That is why some of the ancients conceived the *void* as the principle of motion, for they rightly saw the moving principle as the *negative*. . . .[19]

Thus Hegel criticizes the idea that subject and object are each simple, immediate identities which exist in opposition to each other, and argues that the movement of negativity in fact precedes and produces every identity.[20]

But Hegel finishes the sentence with the observation that what "the ancients" failed to grasp is that "the negative is the self"—i.e., the otherness of the object is negated through thought, and therefore the source of negativity is the Subject. For Derrida, this negation of otherness is a repression. With the idealist understanding of "the Subject" as the source of negativity, the movement of negativity is resolved back into identity. And, he argues, rather than rejecting oppositional logic altogether, Hegel accepts it as the logic which contains the movement of negativity, and which ultimately resolves this movement into the the stasis of identity. Thus, with Hegel, negativity is resolved again into the opposition which underlies and produces identity, which, for Derrida, *is* the appropriation and subsumption of otherness by the same. Otherness becomes merely the other-of-the-same—its reflection, its mirror-image, its "negative." Thus, the true otherness of the other is repressed and denied, as the movement of negativity which precedes identity—which produces it and calls it into question—is closed off. This is the story of all of western philosophy: rather than opening up to the difference of its object, philosophy masters the object, imposes itself upon it, and thus negates and erases all difference. Against Hegel, then, Derrida argues that negativity must be sustained without resolution. And this sustaining of the movement of negativity is the basis of Derrida's concept of différance.

> I have attempted to distinguish *différance* (whose *a* marks, among other things, its productive and conflictual characteristics) from Hegelian difference, and have done so precisely at the point at which Hegel, in the greater Logic, determines difference as contradiction only in order to resolve it, to interiorize it, to lift it up (according to the syllogistic process of speculative dialectics) into the self-presence of an onto-theological or onto-teleological synthesis.[21]

The movement of différance, then, is the logic of negativity, but without the resolution of difference into identity—without the ultimate subsumption of otherness into the same, and without the fall back into the oppositional structure which underlies identity and hence domination. This requires an endless deferral of meaning, an endless refusal to accept a single meaning or position, for to do so would be to repress the other of meaning. Différance, then, entails a constant oscillation between different possible meanings—or rather, between meaning and its other, non-meaning—always sustaining the difference between them, never accepting their resolution into a single identity.

For an understanding of identity as repression, Derrida turns from Hegel to Freud.

> [T]he Hegelian concept of contradiction ... is constructed in such a way as to permit its resolution within dialectical *discourse* ... [whereas] the "undecidable," which is not contradiction in the Hegelian form of contradiction, situates, in a rigorously Freudian sense, the *unconscious* of philosophical contradiction, the unconscious which ignores contradiction to the extent that contradiction belongs to the logic of speech, discourse, consciousness, presence, truth, etc.[22]

Here, Derrida draws on Freud's concept of repression to describe the process of mastery which underlies all western philosophy. Deconstruction is, then, "the analysis of a historical repression and suppression of writing since Plato. This repression constitutes the origin of philosophy."[23] Nevertheless, Derrida insists that, "Despite appearances, the deconstruction of logocentrism is not a psychoanalysis of philosophy."[24] And this is because the ultimate aim of psychoanalysis is to restore the identity of the subject: to make the unconscious conscious, to resolve the force of negativity into a simple presence, to resolve all difference into a coherent unity. Thus, Freud capitulates to the logic of logocentrism: the affirmation of the identity of the subject as a normative ideal is merely a reassertion of the will to mastery, the law of identity which represses difference.

Derrida's analysis of Freud, then, follows the same lines as his analysis of Hegel. He argues that Freud uncovers and explores the unconscious as that which calls into question the identity of the self, but, like Hegel, Freud uncovers difference only to reestablish identity: he uncovers the unconscious only to bring it under the mastery of the rational consciousness, to restore the identity of the subject. Thus, Freud exposes repression only in order to reaffirm its necessity.

Derrida is not, however, arguing for the "liberation" of the unconscious. The concept of the unconscious as an entity, like the concept of the subject, is based, he argues, on a metaphysics of presence.

The concept of a (conscious or unconscious) subject necessarily refers to the concept of substance—and thus of presence—out of which it is born.

Thus, the Freudian concept of trace must be radicalized and extracted from the metaphysics of presence which still retains it (particularly in the concepts of consciousness, the unconscious, perception, memory, reality)....[25]

[A]ll these concepts, without exception, belong to the history of metaphysics, that is, to the system of logocentric repression which was organized in order to exclude or to lower (to put outside or below), the body of the written trace as a didactic and technical metaphor, as servile matter or excrement.[26]

Thus, Derrida warns against valorizing the repressed term—the other over the same, or the particular and concrete over the universal and general—not because this would merely reverse the opposition, but because this would once again affirm the truth of an identity, and thus would be to fall back into the "metaphysics of presence." On the basis of this position, Derrida rejects any recourse to empirical explanation. Following Husserl, he rigorously maintains a transcendental standpoint with regard to "the object," whereby any assertion regarding an object of knowledge must be suspended and referred back to a questioning of the meaning of objectivity.

Derrida's rigorous refusal of presence, of identity, also precludes any recourse to relativism, and any valorization of the particular and concrete over the universal and abstract. Thus, those of Derrida's American followers who claim to draw on his theory to affirm the experience of particular minorities against the false universals of the dominant order, to affirm a multiplicity of possible meanings and identities against the attempt to subsume these under a false and repressive unity, base their arguments on a misreading of Derrida. Derrida's refusal of identity—any identity—precludes the affirmation of specific differences against dominant universals. And he recognizes that if we are going to repudiate identity as intrinsically repressive, it is incoherent to affirm particular specific differences against universal identity, for this is merely to affirm smaller identities against a larger one.

There are dangers, of course, in this position. For one thing, it becomes difficult to avoid valorizing an abstract notion of "nonidentity," an absolute otherness, in opposition to identity, and thereby instating another metaphysics.[27] Derrida argues that with his concept of différance he avoids this danger. In fact, however, precisely because he equates any and every identity with the repression of difference, he falls back into an oppositional model, whereby identity and différance, or identity and negativity, are necessarily and absolutely opposed, and constitute an eternal duality.

Indeed, Derrida's opposition between identity and negativity bears a striking resemblance to Kojève's "dualist ontology." In his affirmation of negativity, in constant vigilance against identity, Derrida echoes Kojève's assertion that "Identity is not at all dialectical," but is merely positive. Only Negativity is dialectical.[28] But Derrida moves from the claim that identity is merely positive to the claim that identity is the expression of a will to domination. And this leads to the other danger in Derrida's position: it is difficult for him to avoid the charge of nihilism. Once it is assumed that any identity is produced through a logic of domination, or repression, of nonidentity, then the logic of negativity, of différance, becomes imbued with an ethical and political legitimacy: the deconstruction of identity becomes the subversion of the Law of the Father, of the logic of phallogocentrism which has so far dominated western culture. But as nothing can be identified as the object of repression, and nothing can be affirmed as an alternative, Derrida cannot move beyond Kojève's affirmation of pure negativity against identity: he cannot move beyond the simple negation of what is.

Thus Derrida, like de Beauvoir, is still stuck in the situation of the Unhappy Consciousness. Imagining that identity and difference are absolutely irreconcilable, Derrida can only oscillate back and forth between the two. Still obsessed with the impossibility of an impossible identity, he cannot conceive of a relationship between identity and difference, identity and nonidentity, which is non-repressive, non-dominating. Imagining that the empirical, the material, must be rejected as merely positive, he can never get beyond the fundamental division, the irreconcilable dualism of transcendental abstractions. Against a dream of oneness and perfection, absolute identity, he can do nothing but repeat his negation of the presence, the identity, the determinate content of things. He can only affirm the absoluteness of différance, negativity.

Derrida's limitation is his assumption that identity equals the negation and repression of all difference. Viewed from the perspective of Hegelian theory, Derrida's understanding of identity is appropriate only to immediate, abstract identity. Hegel argues that fully developed and differentiated identity entails not the repression but the expression of difference. Like Derrida, Hegel criticizes any attempt by philosophy to impose identity, or unity, by repressing difference. And, from the perspective of Hegel's theory, it is Derrida's position which, in its refusal of the validity of empirical knowledge, represses difference. Unable to recognize the concrete particularity and specificity of things, unable to recognize any difference or otherness from abstract formulations of identity and negativity, Derrida is unable to conceive of the capacity for the expression of a universal in a particular without the inevitable collapse of difference into identity. Insisting that the affirmation of differences is merely another affirmation of identity, all he can do is impose abstractions upon differences, rendering everything identical. Unable to recognize differences, he can only affirm absolute différance.

At this point, it is useful to recall Hegel's critique of Schelling: in Schelling's theory, Hegel writes, we encounter

> the shapeless repetition of one and the same formula, only externally applied to diverse materials, thereby obtaining merely a boring show of diversity.... When the knowing subject goes around applying this single inert form to whatever it encounters, and dipping the material into this placid element from outside, this is no more the fulfilment of what is needed, i.e. a self-originating, self-differentiating wealth of shapes, than any arbitrary insights into the content. Rather it is a monochromatic formalism....
>
> Yet this formalism maintains that such monotony and abstract universality are the Absolute, and we are assured that dissatisfaction with it indicates the inability to master the absolute standpoint and to keep hold of it ... to pit this single insight, that in the Absolute everything is the same, against the full body of articulated cognition, which at least seeks and demands such fulfilment, to palm off its Absolute as the night in which, as the saying goes, all cows are black—this is cognition naively reduced to vacuity.[29]

Derrida's conviction that identity is always the product of repression leaves him with a theory of absolute différance in opposition to an absolute identity. Trapped in that opposition, thus, he is unable to conceive of forms of identity which could include and facilitate difference. He is unable, then, to understand the identity of the subject as anything other than a product of repression.

In the next section, I shall take up a very different approach to the question of subject identity: Jessica Benjamin theorizes the development of the self through the Hegelian model of intersubjective recognition. As I have suggested, Hegel's theory provides a way to begin to think about subject identity as a product of the realization and expression of difference, governed by an empirical process and normative ideal of intersubjective recognition. As I shall argue, Benjamin fails to realize the potential of this perspective, and to move beyond Hegel, because she shares Derrida's assumption that self-identity is necessarily a product of domination.

The Reconstruction of Identity in Paradox: Jessica Benjamin

In her ambitious and insightful book, *The Bonds of Love,* Jessica Benjamin draws on feminist criticism and reinterpretation of psychoanalytic theory to develop an analysis of the problem of domination. Benjamin takes as her starting point Simone de Beauvoir's analysis of gender relations in terms of the subject-object, or self-other, relation.

> The point of departure for this reexamination of the problem of domination is Simone de Beauvoir's insight: that woman functions as man's primary other, his opposite—playing nature to his reason, immanence to his transcendence, primordial oneness to his individuated separateness, and object to his subject.[30]

Thus, Benjamin sets out to find an explanation for the "psychological persistence" of the gender roles which define man as subject and woman as object/other. To do this, she must attempt to understand "the genesis of the psychic structure in which one person plays subject and the other must serve as his object" [7]. Her stated purpose is "to analyze the evolution of this structure and show how it forms the fundamental premise of domination" [8].

Benjamin's thesis is that "domination and submission result from a breakdown of the necessary tension between self-assertion and mutual recognition that allows self and other to meet as sovereign equals" [12]. For Benjamin, then, it is the inability to sustain the tension between self-assertion and mutual recognition that produces the subject-object model of identity, wherein the subject develops through opposition to and domination of an object.

Benjamin argues that Freudian theory takes no account of the subject's need for intersubjective recognition, but theorizes the self only as an atomistic individual, who develops through opposition to an object/other. For a theory of mutual recognition, Benjamin turns to Hegel. But she argues that Hegel himself was unable to sustain the tension between self-assertion and recognition in his theory: for Hegel, recognition was essentially only a means to self-assertion.

Thus, Benjamin argues that both Freud and Hegel are unable to sustain the tension between self-assertion and recognition in their theories, and thus they begin and end with the affirmation of the isolated, autonomous subject. Both, then, accept the subject-object model of self-identity as being necessary and inevitable.

> Hegel posits a self that has no intrinsic need for the other, but uses the other only as a vehicle for self-certainty. This monadic, self-interested ego is essentially the one posited in classical psychoanalytic theory. For Hegel, as for classical psychoanalysis, the self begins in a state of "omnipotence" (Everything is an extension of me and my power), which it wants to affirm in its encounter with the other, who, it now sees, is like itself. But it cannot do so, for to affirm the other would be to deny the absoluteness of the self. The need for recognition entails this fundamental paradox: at the very moment of realizing our own independence, we are dependent upon another to recognize it. [33]

Benjamin's central argument against Hegel is that, according to Hegel, tension must always be resolved. Therefore, the "fundamental paradox" of independence and dependence, of self-assertion and mutual recognition, cannot be sustained but must inevitably be resolved. Therefore, domination is inevitable.

Like de Beauvoir, Benjamin assumes that Hegel's master-slave story is definitive of his theory of subjectivity; she reads the story as Hegel's description of a universal human psychology.

> The conflict between assertion of self and need for the other was articulated long before modern psychology began to explore the development of self. Hegel analyzed the core of this problem in his discussion of the struggle between "the independence and dependence of self-consciousness" and its culmination in the master-slave relationship. He showed how the self's wish for absolute independence clashes with the self's need for recognition. In Hegel's discussion two hypothetical selves . . . meet. The movement between them is the movement of recognition; each exists only by existing for the other, that is, by being recognized. But for Hegel, it is simply a given that this mutuality, the tension between asserting the self and recognizing the other, *must* break down; it is fated to produce an insoluble conflict. The breakdown of this tension is what leads to domination. [31–32]

In a footnote, Benjamin adds:

> The reader may ask, Why does this tension have to break down? The answer is, for Hegel every tension between oppositional elements carries the seeds of its own destruction and transcendence (*Aufhebung*) into another form. That is how life is. Without this process of contradiction and dissolution, there would be no movement, change, or history. [32]

Clearly, then, Benjamin objects to even the momentary or temporary resolution of tension which, for Hegel, produces a new tension, and hence, history. For Benjamin, any resolution of tension is a form of domination.

Benjamin's critique of Hegel's dialectical logic is here very similar to Derrida's. Benjamin's claim that the resolution of tension produces the subject-object model of subjectivity, wherein the subject develops through domination of the other/object, is very close to Derrida's claim that the resolution of negativity or différance produces the oppositional model of identity, wherein the concept of the subject is based on the repression and appropriation of the difference of the other. Both are criticizing the subject-object model as a structure of domination. In both cases, the moment of identity—that is, of resolution of difference, conflict, negativity—is equated with mastery, with domination of otherness. In both cases, it is argued that this moment of identity must be renounced in favor of a constant tension, a constant movement of negativity, which forever defers resolution.

Both Derrida and Benjamin, then, reject de Beauvoir's affirmation of a subject who develops through the negation of the other/object. But, in arguing for the maintenance of constant negativity, both of them accept de Beauvoir's and Kojève's premise that pure negativity—the constant negation of what is, and the refusal of resolution—is the principle of freedom. Just as, for de Beauvoir, negativity produces freedom from mere being, for Derrida and Benjamin, negativity produces freedom from the domination of stasis, closure.[31]

Benjamin's position is, of course, also very different from Derrida's. For Benjamin, the concept of the identity of the self represents not a repression of nonidentity but a repression of connection, of the self's need for the other. And thus, for Benjamin, the tension which must be sustained is not the tension of unending différance, but the tension of a fundamental ontological duality between self-assertion and mutual recognition. This duality is unavoidable; all we can hope to do is to shift the distribution. Thus self-assertion and recognition must no longer be divided between two subjects, one who asserts and one who recognizes, but must be maintained within each subject. The relationship of domination and submission develops, Benjamin argues, only when "the basic tension of forces *within* the individual becomes a dynamic *between* individuals" [62]. Ultimately, then, Benjamin upholds a model of the subject who is unified-in-division—who embodies the fundamental paradox, and thereby forms a unified whole. "Wholeness can only exist by maintaining contradiction" within each subject [63]. Thus, Benjamin's ideal is not the deconstruction of the subject but the reconstruction of the self as a fundamental paradox.[32] And in this, her model looks once again, a lot like de Beauvoir's. For Benjamin, as for de Beauvoir, the "mutual recognition" between subjects can be achieved only through the affirmation of a paradoxical oscillation between two irreconcilable aspects of the self. For, like de Beauvoir, Benjamin understands "mutuality" between subjects to be fundamentally contradictory. It is fundamentally paradoxical that the assertion of the self requires being recognized by the other. And the assertion of oneself and the recognition of another as a subject are fundamentally contradictory acts.

The question is, why are self-assertion and mutual recognition necessarily contradictory and paradoxical? Why is the recognition and assertion of self and other as both human individuals, both members of a human community, fundamentally paradoxical? Why should the recognition of our likeness, our "universality," necessarily contradict our difference from each other? Why should the recognition of the other's subjectivity be threatening to mine? And why should the recognition of our interdependence present a paradox?

In fact, there is no fundamental contradiction between recognition and self-assertion. The contradiction arises only when self-assertion is equated with negation of the other. Thus, the contradiction or paradox which Benjamin believes is fundamental to mutual recognition in fact arises only because she accepts the equation of self-assertion with the negation of the other. Thus, she accepts de Beauvoir's model of the self as a product of opposition to and will to mastery of the other, which must constantly be checked by the need to recognize the other. But isn't this the same subject-object model that Benjamin criticizes in Freud and Hegel? How can Benjamin hold to the model of self-assertion as negation of the other, when that is precisely what she is criticizing? To answer these questions, we need to examine more closely Benjamin's critique of Hegel's subject-object model.

Benjamin argues that Hegel understands self-development not in terms of the intersubjective relationship between subjects, but only in terms of the intrapsychic struggle of the isolated individual. Hegel is primarily concerned not with mutual recognition, but with the individual's struggle for self-consciousness, of which mutual recognition is merely an incidental requirement. "Hegel posits a self that has no intrinsic need for the other, but uses the other only as a vehicle for self-certainty" [33].

Thus, Benjamin's reading of Hegel is the same as de Beauvoir's. Only the valuation has changed. Like de Beauvoir, Benjamin fails to recognize that for Hegel the master-slave story represents just one moment in the history of the development of the human subject. The story of the master and slave is incomprehensible outside the context of the *Phenomenology,* which is the story of the overcoming of false oppositions through the recognition of the fundamental unity of subject and object, of universal and particular. In this context the master-slave story serves as an explicit critique of the view of the human self as a particular, isolated individual who exists in opposition to, and through competition with, other particular, isolated individuals. For Hegel, this sense of ourselves as particular and opposed to otherness is a stage which must be transcended; human beings must come to recognize our universality as human beings, as members of the human community. This requires a recognition of our sameness with others—we are all human subjects—which necessarily entails a recognition of our differences—the other, like myself, is a unique individual. Thus, Hegel's story of the master and slave must be understood as only the first step towards the ultimate goal of mutual recognition. And it is only at this first stage that there is a contradiction between self-assertion and recognition.

> The contradiction arises when men at a raw and undeveloped stage of history try to wrest recognition from another without reciprocating. This is at a stage when men have not recognized themselves as universal, for to have done so is to see that recognition for me, for what I am, is recognition of man as such and therefore something that in principle should be extended to all. But here we have man as a particular individual (Einzelnes) who strives to impose himself, to achieve external confirmation. [Taylor, 153]

It is clear, then, that in Hegel's view the human subject is not doomed to a constant struggle between the eternally contradictory acts of self-assertion and recognition, and hence is not doomed to resolve this tension in an endless repetition of the relationship between domination and submission. In fact, the human subject does have, in Benjamin's words, "an intrinsic need for the other" [33]. And this need is not only a need to be recognized by the other, but is equally a "need to recognize the other" [23] as a subject like (and different from) oneself.

This is true, of course, only on the assumption that the term "need" in this context refers to social needs, and thus incorporates a normative dimension. But it is not entirely clear that Benjamin is using the term in this way. In fact, there is a fundamental confusion in Benjamin's work with respect to the use and meaning of the term "need" and its relationship to desire and to norm.

This confusion emerges when we try to analyze Benjamin's critique of Hegel's and Freud's subject-object models. There are, in fact, three different critiques: 1) a critique of the assumption of a "fundamental desire" for negation of the other—i.e., primary aggression. Benjamin argues that we need to begin from the assumption of a fundamental need for the other. (This is a critique of the conception of human nature.) 2) a critique of the narrative of self-development as a process of separation from—i.e., negation of—the other, to produce an atomistic individual. Benjamin argues that the development of the self is better understood as the development of a capacity for intersubjective relationship. (This is a critique of the normative model.) 3) a critique of the understanding of the process of self-development only in terms of the individual, in the relation of the subject to objects, rather than in terms of intersubjective relationships. (This is a critique of the analytical model.)

All of these criticisms are important, but Benjamin does not clearly differentiate one from the other, and hence her position continually shifts among a series of different arguments. Sometimes Benjamin argues that there is no fundamental aggression or desire for negation of the other; sometimes she argues that the desire for negation of the other and the desire/need for recognition are equally fundamental; sometimes she argues that self-development is a learning process, wherein the child moves from a desire for self-assertion through negation of the other to a recognition of the other's subjectivity as necessary to one's own; sometimes she argues that the entire process of self-development must be understood as a process of mutual recognition.

Benjamin refers to the desire for self-assertion through negation of the other as the desire for "omnipotence":

> the wish for absolute assertion of oneself, the demand to have one's way, the negation of the outside—all that Freud understood as aggression and omnipotence.... [39]

And her position as to the validity of a theory of a desire for omnipotence continually changes. At times, she argues that it is wrong to posit a fundamental desire for omnipotence. Sometimes she makes this argument by claiming that the desire for omnipotence is an effect, not a cause.[33]

> Omnipotence is a meaningful idea not as the original state, but as a fantasy that children construct in the face of disappointment, a reaction to loss—indeed, it is usually derived from a perception of the parent's power.... Omnipotence describes a defensive wish, buried in every psyche, that one will have a perfect world, will prevail over time, death, and the other—and that coercion will succeed. [256–257, n.]

Given that omnipotence, or the desire for self-assertion through the negation of the other, is "buried in every psyche," it seems to me that the question as to how it got there is irrelevant. The point is that, according to Benjamin, it is universal. And, it would seem, ineradicable. For it is difficult to imagine a childhood without disappointment, loss, or parental power.

But in other places, Benjamin argues that the very concept of a desire for omnipotence must be replaced:

> One of the most important insights of intersubjective theory is that sameness and difference exist simultaneously in mutual recognition. This insight allows us to counter the argument that human beings fundamentally desire the impossible absolutes of "oneness" and perfection with the more moderate view that things don't have to be perfect, that, in fact, it is *better* if they are not. [47]

Now, in fact, our rational recognition that it's better if things aren't perfect allows us to say absolutely nothing about what human beings fundamentally desire. But Benjamin frequently conflates "fundamental desires" with "what is better." In other words, she often simply substitutes a normative ideal for an analysis of human desire and human development. Or she assumes an immediate identity of desire and normative ideal, defined as need.

This is evident once again in her discussion of the role of aggression in the process of recognition. Here, Benjamin argues once again that there is in fact a basic desire for omnipotence, or self-assertion through negation of the other, but Benjamin argues, following Winnicott (whose theory, she asserts, is "in many ways, a modern echo of Hegel's reflections on recognition" [37]), that the true aim of aggression against the other is the recognition of the other as a subject who can recognize oneself.

> [T]he object must be destroyed *inside* [in fantasy] in order that we know it to have survived *outside;* thus we can recognize it as not subject to our mental control.... For if I completely negate the other, he does not exist; and if he does not survive, he is *not there* to recognize me. But to find this out I must *try* to exert this control, *try* to negate his independence. [38]

> The meaning of destruction is that the subject can engage in an all-out collision with the other, can hurtle himself against the barriers of otherness in order to feel the shock of the fresh, cold outside. [40]

Thus Benjamin gives us what is in fact a teleology of aggression: the real meaning of aggression against the other is the recognition of the other; the purpose of aggression is to recognize that the other is independent of the self. In other words, the purpose of our *desire* for omnipotence is the discovery of our *need* for recognition.

It seems to me that Benjamin has so much difficulty with the notion of "omnipotence" because she believes that human aggression and mutual recognition are fundamentally incompatible. Once it is acknowledged that there is an element of aggression in human beings—and, for a psychoanalyst, the acknowledgment is difficult to avoid—the only solution seems to be the affirmation of paradox. And what becomes apparent through her discussions of omnipotence is that she *equates* omnipotence, or the will to negate the other, with self-assertion. And, as we have seen, she equates the identity and autonomy of the self with self-assertion. Like de Beauvoir and Derrida, Benjamin still conceives of the self—of self-assertion and self-identity—as a negation of the other. Thus, Benjamin has been unable to successfully integrate the insights of psychoanalysis with those of intersubjective theory, but has maintained a dualism between the two. She accepts the subject-object model of self-assertion through negation of the other, and simply argues that we must add on a concept of mutual recognition. Therefore, intersubjective recognition requires the preservation of a constant oscillation between recognition and self-assertion. And if self-assertion and mutual recognition are mutually contradictory, and paradoxical, then clearly Benjamin assumes that intersubjective recognition entails a repression or negation of self-assertion; in other words, the recognition of our universality entails a repression of my particular individuality, my specific difference.

As it turns out, Benjamin has been unable to live up to her own critiques of the subject-object model in Freud and Hegel. 1) Against her own critique of the assumption of a fundamental desire for negation of the other, she herself sees the will to negate the other as definitive of self-assertion, as one pole of the paradox of human nature. 2) While she argues that the normative ideal of the self as an atomistic individual must be replaced with the ideal of intersubjective recognition, Benjamin's normative ideal turns out to be not intersubjective recognition but the preservation of a paradox between self-assertion and recognition. 3) Against her argument that the subject-object model must be replaced with an intersubjective model, Benjamin ends up affirming a fundamental ontological duality between self-assertion and recognition.

Benjamin's theory slides back behind her own arguments because her model of the self lacks any concept of mediation. She fails to develop a theory of mutual recognition as a capacity to mediate between the assertion of the self and the recognition of the other. For Benjamin, mutual recognition is not understood to be capable of mediating paradox: rather, the need for recognition is what produces paradox. And thus, rather than developing Hegel's analysis of mutual recognition to move beyond Hegel, Benjamin regresses back behind Hegel to an affirmation of a fundamental ontological duality between self-assertion and recognition, between independence and dependence, between subject and object.

For, contrary to Benjamin's claim, Hegel does not argue that the only way out of duality is through domination. In assuming that the master-slave relation is the end of Hegel's story, Benjamin misses the point of Hegel's theory: the attempt to expose dualities, or simple paradoxes, as false concepts, as products of an incapacity for mediation. Thus, for Hegel, the concept of the atomistic individual represents a failure to recognize human community, and human universality. On the other hand, the concept of simple unity or homogeneous community represents a failure to recognize individual autonomy, and a resolution of difference into domination. And if Hegel himself can be accused of failing to sustain mediation, and of collapsing difference into unity (and Benjamin does not address this aspect of Hegel's theory at all), the solution cannot be a return to paradox. Hegel at least offered an alternative to either paradox or domination, with the concept of mutual recognition as intersubjective mediation.

Thus, against Benjamin's normative ideal of a paradoxical tension between self-assertion and recognition, and against Derrida's normative ideal of a dissolution of identity in the name of nonidentity, I want to argue for a normative ideal of mutual recognition which can accommodate the reality of human aggression and human difference. This ideal of mutual recognition must be realized both in the subjective knowledge of intersubjective relationship and in the active practice of intersubjective dialogue.

This requires a concept of individual self-identity not as a negation of the other but as a capacity for mutual recognition; and not as a negation or repression of nonidentity or difference, but as a capacity for the realization and expression of nonidentity and difference through the realization and expression of a social self.[34] I shall attempt to develop these ideas in the chapters which follow.

2

Separation as Domination

Nancy Chodorow and the Relational
Feminist Critique of Autonomy

The struggle for individual autonomy has always been, and remains, crucial to feminist politics: the right of all women to self-governance, to make individual life choices freely and independently, is an ideal which guides most of our collective political struggles. At the same time, the critique of the ideal of autonomy, often leading to its outright rejection, is also central to feminist theory and practice. The critique of autonomy, associated with critiques of liberal individualism, comes from several different directions. The combination of the socialist critique of the liberal ideology of competitive individualism and radical and socialist feminist analyses of the sexual division of labor leads Alison Jaggar, in her classic overview of feminist arguments, *Feminist Politics and Human Nature,* to assert that the ideal of individual autonomy is "characteristically masculine as well as characteristically capitalist," and ought to be rejected altogether by feminists.[1] Poststructuralist and Freudian feminist theorists argue that the ideal of individual autonomy is a fiction that covers up the structures of language, power, and embodiment that construct us. Relational (communitarian, cultural, maternal) feminists argue that the concept of the independent, autonomous ego contradicts the empirical reality of our embeddedness in and dependence upon relationships, and that the normative ideals of self-fulfilment and individual rights must be replaced with a stress on the value of social relationships and the well-being of communities. And cultural relativists argue that the ideal of individual autonomy reflects values which are specific to white western male-dominant culture, and that to hold it up as a universal ideal is to obscure the reality and importance of cultural and historical differences. What unites all of these arguments is a critique of the construction of the subject as an "abstract individual," and an insistence on an understanding of the subject as a social and cultural product, embodied and embedded in relationships with others, and in specific historical and political contexts.

The upshot is that individual autonomy is very commonly rejected by feminists as an ideal. And this produces a paralyzing impasse at the core of feminist theory and practice: on one hand, the ideal of autonomy is rejected as a liberal ideology, as a product and underpinning of capitalist patriarchal society and of phallogocentric culture; on the other hand, we cannot avoid continually reaffirming the ideal of autonomy—of freedom of thought, choice, and action—in everyday personal and political struggles.

It seems to me that the only way out of this paradox is to reformulate our conception of autonomy—to develop a conception of autonomy which does not conflict with our social construction, our embodiment and embeddedness. But while a great deal of feminist scholarship has been directed toward reformulating the *self,* as an embedded and relational self (or as a multiple and fragmented self), the problem of *autonomy* tends to be set aside. Very often, theorists, when faced with the unavoidable necessity of acknowledging the importance of autonomy, fall back into a simple reaffirmation of an un-reformulated conception of autonomy.[2]

In this chapter, I shall analyze the critique of autonomy—and the rather half-hearted attempt to reformulate it—in what I shall call "relational feminist" theories. Theorists such as Carol Gilligan, Evelyn Fox Keller, Susan Bordo, Jane Flax, Nancy Hartsock, and Sandra Harding all draw on Nancy Chodorow's psychoanalytic account of human self-development to ground their understanding of gender relations and male dominance in terms of an opposition between separation and connection.[3] Important critiques of these theories have focussed on their tendency to universalize and essentialize male and female qualities, on the circularity of the arguments, and on the problems inherent in revaluing feminine qualities which are products of oppression.[4] From a different perspective, Freudian and Lacanian feminists criticize Chodorow for failing to problematize the identity of the self—for ignoring the role of unconscious sexuality and aggression, and of symbolic structures of power, in human development.[5] I want to shift the focus, to attempt to develop an immanent critique of the conceptual claims made by these theories. Focussing on Chodorow's model of self-development, I shall argue that the assumption of a transcendental opposition between separation and connection, and the equation of separation with domination, pushes Chodorow into the paradoxical position of having both to affirm and to reject autonomy.

I shall preface my analysis of Chodorow's work with a brief discussion of Simone de Beauvoir's influence on relational feminism and of Carol Gilligan's reflection of that influence.

To get at the roots of the paradoxical construction of autonomy, we need to reconsider the ways in which Simone de Beauvoir's analysis of women's status as Other to man's Self has influenced feminist theory. In the previous chapter I tried to show that de Beauvoir's Kojèvian, existentialist model of the subject, according to which the self is defined only in terms of negativity, of constant opposition to and will to dominate an object/other, allows no possibility of a relationship between identity and nonidentity within the subject, or of a non-oppositional relationship between subjects. Here I want to argue that relational feminist critiques of the oppositional subject-object model of the self espoused by de Beauvoir have in fact failed to challenge this oppositional model, and have simply repudiated it as a typically male model. As I shall argue, de Beauvoir's model of autonomy as a product of opposition to an other and of a struggle for domination is typically accepted as: 1) an accurate empirical description of the (modern) masculine self, and 2) the definitive conceptual model of the separate, autonomous self. Moreover, de Beauvoir's transcendental opposition between this autonomous self and a purely relational other, defined as being-for-self and being-for-other, is accepted as a universal truth, and translated into an opposition between separation and connection. It is no coincidence that this oppositional model reflects de Beauvoir's analysis of the relation between Man and Woman as an opposition between Self and Other.

De Beauvoir argues that the modern woman is caught in a conflict between her aspiration to be an autonomous subject and the social requirement—often internalized as a personal desire—that she take up the role of Other.

> The drama of woman lies in this conflict between the fundamental aspirations of every subject (ego)—who always regards the self as the essential—and the compulsions of a situation in which she is the inessential.[6]

The "drama of woman" is then, in Sartrean terms, her entrapment in the conflict between being *pour-soi* (for self) and being merely *pour-autrui* (for others).

> But most often woman knows herself only as different, relative; her *pour-autrui*, relation to others, is confused with her very being. [678]

For de Beauvoir, women's lapse into being-for-others is typical of romantic love. In love, man reaffirms himself and his own "sovereign subjectivity" through experiencing and being recognized by an other; woman does not reaffirm herself, but abandons herself to love, to the experience of loving and of being loved. He remains and affirms himself; she is other, self-less, relative.

Genuine love, for de Beauvoir, would be an equal relationship of "the mutual recognition of two liberties" wherein lovers "experience themselves both as self and as other: neither would give up transcendence, neither would be mutilated" [677]. But, as it turns out, de Beauvoir's model of genuine love is based on her understanding of "what *man* demands of love" [677]. And what man demands of love is, according to her sources, self-knowledge and self-affirmation. She quotes George Gusdorf, who claims that "Woman plays an indispensable and leading role in man's gaining knowledge of himself" [677]. And de Beauvoir wants the same for women. Ideally, then, genuine love serves as an intermediary between oneself and oneself.

What is of course left out of de Beauvoir's model is the value of recognizing, caring for, and coming to know an other as an end in her- or him-self, and not merely as a means to the affirmation of self.[7] Relational feminists such as Chodorow and Gilligan argue that while the "being for others" which has been upheld as the ideal of femininity has served to oppress women, it incorporates some very positive values—nurturance, caring, empathy, connection to and attentiveness to the particularities of specific, concrete others—which would be lost if women were to embrace the ideal of individual autonomy. These theorists call attention to and describe a modern (western, capitalist) split between opposing self-identities and value orientations—a masculine orientation toward autonomy and a feminine orientation toward being-for-others—and its relation to the public-private division of men's and women's work. While their attempt to revalue "feminine" qualities leaves these theorists open to the criticism that they are romanticizing qualities born of oppression, it can hardly be denied that empathy, caring, and attentiveness to others are important qualities which do need to be valued. And in fact, both Chodorow and Gilligan argue that it is necessary to go beyond revaluing "feminine" qualities to transcend the oppositions.

But this ideal is difficult to reconcile with their conceptual framework. Relational theorists tend to accept de Beauvoir's assumption that autonomy and relatedness—being-for-self and being-for-others—are absolutely opposed. For example, Carol Gilligan argues that her studies of moral reasoning uncover two images of self—self as a separate and autonomous individual and self as connected to others—which are "fundamentally incompatible."[8] Gilligan uses the imagery of the duck/rabbit picture—one can see either the duck or the rabbit, but never both together—to represent these two conceptions of self. In Gilligan's terms, there is no room for a conception of self as both separate and autonomous and fundamentally connected to others; these two orientations are mutually exclusive, inextricably embedded in two fundamentally incompatible worldviews. This does not necessarily mean that it is impossible for one person to understand or use both orientations: one can switch between seeing a duck and seeing a rabbit. It does mean, however, that the two perspectives must always be opposed, always competing for priority.

What Gilligan has done is to turn a very difficult practical problem —the problem of how to work through the existing conflict between autonomy and care for others—into an eternal opposition, the resolution of which is rendered impossible. Nevertheless, at the end of this article Gilligan is able to write:

> Two ways of defining the self—by submission and by detachment—have created an obstacle to attachment that begins to give way when dialogue replaces reflection and blind commitment yields to response. Like searchlights crossing, these transformations of self intersect to form a bright spot of illumination, making it possible to join self with other and other with self. [18]

Here, Gilligan is cheating with her categories: suddenly, the poles of separation and connection (or detachment and attachment) have been replaced by poles of detachment and *submission,* and it is attachment which can transcend the opposition. And it might well be asked how it is possible to hold a dialogue between two perspectives which have been defined as fundamentally incompatible. Given the fundamental incompatibility of the two perspectives, the claim to a harmonious resolution is rather facile, and in fact minimizes the reality of the struggle between being-for-self and being-for-others that women do experience in our culture.

The belief in the fundamental incompatibility of autonomy and care for others surely has its roots in the experience which de Beauvoir so perceptively, if a little theatrically, describes as "the drama of woman"—the experience of conflict between aspiring to a universal ideal of autonomy and aspiring to a feminine ideal of being for others. It is this experience, I think, which is frozen into an eternal opposition by both de Beauvoir and Gilligan. But Gilligan's claim that women generally tend to value connection rather than autonomy denies the very existence of this conflict.[9]

For an account of the social and psychic origins of the two different senses of self which she identifies, Gilligan turns to Nancy Chodorow's psychoanalytic developmental model of male and female self and gender identity. Chodorow follows object relations theorists in replacing Freud's emphasis on erotic and aggressive drives with an emphasis on social relationships, and in shifting from

Freud's focus on the Oedipal complex as the site of the formation of the autonomous self, through internalization of paternal prohibitions, to a focus on the development of self through pre-oedipal connection to the mother. She thereby claims to replace an oppositional view of development with a relational one. As I shall argue, however, she actually fails to challenge Freud's (or de Beauvoir's) conception of the autonomous male self, based on opposition to an other.

Chodorow's thesis is that masculine and feminine gender identities, and male domination and female subordination, are produced by the social institution of female mothering. Because in virtually all known societies the caretakers of small children are women, both male and female children develop their self-identities primarily in relation to a woman—to their mother. Both sexes initially identify with the mother, but a boy has to develop his self-identity through separation from his mother, negation of his identity with her, and secondary identification with his father. Since men and fathers are largely absent from childrearing, the boy typically identifies with an abstract role rather than with a whole personality. The boy defines himself primarily as not-mother, and his connection to his mother must be repressed and denied. This repression of connection translates into objectification and domination—not only of the boy's own mother but, by extension, of all women. The girl, on the other hand, defines her self-identity through maintaining her identification with her mother. Thus her sense of self is more holistic and diffuse; her self-identity is inextricably embedded in her relationship with her mother, and by extension, with others. Consequently, however, the boundaries between herself and others tend to be rather fuzzy, and she has no clear sense of her self as separate, individuated. A girl's sense of autonomy and independence—of her own agency—tend to be relatively weak. Thus, it could be said that Chodorow sees normal male and female development as essentially pathological: boys are atomistic individuals who objectify women and have repressed all connections with others; girls are connected, but have trouble seeing themselves as autonomous and separate from others. Chodorow's solution to this pathological condition would be a society where both men and women share equally in parenting, so that both sexes could develop separate but relational selves. But this ideal of a happy balance between connection and separation is rendered untenable by Chodorow's own arguments: as I shall show, because Chodorow equates separation with domination, her attempt to reformulate autonomy lapses into paradox.

Chodorow claims that her aim is to provide an explanation for the differences between male and female self-identities—an explanation which goes beyond role theory to analyze "social structurally induced psychological processes."[10] To do so, she draws on object-relations theories to shift from Freud's focus on infantile drives to an analysis of relationships between parents and children. Unfortunately, in doing so, she tends to omit any analysis of how social relations are mediated through the human unconscious. Chodorow's central thesis—that women's mothering produces a sense of self as separate in boys and connected in girls—is ultimately based on her claim that mothers *treat* girls differently from boys.

> Because they are the same gender as their daughters and have been girls, mothers of daughters tend not to experience these infant daughters as separate. . . . Primary identification and symbiosis with daughters tend to be stronger, . . . with cathexis of the daughter as a sexual other usually remaining a weaker, less significant theme. [109]

> Because they are of different gender than their sons, by contrast, mothers experience their sons as a male opposite. Their cathexis of sons is more likely to consist from early on in an object cathexis of a sexual other. . . . [110]

But while Chodorow discusses at length various psychoanalytic analyses of the *consequences* of this difference, she provides no analysis of how the child *learns* its gender—that is, the social significance of its anatomical sex—and constructs its sexual identity. There is no discussion of the psychic mechanisms involved in the formation of sexual identity. Rather, the child's identity formation is seen as a simple response to the mother's treatment. The girl is treated as female-same-connected; therefore, she experiences herself as female-same-connected. The boy is treated as male-separate-opposite; therefore, he experiences himself as male-separate-opposite.

Moreover, Chodorow's theory is based not only on the assumption of the mother's heterosexual orientation, but on the assumption that the mother's feminine gender identity and heterosexual orientation are fixed and unwavering, and that these are simply and unproblematically transferred to the child. The mother's relation to the boy, but not the girl, is eroticized. In a note, Chodorow adds: "I must admit to fudging here about the contributory effect in all of this of a mother's sexual orientation—whether she is a heterosexual or lesbian" [110]. But whether the mother "is" a heterosexual or a lesbian is not the point. Chodorow assumes that the mother's heterosexual orientation, once established, is unambiguous and unproblematic. But, as Jacqueline Rose points out, this assumption misses the point of psychoanalytic theory.

> What distinguishes psychoanalysis from sociological accounts of gender ... is that whereas for the latter, the internalisation of norms is assumed roughly to work, the basic premise and indeed starting-point of psychoanalysis is that it does not. The unconscious constantly reveals the "failure" of identity. Because there is no continuity of psychic life, so there is no stability of sexual identity, no position for women (or for men) which is ever simply achieved.[11]

What psychoanalysis has been able to show is that gender roles, sexual identities, and sexual orientation are never unproblematic, never "simply achieved." The assumption that mothers' treatment of their children will simply conform to socially acceptable gender roles, and that children will learn those roles automatically and without conflict, is exactly what psychoanalytic theory calls into question.

The contribution of Freudian theory is precisely its critique of the assumption that fixed and unambiguous gender roles and heterosexual orientation are natural or "normal." According to Freud, all human children are born with the same range of drives and make no distinction as to the gender of the object. Gender identity and sexual orientation are produced through a combination of "constitutional" and social influences.

> [P]sychoanalysis considers that a choice of an object independently of its sex—freedom to range equally over male and female

objects—as it is found in childhood, in primitive states of society and early periods of history, is the original basis from which, as a result of restriction in one direction or the other, both the normal [heterosexual] and the inverted [homosexual] types develop. Thus from the point of view of psychoanalysis the exclusive sexual interest felt by men for women is also a problem that needs elucidating and is not a self-evident fact based upon an attraction that is ultimately of a chemical nature. A person's final sexual attitude is not decided until after puberty and is the result of a number of factors, not all of which are yet known. . . .[12]

There is, Freud argued, no simple or natural relationship between sexual orientation and gender identity.[13] Moreover, once produced, neither gender identity nor sexual orientation is ever fixed and unambiguous. Thus, Freud writes:

[N]o individual is limited to the modes of reaction of a single sex but always finds some room for those of the opposite one. . . . For distinguishing between male and female in mental life we make use of what is obviously an inadequate empirical and conventional equation: we call everything that is strong and active male, and everything that is weak and passive female.[14]

And against researchers who have regarded deviations from "normal" heterosexual practices to be "indications of degeneracy or disease" Freud argues that such "deviations," including homoerotic attraction, must be understood to be included within a spectrum of dispositions and practices which are part of normal human sexuality. They are, he argues, "constituents which are rarely absent from the sexual life of healthy people" [74]. It follows that even a heterosexual mother cannot be expected to relate to her daughter only in ways which will conform to norms of heterosexual behavior.

Indeed, against Chodorow's assumption that the relation between a girl and her mother has little or no erotic component—i.e., that it simply conforms to the conventions of heterosexual normalcy— Freud argued that the relation between a girl and her mother is normally sexualized, for the mother is the first object of libidinal drives for both boys and girls.[15]

It is of course well known that Freud's own biases with regard to what constitutes normalcy constantly came into conflict with his problematization of normal sexuality, and his critique of the reduction of sexual and psychical matters to matters of biology is undermined by his own not infrequent appeal to some ultimate biological destiny. The point is that while Chodorow's account of the development of gender identity relies on an assumption of the normalcy, fixity, and stability of masculine and feminine gender identities and heterosexual orientation, for Freud this assumption is precisely what is open to question.[16]

Finally, Chodorow's explanation of the development of gender roles depends upon an unexamined assumption that being "the same" necessarily translates into being not separate, or connected, and that difference necessarily entails opposition. Because they are the same gender, mothers experience daughters as not separate. Because they are of a different gender, mothers experience their sons as opposite. But where does this understanding of sameness and difference come from in the first place? Chodorow provides no analysis of how being the same comes to be equated with being not separate, or of how being different comes to mean being opposed. These equations are simply taken for granted. But the question of how sex difference comes to mean opposition is precisely what has to be questioned by feminists.

It can be argued that Chodorow is simply saying that in a society which defines difference as opposition, mothering reproduces this definition. In fact, there is a deep ambivalence in Chodorow's work: on one hand, she argues that her analysis is restricted to modern capitalist society, and to the role of exclusive mothering in reproducing already-existing gender roles and male dominance in this society; on the other hand, she aspires to an account of how women's mothering, "one of the few universal and enduring elements of the sexual division of labor,"[17] actually produces virtually universal gender roles—mothering, in other words, is seen as a root cause of male dominance.

Perhaps Chodorow's own self-description should be taken as authoritative here. In the introduction to her more recent collection, *Feminism and Psychoanalytic Theory,* Chodorow writes that in *The Reproduction of Mothering* she "implied that women's mothering was *the* cause or prime mover of male dominance."[18] She now feels that male dominance is multiply caused;[19] but she remains convinced that women's mothering is *one* primary cause of male dominance. If anything, Chodorow now presents even more strongly the position that women's mothering helps to produce, rather than simply reproduce, male dominance.

But if this is so, then Chodorow must be making the claim that the equation of difference with opposition is a natural and inevitable one. For according to Chodorow, the male oppositional personality is a foundation of male dominance, and mothering produces the oppositional male personality. If boys differentiate in relation to mothers, they will have to define their sense of self as being not-mother, as being opposed to mother, and hence to all women, who are "the same" as mother. And this is so because mothers and boys are of different genders. The explanation works only if the equation of difference with opposition is assumed, *a priori*.

As Linda Nicholson and Iris Young have pointed out, Chodorow's explanation of male dominance entails a logical circularity.

> On the one hand, Chodorow wishes to explain male dominance as a consequence of female parenting. However, to make her argument work she implicitly must appeal to such dominance. Thus she notes that men, to achieve gender identity, must renounce their early identification with their mothers. However, is not the disdain that is a part of this renunciation itself a consequence of existing ascribed inferiority?[20]

Nicholson and Young are right to point to an apparent circularity in Chodorow's theory. But this circularity needs to be considered in the context of the psychoanalytic concepts that Chodorow is using. The strong claim that Chodorow is making—and the only one that can release her from the charge of circularity—is that separation in itself produces domination. The importance of this assumption emerges upon closer examination of Chodorow's account of the development of the self.

Chodorow argues that self-identity has a twofold origin. One origin is "an inner physical experience of body integrity and a more internal '*core* of the self.'"[21] The development of this "core of self" depends upon "the provision of a continuity of experience" [68]. The other origin of self-identity is a differentiation or demarcation of self from the object world, through which the child develops a sense of separate self. Both of these tracks of development derive from the child's early relational experiences. "It is the relation to the mother, if she is primary caretaker, which provides the continuity and core of self" [71]; and "The infant achieves a differentiation of self only insofar as its expectations of primary love are frustrated" [69].

This concept of "primary love" is crucial to Chodorow's theory. Chodorow rejects Freud's claim that infants are motivated primarily by erotic and aggressive drives and, following object-relations theorists, argues instead that there is a "primary and fundamental sociality," first experienced by a child in relation to its mother [63]. Thus, what Freud called primary narcissism is reinterpreted (not unreasonably, I think) as a prototype of social relations. For Chodorow, then, it is this primary attachment to the mother that provides the continuity essential for the development of the "core" of self in the child.

But it is only through the frustration and subsequent repression of this primary attachment that babies develop a sense of self as separate from others. And in this, Chodorow agrees with Freud. Thus, while Chodorow differs from Freud in her conception of exactly what must be frustrated for the development of a separate self, she agrees with Freud that the essential component of that development is frustration and repression.[22] It seems odd that while Chodorow rejects so many of the assumptions central to Freud's theory, she accepts completely the psychoanalytic truism that the essential component of the differentiation of the self is repression.

But whereas for Freud individuation required frustration and repression of the drives, which the mother cannot always satisfy, for Chodorow individuation is the product of the frustration and repression of the mother-child relationship itself. Ironically, the effect of the shift to a theory of primary sociality (given the maintenance of the theory of individuation through frustration/repression) is that *individuation is seen to be in fundamental opposition to relationships with others.*

Moreover, with her two tracks of self-development—the core of self established through the sense of continuity provided by connection with the mother, and the sense of separateness established through separation from her—Chodorow seems to naturalize and universalize the opposition between autonomy and connection to others that is stereotypical of male and female roles in modern western societies. Thus, rather than questioning this opposition, she accepts it as a natural and universal fact. Given that Chodorow's theory is intended to be a corrective to Freud's projection of stereotypes of masculinity and femininity and of competitive individualism into facts of nature, this is a serious charge.

Finally, according to Chodorow's understanding of psychoanalytic theory, the repression that is necessary for separation leads directly to domination. Since the child develops a sense of separate self only through frustration and repudiation of primary connection with the first caretaker, the first caretaker comes to represent the dependence and helplessness that the child itself has experienced in this primary relationship. Because women are the primary caretakers, it is women who are associated with dependence and powerlessness, and hence mothering produces male dominance.

> The fact that the child's earliest relationship is with a woman becomes exceedingly important . . . ; that women mother and men do not is projected back by the child *after* gender comes to count. . . . Girls and boys expect and assume women's unique capacities for sacrifice, caring, and mothering, and associate women with their own fears of regression and powerlessness. [83]

It is important to note, then, that Chodorow is not saying that mothers come to symbolize regression and powerlessness because women are culturally defined as such. She is saying, rather, that the first caretaker will inevitably be associated with the passivity that the child itself has experienced in the primary relationship. But there is a problem with this claim:

> Children wish to remain one with their mother, and expect that she will never have different interests from them; yet they define development in terms of growing away from her. In the face of their dependence, lack of certainty of her emotional permanence, fear of merging, and overwhelming love and attachment, a mother looms large and powerful. Several analytic formulations speak to this, and to the way growing children come to experi-

ence their mothers. Mothers, they suggest, come to symbolize dependence, regression, passivity, and the lack of adaptation to reality. [82]

Here, Chodorow moves directly from the claim that mothers are experienced as "large and powerful" to the claim that they symbolize dependence, regression, and passivity, with no explanation as to what exactly tips the balance, causing the latter to win out over the former. Why should mothers, and hence women, be associated with passivity and powerlessness, rather than with power and omnipotence? Why would the dread and fear of the mother's power not produce a society where women are dominant? The fact that Freud posited the dread of the real father's power as an explanation for the continued existence of patriarchy underlines the problem: the argument from an original state of dread and fear of the powerful parent can be used either way—to explain either the dominance or the subordination of "the dreaded sex."[23] The key to Chodorow's explanation, then, is her assumption that the child can develop a *separate* self only by repudiating and denying the first caretaker's (mother's) power, and by associating her with the state of dependence, of nondifferentiation, which must be rejected. What she is saying is that mothering produces male dominance because *separation* necessarily produces the repression of connection to and will to dominate the first caretaker. Thus, the real issue here is not mothering but separation. Mothers are just the scapegoats for the problem of separation, which necessarily produces domination.

I do not want to suggest that Chodorow minimizes the complexity of the primary relationship; in fact, she identifies a number of conflicting sources of the repudiation of the first caretaker. As the representative of primary connection, the primary caretaker represents both omnipotence and dependence, and both qualities elicit both desire and dread in the child. And because the primary caretaker is also the one who forces the child to separate, she represents not only connection but its loss, and she thus arouses the child's hostility and rejection (but not, it seems, the child's love and idealization). The question remains as to why out of all these conflicting feelings hostility wins out and produces male dominance.

For Chodorow, it is separation that produces, after the fact, these negative valuations of connection, and of the mother. But she cannot explain why it is that primary connection necessarily comes to be perceived as dependence. Nor does she explain why it is assumed to conflict with, and to pose such a threat to, separation. And while the desire for connection is assumed as an *a priori* fact, no positive motive is ever given for the desire for separation, which seems to be purely defensive. It is difficult to understand, then, how it comes to be such a powerful motivating force.

The argument seems to be circular, and not only because, as Nicholson and Young point out, women's subordination must be already assumed. Chodorow's argument doesn't work unless we posit a defensive autonomous ego which is established through the repression of connection. That is, unless we already assume that individuation—the development of a sense of self as separate—necessarily requires the repression of connection to others.

Chodorow's equation of separation with repression and domination renders her solution to the problem of gender inequality less than adequate. Her argument is that if men and women were to share parenting equally, then both male and female children would develop in a more balanced way.

> Children could be dependent from the outset on people of both genders and establish an individuated sense of self in relation to both. In this way, masculinity would not become tied to denial of dependence and devaluation of women. Feminine personality would be less preoccupied with individuation, and children would not develop fears of *maternal* omnipotence and expectations of *women's* unique self-sacrificing qualities. This would reduce men's needs to guard their masculinity and their control of social and cultural spheres which treat and define women as secondary and powerless, and would help women to develop the autonomy which too much embeddedness in relationship has often taken from them. [218]

The ideal of a balance between separation and connection, made possible through shared parenting, sounds lovely, but given Chodorow's central argument—that separation is essentially the repression of connection, and necessarily produces domination—it's difficult to see how shared parenting could produce the harmonious balance between separation and connection that Chodorow envisions. Like Carol Gilligan's simple reconciliation of fundamentally incompatible world views, Chodorow's affirmation of a happy balance rings false. Once it has been demonstrated that separation is the foundation of the will to domination, the simple reaffirmation of separation, however balanced, as a developmental goal is incomprehensible.

And indeed, against this model of a desireable balance between separation and connection, Chodorow often argues that we need to reject separation as a developmental goal. In her article, "Gender, Relation, and Difference in Psychoanalytic Perspective," Chodorow rejects separation as an ideal, and argues that it must be not balanced but replaced by connection. But she gets caught up in the logical difficulties entailed by her attempt to distinguish separation, which must be rejected, from the differentiation of self, which, as she has to acknowledge, is necessary and unavoidable. In this article, Chodorow attempts to clarify her position on "difference"—but what emerges is in fact contradictory and confusing. In one passage, she begins by distinguishing between differentiation or separation, which is okay, and difference, which is bad: "it is possible to be separate, to be differentiated, without caring about or emphasizing difference."[24] Then she makes a distinction between differentiation, which is okay, and separation, which is bad: "Differentiation is not distinctness and separateness, but a particular way of being connected to others"; and "to single out separation as the core of . . . the process of differentiation may well be inadequate" [107]. At one point, she equates autonomy and separateness, seeing both as negative: "This inquiry suggests a psychoanalytic grounding for goals of emotional life other than autonomy and separateness. It suggests, instead, an individuality that emphasizes our connectedness" [108]. Then she distinguishes between autonomy, which is okay, and distinction, which is bad: "autonomy . . . need not be based on self-other distinctions, on the individual as individual"; and then she affirms the concept of a "nonreactive separateness" [108].

While this may appear to be mere niggling over semantics, I think that Chodorow's equivocation with these terms demonstrates the impossibility of affirming any concept of a differentiated self while holding to the claim that separation is the source of domination. Chodorow is trapped within the paradoxical construction of autonomy in feminist theory; faced with the necessity of affirming the differentiation of the self, and, moreover, of affirming some form of autonomy, she is unable to provide any basis for working through the paradox, but can only repeat it: the equation of separation with repression and domination pushes her into the paradoxical position of having to both reject and reaffirm separation, and autonomy. As long as separation is equated with the repression of connection, which leads to domination, any attempt to affirm a differentiated, individuated, autonomous self requires an affirmation of the repression of connection, and an affirmation of domination.

It is important to stress that what Chodorow is attempting to do here is to reformulate self-development—and even autonomy—as a function of relationship. She wants to argue that differentiation is not opposed to relationship but must itself be seen as a relational process. This is, I think, an important argument. But in arguing that "differentiation *is not* distinctness and separateness, but a particular way of being connected to others" [107, my italics] she ends up simply reproducing the opposition between separation and connection. Similarly, in her article "Toward a Relational Individualism," Chodorow posits, against Freud's "focus on individual autonomy," an object-relations theory of the self wherein the self is "not apart from the other."[25] She quotes Joan Rivière, who asserts that "there is no such thing as a single human being, pure and simple, unmixed with other human beings" [158]. Here, Chodorow is setting up a false dichotomy: either one can be a distinct, separate, individuated person, or one can be connected to others. Moreover, she is moving from an opposition between separation and connection to an opposition between being an individual and being a part of a whole. But in fact, being distinct and being connected, or being an individual and being a part of a whole, are not mutually exclusive. The fact that this dichotomy is all too familiar in our culture, in our daily lives, should not lead us to accept it as an inevitable truth in our theories.

Chodorow has another—and again, contradictory—alternative. With the rejection of separation, Chodorow falls back on the concept of a "true self" developed through continuity with the mother as the sole requirement of selfhood and of autonomy. In "Gender, Relation, and Difference in Psychoanalytic Perspective," Chodorow writes: "This more internal sense of self, or of 'I,' is not dependent on separateness or difference from an other. A 'true self,' or 'central self,' emerges through the experience of continuity that the mother or caretaker helps to provide...."[26] And it is this "true self" which serves as the foundation for "a relational rather than a reactive autonomy" [107].

Moreover, in this article Chodorow argues that while the separation required of boys in itself produces repression and domination, the connection that characterizes girls' sense of identity becomes a problem only in a male-dominated society. Female "core gender identity" is, according to Chodorow, "not problematic" precisely because it does not entail "difference." Girls "do not define themselves as 'not-men,' or 'not-male,' but as 'I, who am female'" [110]. Thus, a girl's gender identity is free of negativity; it is established through a purely positive, immediate identification. And while girls and women "may have problems with their sense of continuity and similarity, if it is too strong and they have no sense of a separate self," these problems arise only because their "gender category" is "negatively valued" [110].

Chodorow's position on autonomy is, to say the least, confusing. She equates autonomy with separation, and argues that both must be rejected. But she also argues for a reformulation of autonomy, understood as a balance between separation and connection. And she argues that while separation must be rejected, it is really not necessary for autonomy at all. Underlying all these shifts in position is her equation of separation with domination.

This equation is a popular one in feminist theory. For example, in *The Flight to Objectivity,* Susan Bordo argues persuasively that the preoccupation with objectivity, detachment, separation, and autonomy characteristic of modern science and philosophy represents a "masculinization of thought," characterized by an exorcism, transcendence, and domination of "the feminine," and Bordo draws on Chodorow's work to account for this masculinization. Bordo stresses that she is not making a claim for a universal and ahistorical masculinization of culture, but is describing a specifically modern phenomenon. And she reads Chodorow's work as a description of the results of modern western childrearing practices. Moreover, she does not want to make essentialist claims for the existence of masculine and feminine essences, but focusses on the cultural meanings of masculinity and femininity in modern western culture, and particularly in the writings of the philosophers and scientists she takes to be representative of that culture.

But in basing her argument on Chodorow's, Bordo becomes entangled in the circularity which Young and Nicholson have identified. Bordo states her central thesis as follows:

> [B]ecause a more rigorous individuation from the mother is demanded of boys (as a requisite to their attaining a 'masculine' identity in a culture in which masculinity is defined in opposition to everything that the mother represents), they grow up defining achievement and measuring their own well-being in terms of detachment, autonomy, and a clear sense of boundaries between self and world, self and others. This has resulted, in our male-dominated intellectual traditions, in the fetishization of detachment and 'objectivity' in ethical reasoning and scientific rationality.[27]

It seems to me that the argument made here is that in a culture which fetishizes separation and opposition, male development results in a culture which fetishizes separation and opposition. But beyond the problem of circularity, what I want to note here is Bordo's reduction of objectivity, autonomy, a sense of separate self and "a clear sense of boundaries" to a *fetishization* of detachment, which is the essence of domination. Evelyn Fox Keller, Sandra Harding, Nancy Hartsock and others make similar arguments, and similarly back them up with reference to Chodorow.[28]

The equation of separation and domination is not restricted to theorists influenced by Chodorow. It is the acceptance of this equation (and of the romantic and anti-modernist sentiments it evokes) which underlies not only the popularity of Chodorow's work but the rejection of autonomy which is common to so many feminist theories. For instance, while Alison Jaggar is sceptical as to the explanatory power of Chodorow's psychoanalytic theory, she does not question the assumption that "the insistence on making sharp distinctions" is a primary characteristic of male dominance in western culture.[29]

But the claim that separation produces domination obscures the fact that an inability to recognize another person's separateness or distinctness is itself a basis of domination. Jean Grimshaw makes this point in her critique of the ambiguity of the concepts of separation and connection. Referring to R.D. Laing's descriptions of pathological mother-daughter relationships in *Sanity, Madness and the Family*, Grimshaw notes that in these families, the mothers are unable to recognize their daughters' separateness from themselves; they are, however, "connected" to their daughters in that they see them as projections of a family fantasy, or of their own beliefs or desires. Similarly, referring to Marilyn Frye's concepts of the "arrogant eye" vs. the "loving eye," Grimshaw notes that the man with the arrogant eye can see a woman only in relation to himself, only in his service, only "*for* him"—i.e., only in terms of her *connection* to him—whereas one who sees with a "loving eye" is able to recognize the other's specificity as a *separate* person. "Care for others, understanding of them are only possible if one can adequately distinguish oneself from others."[30] This is the point made by de Beauvoir when she argues that man's inability to recognize woman as anything but his Other, as relative to him, produces a peculiar solipsism which allows him to avoid ever questioning or relativizing his own absoluteness.

Similarly, feminist theorists who have taken up Lacan's rereading of Freud through Hegel's dialectic of recognition argue that the recognition of the other's separateness from the self is a prerequisite to the development of a sense of self which is not based on domination. Thus, in her discussion of the relevance of Lacan's thought to feminist questions, Jacqueline Rose writes that for Lacan, "what matters is that the relationship of the child to the mother is not simply based on 'frustration and satisfaction' ... but on the recognition of her desire."[31] The child, in other words, can recognize itself as a self only by coming to recognize the selfhood of the mother—only by learning to recognize the mother as a separate subject with her own desires.

For these theorists, separation does not translate into domination, nor into atomistic egoism, nor abstract individualism. Separation means, rather, the acceptance that one is not the centre of the world, not omnipotent. The process of separation is the process of relinquishing egocentrism and coming to recognize and accept the reality of the other. Thus, separation leads not to domination, but to its overcoming: to the transcendence of egoism, of the self-centredness which makes relationships with others impossible.

3

The Paradox of the Self

Jessica Benjamin's Intersubjective Theory

Jessica Benjamin is unique in attempting to base a feminist theory of gender relations on an intersubjective theory of the development of the self as a process of mutual recognition. But while she takes the idea of an intersubjective theory from Jürgen Habermas, Benjamin rejects Habermas's overemphasis on rationality, abstraction, and universality. Following Chodorow, Gilligan, and Keller, she argues that, in emphasizing formal procedures and abstraction as the basis for a universal form of recognition, Habermas ends up negating the possibility of the recognition of the other's particular subjectivity.[1] For her theory of intersubjectivity, Benjamin turns to Chodorow.

Before taking up the arguments in Benjamin's book, *The Bonds of Love,* I want to begin with an analysis of her early critique of Theodor Adorno.

The End of Internalization: Benjamin's Critique of Adorno

In her 1977 essay, "The End of Internalization: Adorno's Social Psychology," Benjamin challenges the grim thesis of the *Dialectic of Enlightenment*—that the progression of the rational autonomous self has entailed a progression of domination from which there can be no escape. Essentially, Benjamin seems to agree with the historical diagnosis; she argues, however, that the inability to conceive of the possibility of *change,* of emancipation from the logic of domination, was a product of the early Frankfurt theorists' reliance on Freudian drive theory and Hegelian subject-object theory, and of their inability to come up with an alternative to liberal individualism. In particular, she argues that Adorno's reliance on the internalization of authority as the only means for developing autonomy was responsible for his inability to move beyond his conception of the self as an insurmountable paradox.

The story of the *Dialectic of Enlightenment* closely follows that of Freud's *Civilization and Its Discontents,* with a Marxist and Weberian twist. Horkheimer and Adorno argue that human beings developed the rational autonomous ego to ensure survival, to defend against the wildness and chaos of both external nature and the internal nature of aggressive drives—selfish drives for pleasure and for death, or for the end of pain. The self is constituted by and becomes the agent of the rational control and management of internal and external nature. So, the self is a positive development, which allows us to interact with nature in a constructive way. But, because the rational self is a product of the internalization of authority to control aggressive drives and to control external nature, the instrumental dimension of rationality becomes overdeveloped, and rationally coping and interacting with nature becomes a matter of using reason to dominate nature. (This argument is an extension of Max Weber's analysis of instrumental rationality.) The self becomes all too proficient at the domination of nature, at the repression of drives, at defending identity against otherness, against difference, and against its own pleasure. For, in stopping up the destructiveness of the drives, we also stop up our capacity for pleasure.

Thus, Adorno sees the self as a product of repression. But he does not, like Derrida, conceive of self-identity as simply an instance of mastery or narrative closure, and he does not see the self as entirely determined by the logic of phallogocentrism. He recognizes the positive dimensions of rationality and self-identity, and he stresses the importance of sustaining a tension, an interaction, between identity and nonidentity—in this case, between the rationality of the self and the drives for pleasure. So he argues that the answer to the problem of self-identity cannot lie in simply repudiating identity and going over to the other side, to nonidentity or absolute difference. For the development of self-identity and autonomy is not simply an acceptance of authority. In fact, the autonomy of the self is what ensures some independence from authority: the development of rational autonomy is the development of a capacity for criticism.

Thus, for Adorno, the "dialectic" of the self is in fact a cruel paradox: in developing our selves, we dominate our selves—in developing our rationality, we dominate and repress our inner selves, our desires, as well as each other and nature. (Here, of course, Adorno is echoing Marx, but he's closed off the potential for emancipation in Marx's theory.)

For, however critical he is of this process, Adorno can see no way out. However critical he is of the nineteenth-century bourgeois patriarchal individual, based on internalization of the father, he sees the decline of the patriarchal family as a negative thing; he looks at fascist Germany and the homogenizing culture industry in America and sees people no longer internalizing the father's authority, and thus no longer developing the strong autonomous ego, the independent self which is capable of rational analysis and critique. There is no longer any self to mediate between external authority and primary nature; instead, there is an immediate identification with external authority. So, Adorno gets stuck in the paradoxical position of criticizing the constitution of the self through the repressive internalization of paternal authority, but seeing this as the only way to develop the capacity for a *critique* of authority.

In "The End of Internalization: Adorno's Social Psychology," Jessica Benjamin argues that Adorno gets caught in this tragic paradox because he fails to question the assumption that socialization requires the internalization of authority. Adorno's inability to question the necessity of internalization is a product of his failure to challenge Freud's assumption that human beings are innately aggressive, his inability to conceive of an alternative to the ideal of the liberal bourgeois individual, and his reliance on the Hegelian conception of self-development in terms of a subject-object opposition.[2]

Benjamin argues that rather than accepting the Freudian model of the human being as innately aggressive, and hence requiring the internalization of authority to curb violent and destructive drives, we need to turn to an understanding of the development of the self as an intersubjective process. For Benjamin, this is provided by an object-relations model of the self. According to Benjamin's version of object-relations theory, the integrity or identity of the self is not a product of a social developmental process but a pre-given essence, and aggression is not innate but produced by social domination. Thus, the development of the liberal bourgeois individual is best understood not as a taming of aggressive instincts to produce a coherent rational self, but as the internal fragmentation of an originally coherent self in response to social domination. "The ego was once whole: what is called id are the parts which are split off in early infancy."[3] The splitting of the ego is a defensive mechanism: it is the ego's way of coping with the reality of domination. The only way the child can deal with its terror in the face of the repressive authority of the parents on whom it depends for survival, and for love, is to internalize that repressive authority. Parental authority and parental violence are internalized in an effort to maintain control. And thus, the child represses its knowledge of the reality of domination. Internalization of parental authority results in conformity to parental demands, in an attempt to deny the reality of domination. "Goal rationality and reasonableness, the virtues of the well-socialized bourgeois child, are based upon an underlying irrationality: the perception of parental violence and childish helplessness must be repressed, even at the cost of blaming oneself for disobedience" [57].

Thus, Benjamin understands internalization as an acceptance of domination, an obedience to authority based on a repression of the knowledge of domination. And this opens up the possibility of the development of a self which does *not* require the internalization of authority: in a world without domination, self-development would not be based on internalization.

But Adorno fails to reject the internalization model, Benjamin argues, not only because of his dependence on Freudian drive theory, but because he cannot imagine a world without domination, and therefore cannot envision a form of autonomy different from the liberal bourgeois ideal of self-control, responsibility, and rationality. "The problem is that Adorno sees the principle of self-control and responsibility which underly individuation in this society as constituting real autonomy. He therefore persists in seeing internalization as a vehicle for consciousness rather than the unconscious acceptance of authority" [56]. Despite his exhaustive critique of liberal individualism, Adorno returns to "the ideal of individual consciousness upheld by liberalism" [45], to the mediating agency of the rational ego produced through internalization, as a source of resistance to authority, to rationalization. For Adorno, "the solution to the problem of reason is more reason" [50].

The real problem, Benjamin argues, is that Adorno collapses together the concepts of ego and superego: the concept of a rational ego capable of dealing with the outside world (i.e., capable of acting according to Freud's "reality principle") is conflated with the concept of the superego, based on internalization of authority. "The identification with parental *authority* as super-ego is collapsed into the identification with parental *competence* or the reality of childhood autonomy as ego formation" [55]. Thus, "Adorno does not discriminate between individuation which is imposed from without and that which develops spontaneously, between living up to the standards of a powerful parent and independence which comes from parental recognition of self-activity. There is no basis for distinction between the performance principle and another reality principle, between obedience and spontaneity" [56].

Benjamin is right to argue that Adorno fails adequately to distinguish ego from superego—fails, then, to distinguish a capacity for dealing with reality from an acceptance of authority. And she is right, too, to argue that self-development must be understood not only in terms of the acceptance of authority and the repression of drives, but as a process of the development of competence through spontaneous activity and identification with others. But Benjamin's own model of a self which is born "whole" and which simply and spontaneously asserts itself is, to say the least, problematic. According to Benjamin's model, the only acceptable role for parents is to benevolently recognize the child's spontaneously enacted self, and to serve as role models, as competent egos with whom the child can spontaneously identify. But this model provides no way of dealing with the fact that the development of a rational ego inevitably requires learning *limits* to self-assertion, and *restrictions* to spontaneity. Typically, the child learns these limits through coming to recognize that the parents do not exist solely for the child.[4]

Furthermore, Benjamin's analysis tends to collapse parental power which is violent and dominating with parental power which is normal and inevitable. According to Benjamin, the authority of the parents is internalized in an attempt to defend against feelings of terror and helplessness that result from the perception of the parent's power and the child's dependence. In an ideal society, then, "the absence of authority and power, rather than identification with a powerful father, would form the basis for autonomous ego development. Rather than assuming innate regressive tendencies which must be counteracted by outside pressure, we could imagine that some form of development toward sociability would occur in the presence of other subjects who do not exercise coercion" [59–60]. But it is difficult to imagine a parent-child relationship which would not involve an imbalance of power. And it is just as difficult to imagine a socialization process which would involve no coercion, but merely "the presence of other subjects." Benjamin too easily collapses any power differential between parents and children into a relationship of domination, and any intervention in the child's spontaneity into an act of violence. In Benjamin's ideal world, parental authority would be replaced by parental love. Love, for Benjamin, is the highest form of recognition of another. Thus, love would replace internalization as the basis for intersubjective relations.

It appears, then, that Benjamin's utopian vision of a world without parental power and without coercion is a vision of spontaneous individuals who spontaneously assert themselves and spontaneously "love" each other without ever learning to recognize and accept their dependence on others—or to recognize and accept that those on whom they depend, those whom they love/need/want, are not entirely dependent upon them. It seems to me that Benjamin wants to shift all of the "blame" for normal childhood feelings of fear, pain, and loss—feelings which normally accompany the recognition of the parents' power, and of the parents' independence—onto parental domination.

The problem is that Benjamin sees no alternative between self-development through obedience to authority and self-development through spontaneous self-assertion, no alternative to an individuation which is "imposed from without" and one which spontaneously emerges from within. What these two alternatives leave out is the possibility of a *social* self.

Benjamin believes that internalization is always an acceptance of domination, and thus we need to reject superego formation and rely entirely on the ego as the basis of autonomy and rationality. But when Benjamin discards the concept of internalization she discards also any dimension of autonomy beyond the instrumental capacity to deal with the environment, in accordance with the reality principle.

The problem is that Benjamin herself fails to distinguish between the internalization of authority, which produces a repressive super-ego, and the internalization of the norms and principles of a society, which is essential for socialization. This requires a distinction between an understanding of internalization as a form of social dom-ination, and an understanding of internalization as a process (based on identification with others) of learning the norms, principles, and ideals of a society, and of coming to accept them as one's own. In this latter sense, internalization is a necessary step in coming to understand oneself as a participant in a society—in coming to understand that I am part of the We. And therefore, it is a necessary step in developing any concrete sense of who "I" am. Internalizing the We perspective leads to an understanding of limitations to my own self-assertion not simply as limitations imposed from without but as limitations imposed by We, and not simply as imposed on me, but as generalizable to all.[5]

Conceiving of group norms as my own is a condition—not a sufficient condition, obviously, but a necessary one—of the development of a level of rational autonomy beyond the reality principle, beyond the simple capacity to negotiate the environment. It is a condition of *moral* autonomy as a capacity for ethical action, a capacity for forming moral and ethical judgments, through an appeal to principles, and ideals. For internalization is the basis not only of conformity to rules and norms, but of an understanding of what it means to appeal to a principle. Thus, internalization is the basis of *critique:* of the capacity to question the legitimacy and validity of particular norms. And this of course was Adorno's main reason for holding on to a concept of internalization: for Adorno, internalization was essential to the capacity to *criticize* injustice and domination. But Adorno was unable to separate, conceptually, the internalization of irrational and repressive authority from the internalization of norms and principles which are understood as valid and legitimate criteria for ethical judgments.

Benjamin fails to criticize Adorno's conflation of the internalization of repressive authority and the internalization of norms necessary for moral autonomy, because there is no room in Benjamin's theory for a concept of moral autonomy. For Benjamin, moral autonomy falls under the category of bourgeois liberal ideals. According to Benjamin, all we need is love.

It is not a coincidence, I think, that, having criticized Adorno for failing to work through his paradox of the self, Benjamin ends up arguing in *The Bonds of Love* that the self is essentially paradoxical, and that the paradox of the self simply has to be accepted. Like Adorno, Benjamin is unable to come up with a form of individual autonomy that can mediate between self and other, between self and society, without domination. Once she begins to question the capacity of love to bring peace and harmony to a world of spontaneous and uninhibited egos, she is left with the acceptance of disillusion: there can be no harmony, but only paradoxical oscillation. In the absence of a theory of mediation, self-assertion and love/recognition are now seen as two principles which clash irreconcilably.

The Paradox of the Self: Jessica Benjamin's Intersubjective Theory

In her book, *The Bonds of Love: Psychoanalysis, Feminism, and the Problem of Domination,* Benjamin sets out to understand gender relations through an intersubjective theory of the development of the self. For Benjamin, this entails an understanding of self-development, and of gender relations, in terms of a dialectic of mutual recognition. Benjamin's central thesis is that "domination and submission [and in particular male domination and female submission] result from a breakdown of the necessary tension between self-assertion and mutual recognition that allows self and other to meet as sovereign equals" [12].

The relationship between self-assertion and mutual recognition is described by Benjamin as fundamentally paradoxical, and this fundamental paradox is, for her, the definitive model of the self. It is "the need for recognition," Benjamin argues, which "gives rise to a paradox" [12]. Citing Hegel's analysis of the struggle for recognition, Benjamin argues that "the need for recognition entails this funda-

mental paradox: at the very moment of realizing our own independence, we are dependent upon another to recognize it" [33]. But
Hegel, according to Benjamin, was unable to conceive of the possibility of sustaining this paradox. Against Hegel's conception of history as a process of resolution and renewal of tension, Benjamin
argues that we need to resist the temptation to resolution, and
accept the fundamental and irresolvable paradox which is definitive
of the self. For Benjamin, it is "the inability to sustain paradox" that
"convert[s] the exchange of recognition into domination and submission" [12].

To represent the paradox of the self, Benjamin uses the image of
Escher's pictures of birds which appear to be flying in two directions.
While "traditional theorists of the self" (Benjamin is referring here
specifically to Freud, ego psychologists, and Hegel) have understood
the self in terms of a picture where "relationship is the ground and
separation is the figure" [25], we need, she argues, to be able to see
both at once. Here, it will be noted, the terms of the paradox have
shifted from self-assertion and recognition to separation and relationship. As I shall argue, it is Benjamin's conflation of self-assertion
with separation (and autonomy) and of recognition with relationship (and immediate connection) that produces her model of the self
as paradox.

For why, after all, does Benjamin want to insist on this figure of
the self as a fundamental and irresolvable paradox? I shall argue that
the model of the self as paradox arises from Benjamin's acceptance of
a purely negative concept of individuation as separation (self-assertion) and hence as domination, and, on the other hand, of a conception of intersubjectivity or mutual recognition as a direct and
unmediated affective relationship of mutuality with a concrete other.

Benjamin's work develops out of the conviction that the subject-
object structure of the self is a product of the failure of intersubjective relations, rather than a normal or natural condition. Thus, she
develops her position through the critique of theories of the self
which have naturalized the subject-object relationship. I've been able
to distinguish at least three different arguments, which Benjamin
directs against Freud, ego psychologists, and Hegel. Here, I will
describe the arguments as they apply to Freud.

First of all, there's a critique of the conception of human nature—of the assumption of a fundamental desire for negation of the other. Freud argued that the human infant is primarily motivated by aggressive, selfish drives for pleasure and destruction—for pleasure and death, or the end of pain. Given this conception of human nature, Freud can understand the development of sociality only in terms of an internalization of the father's authority: if we're primarily aggressive, selfish, and destructive, socialization consists essentially of exerting control over our basic drives, of internalizing the father to dominate the wildness in our natures.

Benjamin argues that we have to go back to the basic conception of human nature to reconceptualize the development of the self. We need to postulate not only primary aggression, not only the perception of others as objects that are merely obstacles to or instruments of one's own satisfaction, but also a primary sociality—a primary desire for interaction with others and for mutual recognition.

Secondly, drawing on Chodorow's and Gilligan's feminist theories, Benjamin criticizes Freud's assumption that the normative goal of self-development is separation—i.e., that self-development entails a transition from a state of connectedness or non-differentiation to a state of separation or independence. The assumption is that to become subjects, we have to break away from a state of immediacy or non-differentiation with the mother; we have to move from a state of suffocating connection to a state of independent autonomy, and we can only do that through turning from mother to father, through internalizing the authority of the father. But this description of self-development completely discounts the entire pre-Oedipal process of development through interaction with and relationship to the mother. And the internalization model precludes any understanding of development through connection, or of relationship as a normative goal.

Benjamin argues that we have to reformulate the model of self-development, to see the development of the self not simply as a process of separation of subject from object, but as a process of relationship with other subjects. So the normative goal should be not the achievement of a separate, autonomous self but rather the achievement of intersubjectivity and the capacity for relationship.

Thirdly, following Habermas, Benjamin argues that Freud naturalizes the structure of domination, because he assumes a transcendental antagonism between subject and object. There's a reductive equation of external nature and internal nature, other subjects and social institutions: these are all lumped together into the category of "object," which exists in a relationship of fundamental contradiction, fundamental opposition to the subject.

Benjamin argues that we need to understand human development not in terms of a transcendental subject-object opposition, but in terms of intersubjective relationships.

All of these criticisms are promising, but Benjamin's own theory of intersubjectivity is disappointing. For Benjamin, "intersubjective theory expands and complements [separation-individuation theory], by focusing on the *affective* content of the mother-child exchange" [31]. Rather than focussing on the child's separation from the mother, intersubjective theory focusses on "the sense of shared feeling," on the "emotional attunement" between mother and child, self and other. "Intersubjective theory introduces attunement, or the lack of it, as an important concept" [31]. So for Benjamin, subjects can be intersubjectively related only through the dimension of affect; shared feeling and emotions are the only mediating force. Thus for her, recognition is always and only affective recognition.

"At the same time," Benjamin argues, "the awareness of separate minds and the desire for attunement raises the possibility of a new kind of conflict." The "core conflict between assertion and recognition" arises in the clash between the child's wish to fulfill his own desire (self-assertion) and the wish to remain in accord with the parents' will (attunement) [31].

It seems to me that Benjamin sees this conflict as an ineradicable paradox precisely because she defines intersubjectivity only in affective terms, as attunement or shared feeling; thus, there is no real basis for *mediation* between the wills of self and other. I want to argue that Benjamin falls back on this idea of intersubjectivity as emotional attunement because she accepts a concept of the autonomous self as a form of domination. One of the roots of this concept can be found in Benjamin's acceptance of Simone de Beauvoir's account of self-development and gender identity in *The Second Sex*.

In the introduction to her book, Benjamin notes that she takes as her starting point Simone de Beauvoir's analysis of gender relations in terms of a subject-object, or self-other, relation.

> The point of departure for this reexamination of the problem of
> domination is Simone de Beauvoir's insight: that woman func-
> tions as man's primary other, his opposite—playing nature to his
> reason, immanence to his transcendence, primordial oneness to
> his individuated separateness, and object to his subject. [7]

Curiously, Benjamin does not mention that her argument also pre-
supposes a feminist critique of de Beauvoir's model of subject development. Many feminist critics have pointed out that while de
Beauvoir criticizes the subject-object structure of *gender relations,*
she fails to criticize the assumption that the subject-object structure
is essential to *self-development.* De Beauvoir argues that the self can
be posited only through opposition to, and negation of, an other;
thus, if women are to assume full subjectivity, women must join in
the battle, as it were, and define themselves as subjects against an
object/other. Against this position, Benjamin's work develops out of
a tradition of feminist theory that criticizes the assumption that the
self must be posited through opposition to an other, and argues that
we need to understand the self not in terms of opposition to an
object, but in terms of relationship to other subjects. However, while
the necessity, universality, and transhistoricality that de Beauvoir
claims for the subject-object model are sharply criticized, the accu-
racy, and adequacy, of the model as a description of (modern) male
self-development is often uncritically accepted as a fundamental
truth. Thus, for Benjamin, the normal development of the male subject is accurately described as a process of repression, domination,
and negation of the other.

One critical link between Benjamin's understanding of the self and
de Beauvoir's is the work of Nancy Chodorow. As I have argued,
Chodorow, far from criticizing de Beauvoir's subject-object model of
self-development, accepts it as an accurate description of the development of masculine autonomy. And Benjamin uncritically accepts
Chodorow's analysis of the development of gender identity, which
she summarizes as follows:

> Since women have almost everywhere been the primary caretak-
> ers of small children, both boys and girls have differentiated in
> relation to a woman—the mother. When we look to the typical

course of male differentiation, we see at once that this creates a special difficulty for boys. While all children identify with their first loved one, boys must dissolve this identification and define themselves as the different sex. Initially all infants feel themselves to be like their mothers. But boys discover that they cannot grow up to *become* her; they can only have her. This discovery leads to a break in identification for boys which girls are spared. Male children achieve their masculinity by denying their original identification or oneness with their mothers. [75]

Thus, Benjamin accepts Chodorow's analysis of self-development and gender relations in terms of the categories of identification and "disidentification".[6] And Benjamin understands her own categories of self-assertion and recognition to be interchangeable with Chodorow's categories of identification and disidentification, or separation and connection.[7]

Following Chodorow, then, Benjamin argues that the fact of women's primary responsibility for childcare is sufficient to explain the development of gender identity in terms of a dialectic of separation and connection, which in turn produces male domination and female submission. This explanation entails a series of problematic assumptions. Individuation is equated with separation, and separation is equated with domination. And this process of individuation via separation as domination can only be balanced by a maintenance of primary unmediated connection, an emotional attunement, which is equated by Benjamin with recognition.

Benjamin describes the process of male self-development, and accounts for male domination, as follows:

The boy develops his gender and identity by means of establishing discontinuity and difference from the person to whom he is most attached. This process of disidentification explains the repudiation of the mother that underlies conventional masculine identity formation. [75–76]

The key word here is "explains": for Benjamin, as for Chodorow, the repudiation of the mother which underlies male domination is adequately accounted for by the fact that boys must separate or disidentify from their mothers. Thus, she argues, "the fact of women's mothering ... explains masculine sadism" [78]. At times, Benjamin comes close to claiming that this process of male self-development through separation-domination is an inevitable result of the natural, and unchangeable, fact that it is women who bear children. "The assignment of subject status to male and object status to female follows from the seemingly unavoidable fact that the boy must struggle free with all the violence of a second birth from the woman who bore him. In this second birth, the fantasy of omnipotence and erotic domination begins" [81]. More consistently, however, Benjamin stresses that this is a social, not a natural, fact: male domination is not inevitable but a result of the fact that in most societies mothers are the primary caretakers of children.[8] In any case, she accepts the equation of separation from the mother and male domination, and she shifts this equation into the framework of her theory of mutual recognition, and its failure: separation from the mother is now understood as a replacement of mutual recognition with a subject-object relation.

> The need to sever the identification with the mother in order to
> be confirmed both as a separate person and as a male person ...
> often prevents the boy from recognizing the mother.... An
> objectifying attitude comes to replace the earliest interactions of
> infancy in which mutual recognition and proud assertion could
> still coexist. [76]

Here (once again) Benjamin's explanation begs the question as to *why* the severance of primary identification should necessarily produce an objectifying (and hence dominating) attitude. The causal relation is simply assumed.

> In breaking the identification with and dependency on mother,
> the boy is in danger of losing his capacity for mutual recognition
> altogether. The emotional attunement and bodily harmony that
> characterized his infantile exchange with mother now threaten
> his identity.... When this relationship with the other as object is
> generalized, rationality substitutes for affective exchange with the
> other. [76]

Here, rationality is seen as the denial and repression of mutual recognition or intersubjectivity, which Benjamin equates with "emotional attunement," "bodily harmony," and "affective exchange." So, male identity is established through separation from the mother, which produces objectification and the development of rationality, which are equated with domination.

In her concluding chapter, "Gender and Domination," Benjamin outlines the effects of this path of male development on modern society. The form of modern domination which Max Weber and the early Frankfurt theorists identified as rationalization can, she argues, be traced to the development of the male self through repudiation of the mother.

> Feminist criticism in many disciplines has demonstrated that the concept of the individual is really a concept of the male subject. Likewise I will argue that the principle of rationality which social theorists since Weber have seen as the hallmark of modernity—the rationality that reduces the social world to objects of exchange, calculation, and control—is in fact a male rationality. Rationalization, at the societal level, sets the stage for a form of domination that appears to be gender-neutral, indeed, to have no subject at all. Yet its logic dovetails with the oedipal denial of woman's subjectivity, which reduces the other to object. [184–85]

Benjamin argues that in the modern world, the two principles of self-assertion and recognition have been split between the public world of men and the private world of women and children.

> The psychic repudiation of femininity, which includes the negation of dependency and mutual recognition, is homologous with the social banishment of nurturance and intersubjective relatedness to the private domestic world of women and children. The social separation of private and public spheres—long noted by feminists as the crucial form of the sexual division of labor and thus the social vehicle of gender domination—is patently linked to the split between the father of autonomy and the mother of dependency. [185]

Again, Benjamin attributes this split to a breakdown of tension. Thus, "the principle of pure self-assertion comes to govern the public world of men," and "private life ... preserves authorship and recognition" [185]. But the instrumental principles based on self-assertion, which dominate the public world, also subvert the values of private life, and thus threaten "the maternal aspects of recognition: nurturance (the recognition of need), and attunement (the recognition of feeling)" [185].

In arguing that the increasing rationalization of modern society has driven recognition out of the public world and into the private, Benjamin gives the distinct impression that she believes that there was a time when human beings were more truly recognized as themselves in the public sphere. More importantly, Benjamin makes it clear that her model of recognition is based on an ideal of maternal nurturance. Recognition, for Benjamin, is the maternal care for the needs and feelings of particular others, which only happens, and then only if we're lucky, in the private realm. Thus, because "the public world is conceived as a place in which direct recognition and care for others' needs is impossible" [197], the recognition of others does not occur in the public world. "The public sphere, an arrangement of atomized selves, cannot serve as the space between self and other, as an intersubjective space; in order to protect the autonomy of the individual, social life forfeits the recognition between self and other" [197].

Thus, for Benjamin, recognition is the direct apprehension of the needs and feelings of particular others. And this form of recognition is diametrically opposed to, indeed precluded by, the apprehension of human beings as autonomous individuals. The apprehension of another person as an autonomous individual does not count, for Benjamin, as a form of recognition. But this introduces serious problems into a theory of mutual recognition. For any recognition of another which does not take into account the other's *autonomy* thereby reserves the capacity for interpretation solely for the subject-observer—for, in this case, the mother. In this sense, this "maternalistic" recognition of the particular needs and feelings of the other corresponds to a paternalistic recognition of others' particularities (for example, their color, their gender, their social position) as the basis for extension and limitation of privileges. The move beyond paternalism and maternalism requires a recognition of others as autonomous subjects capable of critical reflection—capable, in particular, of interpreting and defining what their own needs and feelings are, and of deciding which particularities they want recognized. Thus the modern ideal of the autonomy of the individual, which underlies the principle of universal equal rights, can be understood as upholding the right of each person—each "other"—to be recognized as capable of making her or his own choices, and of participating in public dialogue on that basis. And surely this is the only legitimate basis for the public recognition of not only individual but collective particularities: social groups (such as women, blacks, natives, gays, and of course, all of the groups within the groups) must be recognized as capable of participating in the determination of which particularities they want recognized, and what form that recognition should take—must be recognized, then, as legitimate participants in a public dialogue.

But for Benjamin, the abstraction from particularities, from direct and immediate recognition, to "formal legal principles of equality and justice" which uphold the equal rights of autonomous individuals, is the crux of male violence and domination. "It is difficult to grasp the fact that the center of male domination lies not in direct expressions of personal violence (rampant though they are) but in the societal rationality which may or may not be defended by men. Male domination, as Weber said of rationalization, works through the hegemony of impersonal organization: of formal rules that refer to the hypothetical interaction of autonomous individuals" [216]. Thus, Benjamin argues, theorists like Catharine MacKinnon do not go far enough in their argument that "formal legal principles of equality and justice" work to cover up male violence and domination. In fact, these principles, enshrined in "impersonal legal structures," are not merely a cover for violence: rather, they are themselves the prime expression of male violence [216].

Again, it is the impersonality, the abstraction from particularities to universal principles, which Benjamin perceives as an act of domination. And she cites the work of Evelyn Fox Keller and Carol Gilligan as corroborating the view that domination can be traced back to a form of self-development that has been centred on the goal of separation, rather than on the preservation of connections. Gilligan, she argues, "shows how Kohlberg's conception of moral reasoning is grounded in a notion of abstract formal recognition independent of specific needs or ties" [194]: the other is recognized only as having the same rights as the self. Thus, in Kohlberg's model, "the particular other is subsumed by the universal 'generalized other'" [194]. But, as I have argued, only the recognition of others as having universal, equal rights to determine and articulate *which* particularities they want recognized can ensure the fair recognition of others as not only generalized but concrete, particular others, in a way that avoids the maternalism/paternalism of deciding for others which of their particularities will be recognized, and how. Thus, Gilligan's "ethics of care and responsibility" is, arguably, a more self-centred ethics than the "ethics of rights and justice" she criticizes, for only the latter explicitly grants to *others* the capacity to make their own moral choices.

Benjamin's alignment of autonomy, rights, and justice with the affirmation of pure self-assertion is the effect of the absence of a concept of mediation in her theory. Her model of the self lacks any theory of how a subject can move from the clash between "pure self-assertion" and "direct recognition" to the capacity to act responsibly to both self and others as a participant in a social world. Such a theory of mediation can be provided by a concept of autonomy as a capacity for participation, which includes a capacity to interpret, abstract from, and reflect upon particularities through an appeal to universal principles—which includes, therefore, a capacity for critique. Because she defines autonomy only negatively, as self-assertion and separation, rather than as the capacity to participate in a social world, Benjamin falls back on emotional attunement as the only available mediating force—but it is a force incapable of mediating the paradox of the self.

As I have argued, the separation/identification model is inadequate to explain the development of masculine autonomy. The inadequacy of the model is further evident in Benjamin's description of female self-development. In contrast to the boy, she notes, a girl "requires no such shift in identification away from her mother. This makes her identity less problematic, but it is a disadvantage in that she possesses no obvious way of disidentifying from her mother, no hallmark of separateness" [78]. But what kind of "identity" are we talking about here? Feminine identity is apparently indistinguishable from primary identification. And indeed, Benjamin defines identity solely in terms of identification. Gender identity, she argues, is explained by the fact that "girls sustain the primary identification with the mother while boys must switch to an identification with the father" [90]. Thus, against Freud's attempt to theorize feminine gender identity as socially and symbolically mediated, Benjamin accepts the counter-claim (made by Chodorow and others) that "girls develop their femininity through direct identification with the mother" [91].

Even when Benjamin attempts to go beyond the analysis of feminine gender identity as a product of direct identification, to inquire into "women's desire," she in fact remains within the identification paradigm: she argues that girls want to identify with the father as a model of separate subjectivity or autonomy, but when the father fails to recognize his daughter as a separate subject like himself, the girl takes up the position of sexual object, as compensation: unable to be a subject, she settles for having (or being had) by one. Correspondingly, Benjamin argues that the girl's "identity" as object, rather than subject, is in fact established through identification with the mother's lack of self, and lack of desire. "Thus, the fact of women's mothering not only explains masculine sadism, it also reveals a 'fault line' in female development that leads to masochism" [78].

The upshot of all this is that both girls and boys need to be able to recognize and directly identify with both mother and father as separate autonomous subjects. Given the current structure of gender relations, boys assert their own separate selfhood only by denying the mother's separate subjectivity, and girls never assert themselves, but simply identify with the mother's lack of self. Neither girls nor boys are able to recognize the mother as a separate, autonomous self—and this, Benjamin argues, is precisely because she isn't one.

The only solution Benjamin can come up with is that mothers need to BE subjects. But while it is probably true that being a subject is a prerequisite to being recognized as one, this fails to address the problems of what it means to be a subject, how women are to become subjects (if indeed they are not subjects already), and what it means to recognize another person as a subject. The assumption, apparently, is that once one is a subject one will automatically be recognized as one.

The relationship to the father raises the opposite problem. Fathers are recognized as autonomous subjects; the problem is establishing some sort of connection with them. Benjamin argues that both boys and girls want to identify with their fathers, who represent autonomy and separation. Against the Oedipal model, which too often defines the boy's identification with his father as a defensive identification based on repudiation of the mother, Benjamin wants to develop the importance of narcissistic identification as a positive, pleasureable element of self-development. In other words, she wants to argue that the development of the self should not be seen as a process which is necessarily based on repudiation, domination, opposition to the other/object; rather, we need to see self-development in terms of a connection to another subject—a connection which is desired and pleasurable. Thus, she is attempting to develop a theory of motivation for and pleasure in self-development, through a theory of intersubjectivity as a desire for recognition, a desire both to recognize and to be recognized. Against the stoic/tragic model of self-development as a version of the Fall, against the view that autonomy is established only through the repression of desire, pleasure, nature, Benjamin wants to argue that we *want* autonomy, *want* to be recognized as autonomous subjects. Here, then, her solution to the opposition between autonomy and attunement, separation and connection, self-assertion and recognition, is to theorize the development of autonomy in terms of positive affect.[9]

But, only the affect is "positive." The autonomy which the father represents (and which the mother should represent)—the symbolic meaning of the father—is still, for Benjamin, only the negative freedom of separation. Autonomy is defined as independence, separation, and, occasionally, as confrontation with "the outside world." This version of autonomy inevitably clashes with a capacity for relationship with or recognition of others—and is then, by definition, opposed to intersubjectivity. Thus, it is Benjamin's acceptance of a definition of autonomy as negative freedom which produces the paradox which she believes to be fundamental to the self. But in fact, separation, far from being definitive of autonomy, is only one moment in the development of autonomy. Once autonomy is understood to entail not just the negative freedom of separation but the capacity to participate in a social world, a capacity which requires a cognitive development—the learning of social roles and norms, as the basis of a capacity for reflection—then it is no longer necessary to fall back on emotional attunement and primary identification as the only possible medium of human connection, or intersubjectivity. It is then possible to see affective relations as necessary but not sufficient criteria for intersubjectivity.

This requires, I think, an understanding of the development of the self not only in affective terms, through a model of identification, but in cognitive and normative terms, through a model of internalization. As Jürgen Habermas points out, both Freud and G.H. Mead use the concept of internalization to account for the social constitution of the autonomous self.[10]

But Benjamin resists any recourse to a theory of internalization for an understanding of the relationship of autonomy and intersubjectivity. For Benjamin, the theory of internalization is in fact a theory of domination.

> Most of psychoanalytic theory has been formulated in terms of the isolated subject and his internalization of what is outside to develop what is inside. Internalization implies that the other is consumed, incorporated, digested by the subject self. [43].[11]

Thus, the other is merely used by the subject as an instrument of self-development, as a means of separation, and is not recognized as an other independent self. And thus, internalization theory upholds an ideal of a subject who develops in opposition to, or through the use of, an object. In contrast to internalization theory, Benjamin argues, intersubjective theory emphasizes "the joy and urgency of discovering the external, independent reality of another person" [44].

The affective recognition of the reality of the other is indeed an important aspect of self-development, which has indeed been underemphasized by many theorists. But by defining internalization as domination, Benjamin merely conflates domination and mediation, and thus rejects mediation as a form of domination. Thus, Benjamin's claim that internalization is the consumption of the other by the self in fact amounts to an equation of the sociality of the self with domination. For with her rejection of the theory of internalization as a theory of consumption, Benjamin rejects a theory of the socially mediated development of the self, in favor of a concept of a self which simply asserts itself, and requires acknowledgement of its self-assertion.

And what, after all, is Benjamin's conception of subjectivity? It will be recalled that Benjamin's central thesis is that the subject-object structure of gender relations—that is, male domination and female subordination—is a product of failed intersubjective relations, and that this failure can be traced back to the failure to recognize the mother as a subject. But what does it mean to be—and to recognize another person as—a subject?

Benjamin begins with a concept of the self which is not constituted but which simply asserts itself. This primary, *a priori* self requires the attentiveness or direct acknowledgement of the other in order to flourish. And this attentiveness or acknowledgement is what Benjamin understands to be recognition. At one point, she compares recognition with sunlight: "Recognition might be compared to that essential element in photosynthesis, sunlight, which provides the energy for the plant's constant transformation of substance" [22]. Elsewhere, she calls it love, or the gratification of identificatory (narcissistic) love [146]. Moreover, the self is immediately capable of recognizing itself and the other as a subject. Benjamin argues that, against a theory of internalization, we need to understand subjectivity as something that is pre-given and apprehended directly and immediately by the subject herself. In Winnicott's theory, she argues, "Reality is thus *discovered* rather than *imposed;* and authentic selfhood is not absorbed from without but discovered within" [41]. Similarly, the subjectivity of the other is something that is directly and immediately "discovered" [44].

Thus, Benjamin sets up an opposition between internalization theory and intersubjective theory that is based on the assumptions that intersubjective theory requires seeing all human interactions—including those between parents and babies—as reciprocal interactions between subjects, and in turn on the assumption that to take an "objectifying perspective" toward a person is always bad.

Benjamin makes the mistake of assuming that an intersubjective theory of self-development requires not only the assumption that human beings are fundamentally social, and that mutual recognition is a human need and normative goal, but that human beings are born ready-made subjects with the capacity to recognize themselves and others as subjects. Intersubjective theory, she says, is based on the premise that "from the beginning there are always (at least) two subjects" [24].

> The intersubjective view maintains that the individual grows in and through the relationship to other subjects. Most important, this perspective observes that the other whom the self meets is also a self, a subject in his or her own right. It assumes that we are able and need to recognize that other subject as different and yet alike, as an other who is capable of sharing similar mental experience. Thus the idea of intersubjectivity reorients the conception of the psychic world from a subject's relations to its object toward a subject meeting another subject. [18–19]

> In this sense, notwithstanding the inequality between parent and child, recognition must be mutual and allow for the assertion of each self. [24]

But the assumption that to recognize the other as a subject is a human social need or a normative ideal in no way entails the assumption that we are born with the ability to do so. And this seems to be exactly what Benjamin wants to claim. As already noted, Benjamin argues that in the development of the male self, "an objectifying attitude comes to replace the earliest interactions of infancy in which mutual recognition and proud assertion could still coexist" [76]. And, "the boy is in danger of losing his capacity for mutual recognition" [76]. According to this analysis, the capacity for mutual recognition is an original, innate capacity, and (male) autonomy established through separation is understood as a version of the Fall, as a loss of the original capacity for mutual recognition or intersubjectivity.

Moreover, as the above citations indicate, objectification is seen by Benjamin as, by definition, a form of domination. Intersubjective theory entails always seeing human relationships as relationships between subjects; internalization theory introduces an "objectifying attitude," whereby the subject is seen as developing in relation to an object—thus, internalization theory is merely a repetition of the attitude taken by the boy toward the mother from whom he has "disidentified."

For Benjamin, then, intersubjectivity entails remaining in the dyad of I and Thou, of two selves mutually recognizing each other as particular, concrete selves. Once the objectifying, generalizing, third-person perspective entailed by internalization is introduced, intersubjectivity is destroyed.

In contrast to Benjamin's understanding of internalization as domination, Freud conceives of internalization as mediation. For Freud, the process of internalization is essential to the *constitution* of a self. The passage from drive-governed and instrumental behavior to the capacity to participate as a subject in a social world requires the ability to take an objectifying, third-person perspective, which is in fact the perspective of the first person plural, or "We"—the perspective of society—toward oneself and others. The internalization of the perspective of society is essential for what Lacan refers to as entrance into the universal symbolic order of language—that is, the capacity to communicate through reference to symbols or concepts whose meanings are shared.

The understanding of internalization as mediation is further developed by G.H. Mead. Mead views internalization as a specifically cognitive process which is necessary for the development of the capacity for reflection.

> The essence of the self ... is cognitive. It lies in the internalized conversation of gestures which constitutes thinking or in terms of which thought or reflection proceeds. And hence the origin and foundation of the self, like those of thinking, are social.[12]

For Mead, it is only through the internalization of the perspective of the other, as representative of a generalized social other, that we acquire the capacity to recognize our selves and others as subjects (in the full sense of the word) in the first place. Thus, it is only through internalization that real intersubjectivity is possible.

> The individual experiences himself as such, not directly, but only indirectly, from the particular standpoints of other individual members of the same social group or from the generalized standpoint of the social group as a whole to which he belongs. For he enters his own experience as a self or individual, not directly or immediately, not by becoming a subject to himself, but only inso-

far as he first becomes an object to himself just as other individuals are objects to him or are in his experience; and he becomes an object to himself only by taking the attitudes of other individuals toward himself within a social environment or context of experience and behavior in which both he and they are involved. [202]

Mead's argument that the recognition of the self as a subject requires that one become an object to oneself is based on his assumption that subjectivity is not a primary affective experience, but a cognitive achievement.

Such a perspective avoids the intractability of Benjamin's "paradox of the self." The self is indeed a paradox when it is conceived as a battle between the assertion of the will and the desire for attunement, the negative freedom of separation and the intimacy of affective connection. Once autonomy is conceived as separation/objectification/domination, and intersubjectivity as shared feeling, we are left with no choice but to sustain an absolute, eternal paradox. But once autonomy is conceived as a capacity for full participation in a social context—and thus entails the internalization of social roles and norms and the capacity to relate particulars to universals, and hence to appeal to principles for critical reflection—then the paradox of the self begins to look much less eternal.

4

The Subversion of Identity

Luce Irigaray and the Critique of Phallogocentrism

It is a truism that the object-relations and ego psychology of Nancy Chodorow and the poststructuralist theory of Luce Irigaray are diametrically opposed: Chodorow affirms the importance of a unified self, while Irigaray relentlessly deconstructs it. As I have tried to show, however, Chodorow's repudiation of the separate self as a product of repression of connection, and as the basis of male domination, constantly undermines her affirmation of the integrity of the self, and produces an ambivalence between an attempt to reformulate the autonomous self and a rejection of autonomy as a goal. Ultimately, Chodorow tends to reject individual autonomy in favor of a self which is fundamentally connected to and in fact indistinguishable from the mother. At the root of this tendency is, I argue, a belief that the identity of the separate self is entirely a product of the repression of connection. This goes along with a belief that separation and connection are fundamentally opposed, and a belief that male subjectivity, as separate self-identity, is reducible to a form of violence. Thus, ironically, Chodorow agrees with Simone de Beauvoir that individuation is a masculine prerogative, and that it is necessarily an act of domination.

In this chapter and the next, I will show that the repudiation of identity in the work of Luce Irigaray, as well as that of Judith Butler and other poststructuralist theorists, not only shares the same roots as Chodorow's critique of the separate self, but produces the same paradox: the reduction of identity to repression means that any attempt to affirm any form of identity is rendered paradoxical.

Thus, against the assumption that Chodorow's "cultural" feminism and Irigaray's and Butler's subversions of identity are fundamentally opposed,[1] I want to argue that both positions are based in a critique of identity as a form of violence, domination and repression.[2]

I shall begin with a reading of Irigaray's work which will focus on its similarity to Chodorow's: in particular, I shall argue that Irigaray is not only a theorist of difference, and *différance,* but is also a theorist of connection, and relationship. Thus in Irigaray's work we can see the link between Chodorow's relational feminist critique of the separate self as a source of violence and the Derridean poststructuralist critique of the violence of identity.[3]

Like Nancy Chodorow, Luce Irigaray locates the origins of the separate male self in a denial of connection to the mother. In her critique of Freud, Irigaray argues that the establishment of the unified self, symbolized by the phallus, is in fact a defense against relationship, first to the mother and subsequently to others. And this defensive unity serves to repress desire for and dread of the mother. But Irigaray links this denial of connection to the mother to the repression of negativity, nonidentity, and *différance* which, for Derrida, characterizes the phallogocentric identitarian logic of western thought and culture. Irigaray rereads Derrida's description of the binary logic of identity as a description of the relation of the masculine unified subject to the feminine Other. And like Derrida, Irigaray wavers between the assertion that this Other is only the projected opposite of the Self-Same, and the need to claim that there is an actual otherness which is variously appropriated, assimilated, excluded, and repressed in the service of the maintenance of the Self-Same. Like Derrida, Irigaray develops her position through a series of readings of the texts of western philosophy, demonstrating the obsessive repetition of the logic of the Same in each text.

In her book, *Speculum of the Other Woman,* Irigaray reads Plato's allegory of the cave in *The Republic* as the story of man's repression of his connection to the mother. But the focus here is on *bodily* connection—and what man represses in his search for ideal Truth is his origin in the female body. For Plato the men chained in the cave, seeing only the flickering shadows of reality, represent human beings fixed on the plane of appearances, able to see only material things, which are mere reflections, mere copies of the Ideal. Irigaray agrees with Plato that men are unable to know reality; but she argues, giving a feminist twist to materialist critiques of Platonic idealism, and to the Nietzschean-Freudian critique of the will to Truth as a will to power, that the reality men are unable to know is the reality of human origin in female bodies. The cave which for Plato is a prison is the body, and in particular, the origin of all bodies: the womb. Man's quest for Truth, then, is a relentless struggle to escape and repress his origins in the womb. But Irigaray's position is not quite so simple as a repudiation of the repression of the body by the mind: what she's criticizing here is the refusal to *reflect* on embodiment. Unable to reflect, man is unable to find a path that might link the two worlds—the Ideal and the merely real. Because what is repressed, according to Irigaray's reading, is not only the womb but the vagina, the birth passage, which might represent a path of transition, a connecting link between worlds. What is repressed, then, is connection. In a phallic economy, the vagina is merely a sheath for the penis, merely the negative—a penis turned inside out. Thus, its function as a means of *connection* is repressed, and so is *feminine specificity:* the *difference* of the female body is reduced to a mere mirror-image inversion of the male body.

Irigaray's critique of the representation of the vagina as only a mirror-image of the penis echoes Derrida's critique of the phallogocentric identitarian logic of binary opposites: the other is merely the other of the same, and the *différance,* the relationality, which underlies identity is repressed. For Derrida's concept of *différance,* derived from Saussure's understanding of language as a system of relationships among terms, is very much a concept of repressed relationality: of an infinite relationality which is repressed by the oppositional logic of the Same and its Other.[4] But for Irigaray, what the logic of identity represses is the connection to and the specificity of the maternal and/or female body.

Irigaray continues this line of thought through her analyses, in *Speculum,* of the development of western culture. When the Copernican revolution and the fathers of modern science turn the world upside down, the womb/cave/female body is no longer simply denied and repressed, but is forcibly entered and thoroughly examined—with the same results. Now it is the specular logic, the logic of the gaze, of looker and looked-at, subject and object, which represses any connection between the two. The scientist fails to recognize feminine difference; he appropriates it as nothing but an object of his knowledge. Or, alternatively, he sees there nothing but his own reflection.

Similarly, Freud uncovers the unconscious merely to make it conform to the phallogocentric laws of knowledge and truth. Psychoanalysis is seen as a rape: the feminine unconscious is thoroughly interrogated, its secrets uncovered by the man who must know all—but he never sees what's really there. What he sees is Nothing. Lack. Absence. Into which he projects his own Truth: the unconscious he discovers is always only his own. Thus, he resolves her nonidentity into his identity.

Hegel's account, in the *Phenomenology*, of the Greek transition from matriarchal to patriarchal order, as seen through Sophocles' *Antigone*, is read by Irigaray as a rather melancholic rationalization and affirmation of the repression of blood ties—of the earthly, fluid, bodily connection to the mother—for an identity marked by the Name of the Father. This repression entails neither disavowal nor projection, but assimilation: "The man (father) will persevere in developing his individualization by *assimilating* the external other into and for the self"; "The Father-king [Creon] will repeat the rupture of (living) exchange between man and woman by sublating it into his discourse."[5] But the other cannot be assimilated and sublated without being destroyed. "*At the heart of the dialectic is hypochondria, melancholia*. It can be linked to a clot of blood"—the hardening of the fluids, a clot of blood, represented by the stone which closes Antigone's cave: "the space in which femininity dies" [222]. Drained of blood—the blood that has been used to nourish "the universal consciousness of self"—woman becomes merely man's unconscious, his negative, and, as such, his mediation [225]. (This theme—the replacement of the *connection*, the fluidity of blood ties, with a solidity produced by an abstract *mediation*—is one we will return to. At this point it should be noted that Irigaray's stress on the repression of the fluidity of blood is more Nietzschean than Hegelian.)

Irigaray's readings of the texts of western culture recall de Beauvoir's: woman is defined always and only as the Other, the object, the negative, the inessential—always only in relation to Man. Like de Beauvoir, Irigaray criticizes the construction of woman as Eternal Other, which Man needs in order to affirm him-Self as sovereign, universal, and singular. But while de Beauvoir argues that equality can come only when women succeed in affirming their own sovereign subjectivity through the same oppositional logic—through a struggle for freedom from the immanence of their bodies, and through positing themselves against other subjects—Irigaray argues that this oppositional logic which underlies the positing of identity is a specifically masculine logic which cannot accommodate a reciprocity between male and female, but which in fact depends upon the exclusion, construction, appropriation, assimilation, commodification, and destruction of woman's otherness. The denial and disavowal of woman's body is necessary to the Platonic ideal; the reduction of that body to an object is necessary for the establishment of the male subject as knower; the assimilation of woman's otherness is necessary for the construction of man's unified and universal self; and this self requires the projection of man's own otherness, or of his need for an other, onto woman—the construction of her "otherness," which is only a reflection of himself. In Irigaray's words, "any theory of the subject has always been appropriated by the 'masculine'" [133].

But at the heart of each of these analyses lies a fundamental ambiguity: is Irigaray arguing that male thought represses a real female otherness, or is she arguing that what is repressed is the spectre of femininity and maternity, a feminine otherness imagined by men? Is it woman's otherness that is assimilated or appropriated to form the male unconscious, or is man's unconscious projected onto woman? Does the investigation of woman's body and the analysis of her psyche entail a failure to recognize women's true otherness, or simply a projection of man's otherness onto woman? The question is, is there a real woman behind the texts? Is there an essential Woman as Other behind the masculine projections of otherness? Irigaray is almost always ambiguous about this, and she wants the question to be left unresolved. But a considerable amount of scholarship has been directed toward finding the answer to the question: is Irigaray or is she not an "essentialist"? The question is typically posed like this: Is Irigaray following a Derridean program of deconstruction, speaking in a doubled and ironic voice, deploying the concept of "woman" strategically with the aim of subverting it, speaking the language of phallogocentrism only to undermine and implode it from within? Or does she really think there are women, really? The right answer, as we shall see, is "both at once." But the posing of the question in terms of an opposition between Derridean deconstruction and essentialism overlooks the fact that for Derrida, too, the line between pure deconstruction and essentialism is not so clear: as I argued in chapter one, there is an absolute or essential otherness lurking behind Derrida's attempt to deconstruct all essences. Moreover, as a number of theorists have pointed out, there is an Absolute Woman lurking behind Derrida's deconstruction of her.[6]

That said, it is impossible to deny Irigaray's very explicit focus on the specificity of the female *body* as the incarnation of nonidentity or *différance*. Certainly, the question as to whether there is a real woman behind the texts seems to be answered in Irigaray's celebrated and notorious "two lips" manifesto, where she makes the rather flagrant and scandalizing claim that woman's body is inherently multiple, nonidentical and connected, while man's body leads him inexorably into instrumental and dominating reason.

> Thus, for example, woman's autoeroticism is very different from man's. In order to touch himself, man needs an instrument: his hand, a woman's body, language.... And this self-caressing requires at least a minimum of activity. As for woman, she touches herself in and of herself without any need for mediation, and before there is any way to distinguish activity from passivity. Woman "touches herself" all the time, and moreover no one can forbid her to do so, for her genitals are formed of two lips in continuous contact. Thus, within herself, she is already two—but not divisible into one(s)—that caress each other.[7]

Thus, Irigaray associates the female body with nonidentity, *différance*, connectedness, and the male body with identity, unity, and instrumental mediation. For Irigaray, these two bodies correspond to two different logics, associated with the two primary operations of language identified by Roman Jakobson: metaphor and metonymy. The male body corresponds to the logic of *metaphor,* of sameness and substitution, and the female body corresponds to the logic of *metonymy,* of proximity, nearness, contiguity.

There are at least four ways of interpreting Irigaray's association of the logic of metonymy with the female body. First, there is the *literal* interpretation: Irigaray is saying that women are anatomically predisposed to relationality whereas men are predisposed to instrumental domination. This claim contradicts Irigaray's argument that the masculine obsession with unity entails a *repression* of connection, difference, and nonidentity—a repression which requires constant struggle. If men are already "unified," there would seem to be no need for such a struggle. The fact that these two positions are contradictory, however, provides no assurance that Irigaray does not hold both at once. Second, there is the *metaphoric* interpretation: Irigaray uses the female body as a metaphor for the relational logic of metonymy. This explanation would conflict with Irigaray's repudiation of metaphor as a logic of domination, but, once again, we can't necessarily rule it out. This leads to the third possibility: that Irigaray is arguing for a relation between the female body and metonymic logic and language which is neither literal nor metaphoric, but which is itself *metonymic.*[8] This interpretation is the one most consistent with Irigaray's theory, the most intriguing, and the most difficult to make sense of. Finally, Irigaray's association of the female body and metonymy may be purely *strategic,* an ironic or parodic response to Lacan's obsession with the phallus as the mark of unity. Irigaray's version of *mimesis*—the assumption of the position constructed as feminine, in order to deconstruct it—would fit into this category. All of these intepretations probably have some validity. And Irigaray means for us to understand everything she says as "double-voiced." Or triple or quadruple ... multiple. What does seem to be clear is that Irigaray invokes the image of a subversive female body as the model of an alternative logic, a non-repressive logic which is an alternative to the logic of the Same.

The focus on the question of bodily essentialism has tended to distract attention from an analysis and critique of the nature of this otherness that Irigaray wants the feminine body, in whatever fashion, to evoke. I now want to turn to a closer examination of this other logic, this logic of metonymy, connection, nonidentity, which Irigaray wants to uphold against the logic of metaphor, mediation, and identity.

Connection vs. Mediation: Irigaray's Critique of Lacan and the Dream of an Other Language

As I have argued, for Irigaray, the multiplicity, nonidentity, and constant negativity of *différance* are always tied up with relationality, and with woman's difference. Like Chodorow, Irigaray defines woman's difference as her connectedness or relationality, which is repressed in the service of man's identity, his separate, unitary self. Irigaray associates this dominant masculine identity with the dominance of metaphor in language—the emphasis on substitution, identity, sameness—and she upholds metonymy as a counter-logic. But for Irigaray, metonymy ceases to be simply a linguistic operation. Metonymy becomes the basis of a form of human relationship—a relationship wherein subjects need not define themselves as the same as each other in order to communicate, but can accept each other's difference and simply be near each other, close to each other, touching but neither merging nor opposed.

As we have seen, Irigaray tends to locate this capacity for metonymic connection in the female body, and to posit it against a masculine preoccupation with *mediation*. In Hegel's Antigone story, woman is forced to *be* mediation, to unify human and divine law, individual and community, the male self with himself and with the universal. But in becoming the mediation of differences into a unity, she disappears. The connection she embodies is used to produce unity between opposites, and is thereby destroyed.

Similarly, referring to Lévi-Strauss's thesis that culture is inaugurated and maintained through the exchange of women, Irigaray argues that culture as we know it is fundamentally "hom(m)osexual": women serve only to *mediate* men's relations among themselves. "Woman exists only as an occasion for mediation, transaction, transition, transference, between man and his fellow man, indeed between man and himself."[9]

Again, Irigaray brings it back to the body, claiming that only men have a "need for mediation": "in order to touch himself man needs an instrument" [24]. Woman has no need for mediation, for her body is already relational, already incorporates a metonymic logic of closeness, proximity. Mediation is unnecessary when you already have connection. Moreover, she argues that women's autoeroticism "is disrupted by a violent break-in: the brutal separation of the two lips by a violating penis" [24]. But what is experienced as an intrusion by women is, for man "the encounter with the totally other" necessary for his self-mediation [24].

Irigaray uses this concept of mediation to unify several different ideas: instrumental mediation, the violent use of force, the intervention of an external element which breaks up a dyad, the exchange of commodities which functions to unify a community, the dialectical mediation of opposites, the recognition of self through the mediation of an other, and the substitutional logic of metaphor.

The link between all these ideas is Lacan's reading of the Oedipal phase as the entry into the symbolic order of language. The child's "entry into language" requires the intervention of the "third term" represented by the father/phallus, symbol of the symbolic order, to disrupt the child's fantasy of undifferentiated unity with its mother, to force the child out of its immersion in its body and into the realm of signification, and meaning. Lacan's understanding of language as mediation is particularly Hegelian. For Lacan, language, as the medium of intersubjective communication, is the universal which mediates particulars (i.e., it is that which all have in common and which makes mutual understanding possible). And the capacity to understand and use language requires a break from immediacy—to learn a language is to move from being a creature of needs (and of images) to the acquisition of a capacity to symbolize—to communicate needs as demands, to represent needs symbolically, in a form that can be understood by others. There is, however, always something lost in this communication: following Kojève, Lacan focuses on the alienation required for communication. Language, for Lacan, entails the symbolization of an object which is absent. And thus absence—the gap between what can be said and what is absent, unsayable—is at the center of language. And at the center of the human subject. For the identity of the subject, which is constructed only in language (only through internalization of a "universal" symbolic order) is always a divided identity, at the heart of which lies a constant absence. The acquisition of language entails the recognition and acceptance of the fact that desire cannot be satisfied.

Irigaray is arguing, against Lacan, that the development of the self—or, in any case, of the female self—does *not* require an acceptance of fundamental division which violently breaks apart a primary unity. Like both Chodorow and Benjamin, she is criticizing the representation of the pre-oedipal phase as a simple undifferentiated unity, which has to be broken in order for a separate (but in Lacan's case, fundamentally divided and hence nonidentical) self to develop. This representation of development, she argues, is based on a specifically masculine preoccupation with separation, division, and distinctness, and a specifically masculine need to reject all connection to the mother—and to re-represent this connection as an undifferentiated Whole which is an absence, hole, lack, nothing in opposition to the unitary separate self. For Irigaray, the idea of primal unity and the idea of the separate autonomous self are one and the same: both are fantasies of unity which repress difference and connection.

Thus, Irigaray's image of the two lips is a parody of Lacan's phallus fetish: for Lacan, all desire is always for the phallus—for the unattainable unity of the self, which is simply a reflection of the desire to return to a fantasied primal unity, with no want, no pain, no loss. And socialization, the entrance into the symbolic order, entails an acceptance of castration—an acceptance that one can never have, and never be, the phallus. Becoming a subject, then, means accepting the tragedy of lack. I can never have what I want. And this means accepting the Law of the Father, symbol of the prohibition of desire (which is, initially, for the mother), symbol of domination, through subjection to the order of language. But, for Irigaray, the Law of the Father and the order of language merely repeat the phallus fetish on another level.

Against the Hegelian/Lacanian conviction that the subject desires always and only unity, always and only the phallus, Irigaray argues that this phallus fetish displaces another—more originary? specifically feminine?—logic of desire. For Irigaray, this focus on the desired and impossible phallus is a particularly masculine fetish, and she counters with the image of the violent penis of mediation-as-intervention, the will to unity which breaks up the contiguous contact of the two lips. "The *one* of form, of the individual, of the (male) sexual organ, of the proper name, of the proper meaning ... supplants, while separating and dividing, that contact of *at least two* (lips)" [26]. Irigaray shares Chodorow's and Benjamin's equation of masculine identity, the identity of the self, with a violent separation and division. And like them, she wants to claim that the alternative is not immediacy, primordial merging, fusion into one. For Irigaray, this is simply another masculine fantasy of unity. Rather, there is a (not unsatisfiable) desire for and pleasure in multiplicity, a form of connection that precedes (and renders unnecessary) mediation.

In invoking metonymy as an alternative logic related to the feminine body, Irigaray is criticizing Lacan's claim that it is metaphor—the metaphor of the phallus, the "paternal metaphor"—which institutes language. For Lacan, "metaphor occurs at the precise point at which sense emerges from non-sense."[10] And this point is "the signification of paternity" [158], the birth of the capacity for abstraction (because the recognition of paternity requires a capacity to abstract from the direct bodily experience of maternity). The signification of paternity corresponds to "the poetic spark" which makes it possible for "metaphoric creation" to take place [157]. Irigaray is criticizing this claim, but she is also challenging Lacan to make the transition he himself identifies as the transition from the pre-oedipal imaginary to the symbolic order, understood as a transition from metaphor to metonymy: from the wish to have and to be the phallus (i.e., "the signifier of the desire of the Other"[11]) to the recognition that the phallus is only the signifier of an endless chain of signifiers, that behind language there is no thing that can be wholly possessed. For Lacan, metaphor and metonymy constantly interact in the processes of signification. Against Lacan, Irigaray argues that it is possible to have metonymy without the spectre of the phallus behind it. Without the metaphor, the moment of abstraction; without the tormenting and impossible desire for closure. For metonymy is already there in the feminine body. Pleasure and language are possible without the abyss, without the tragedy.

Lacanian feminists have responded that such an argument is simply a denial of the inevitability of a break with immediacy, of the entrance into language and the symbolic order, and that the claim to a communicative connection which precedes language, and which is rooted in feminine specificity, is a denial of the fact that:

> there is no pre-discursive reality ... no place prior to the law which is available and can be retrieved. And there is no feminine outside language. First, because the unconscious severs the subject from any unmediated relation to the body as such ... and secondly because the "feminine" is constituted as a division in language, a division which produces the feminine as its negative term. If woman is defined as other it is because the definition produces her as other, and not because she has another essence.[12]

Irigaray would respond that this argument falls back into the very opposition of immediacy and mediation that she is criticizing. She is not, she would say, arguing for a retreat back to the immediacy of the body, or to a primordial merging or fusion into oneness with the mother. Rather, she is criticizing the fetishization of separation, and the assumption that the passage to subjectivity is a passage from one unity to another—from the immediate unity of non-differentiation, immersion in the body, and lack of consciousness of difference, to a mediated, divided (and impossible) unity of self. This is a credible argument. But what, in fact, is Irigaray's alternative?

Rather than a transition from immediate to mediated identity, Irigaray envisions a differentiation-in-connection, a relationship between nonidentities that are already differentiated, but not different, and already connected. A "nearness so pronounced that it makes all discrimination of identity, and thus all forms of property, impossible."[13] Like Chodorow and Benjamin, Irigaray apparently believes that *relationship* is possible only once *distinctions* are blurred. The forcible intervention of phallic unity, she argues "supplants, while separating and dividing" the contact of the lips, which "keeps woman in touch with herself, but *without any possibility of distinguishing* what is touching from what is touched" [my italics]. Irigaray continues: "Whence the mystery that woman represents in a culture claiming to count everything, to number everything by units, to inventory everything as individualities. *She is neither one nor two.* Rigorously speaking, she cannot be identified either as one person, or as two. She resists all adequate definition."[14] Similarly, in *Speculum,* Irigaray writes: "For the/a woman, two does not divide into ones. Relationships defy being cut into units."[15] Relationship, then, requires a resistance to individuation.

This idea may have seemed novel once, but by now it is all too familiar, and disappointing. Like Chodorow and Benjamin, Irigaray moves from the insight that individuation in our culture too often entails a fetishization of separation and a denial of relationship to the claim that individuation and relationship are necessarily, logically, mutually exclusive. Thus, the logic of identity must be replaced with a logic of nonidentity, a relational logic which resists identity. Boundaries and distinctions are bad and connection and multiplicity are good. There is no room here for any form of identity which allows for the preservation of nonidentity—for example, of an identity of the self which could accommodate or coexist with multiple roles, affects, and relationships.

Like Chodorow, Irigaray can come up with no way to eliminate domination other than the elimination of distinction: "And how could one dominate the other? . . . One cannot be distinguished from the other."[16] At this point she equivocates, asserting just as Chodorow does that the fact that they cannot be distinguished "does not mean that they are indistinct" [209]. But she offers no explanation as to what she means by this, only a coy shrug: we cannot possibly understand, she says, and we needn't try. All we need to know is that they are Not Ones, cannot be subsumed under the logic of the Same, but are irreducibly nonidentical.

Unlike Chodorow, Irigaray links the rejection of individuality to a rejection of the universality represented by language. Language is seen as an artificial, masculine, instrumental mediation which represses real connection. "For man needs an instrument to touch himself with: a hand, a woman, or some substitute. This mechanism is sublated in and by language. Man produces language for self-arousal."[17] Language displaces relationship, replacing it with masculine autoeroticism.

In her essay, "When Our Lips Speak Together," Irigaray gives us a model of the relationship she idealizes—a relationship between women which does not require the mediation of language, for there is no need of a universal to mediate particulars. The model she presents is a lovers' discourse, and as such, it is quite lovely. But as an alternative to the Lacanian model of language, it is sadly lacking. Against "their violating language"[18] which has never allowed us to "express multiplicity" [210], we need "to find our body's language" [214], which will enable us to "say it all" [212], "without breaks or gaps" [213]. Against their attempt to define us as alike or different, definitions which are "a little abstract" [208], "we can do without models, standards or examples," and, for good measure, without "the right to criticize one another" [217]. We want nothing to "interrupt the flow of our blood" [212], the entirely spontaneous and fluid movement, flux, and flow of our pleasure.

Irigaray's rejection of the division of selves into units, and her rejection of language as a repressive universal, turn out to be based, after all, despite her disclaimers, on a romantic/mystical affirmation of an organic unity defined in terms of the flow of blood and the spontaneity of being. And on an original essence of woman: "Without any intervention or special manipulation, you are a woman already" [211]. It is only after being forced into their language that "you come back, divided: 'we' are no more" [211]. How can Irigaray possibly differentiate this dream of unity from the one she accuses Lacan of upholding? It seems that what Irigaray is criticizing is not so much unity as abstraction.

Moreover, in her attempt to find a form of relationship and mutuality which evades the restrictions of "their language," which is "so limited" [214], Irigaray has simply imposed a new limitation: the scope of this relationship, this language which emerges from the body, is itself restricted to the private realm, to the intimacy of the lovers' discourse. Irigaray is unable to come up with a counter-model to Lacan's which could account for the possibility of a relationship with others beyond the bedroom—or which could deal with conflicts within the bedroom. She evades the problems of intelligibility, of meaning, of mutual understanding among women (not to mention others) with different and conflicting interests, values, and cultures. While a metonymic logic of contiguity, touch, and nearness can and surely does describe some aspects of relationship and language, can this logic serve to *replace* the logic of mediation of differences through an abstraction from particulars to universals?

The problem is that Irigaray fails to challenge the Lacanian conception of language as essentially phallic. For Irigaray is right to criticize Lacan's focus on phallic unity and its absence as the originary foundation of language. But she ends up only repeating that focus on the phallus. She fully accepts Lacan's characterization of language and identity as impositions of a phallic Law of the Father. Only the reaction is different. Instead of stoic acceptance, she advocates a subversion of the Law, through the play, the différance, the relationality of the feminine body. Language and identity must be engaged with only ironically, parodically, strategically, only with the aim of subverting the whole thing. But Irigaray thereby rejects the possibility or value of shared understanding, shared meanings—of the identity or *universality* which is essential to mutual understanding. And she thereby loses Lacan's insight that the development of self-identity and the acquisition of language entail not just the loss of immediacy, not just subjection to the Law, but the capacity—however imperfect— for understanding each other.

For Irigaray, Lacan's concern with the dimension of universality in language only reflects his preoccupation with phallic identity: language is rendered a defensive monologue which silences women's voices, and precludes any possibility of real dialogue, by upholding a deceptive illusion of unity, or shared meaning. But Lacan at least recognized that the movement from narcissistic monologue to the possibility of dialogue requires that participants in dialogue try to understand each other. And that learning a language therefore requires learning to be intelligible, and requires taking responsibility for one's intelligibility in a given social context. Without such a commitment to intelligibility—to identity of meaning as a social value—how are we to articulate differences in a way that the other can understand? But Irigaray has no conception of language as a space of *contested* social meanings, and thus no patience for the idea that identity of meaning—understanding each other—might be an ideal worth striving for.

For Irigaray, any identity of meaning, any abstraction from particulars to universals, any movement from immediacy to mediation, amounts to a movement from the relationality of the feminine body to the Law of the Phallus. But surely this is exactly the assumption that feminists need to challenge. Surely there must be an alternative to immersion in our bodies on one side and accepting the Law of the Phallus on the other. Irigaray's argument that mediation is always a violent intervention, that any universality can only be a crushing and killing of particularity, that any identity of meaning can be only a repression of nonidentity, of metonymy, of the relationality of the body, hides an implicit expectation that language should express everything, and an endless disappointment that it does not. And, as is evident in her lovers' discourse, the expression of everything is precisely Irigaray's dream.

Falling far short of this utopian ideal, the language we have is, for Irigaray, only a tool used against us, and thus can be used by us only strategically. Because she rejects any claim that this language, with its focus on abstraction, identity, universality, might be a medium of intersubjective understanding and relationship, Irigaray must look elsewhere for the possibility of relationship and mutuality. Because she will understand this language only in terms of formal operations of metaphor and abstraction which require a castration, a cutting off of the body, she can only turn to an immersion in the body as an alternative. Because she rejects "the given language" as thoroughly and irredeemably repressive, there is nowhere to go for a theory of relationship, and for a theory and politics of resistance and emancipation, but to a dream of a totally other language, while using this one in way that is purely instrumental.

Because she rejects any form of identity as a form of domination, Irigaray can only turn to pure nonidentity as a way out. And because she wants her theory to ground a theory of women's emancipation, she associates this purity of nonidentity with femininity—and with, in particular, the specificity of the feminine body, now valorized as a source of subversion.

Thus, Irigaray is pushed into a paradox: on one hand, she rejects identitarian thought as essentially phallogocentric; on the other, as the basis of emancipation from the law of identity, she can only assert a feminine identity. That this feminine identity is woman's nonidentity does not deliver her from paradox, but only adds another one. Thus, the only strategy left open is to affirm paradox. And this is exactly what Irigaray does.

Toril Moi and Diana Fuss: On Ahistoricism and Essentialism

Irigaray's paradox—her affirmation of a feminine identity in the face of a rejection of identity as a form of violence—is a constant source of frustration for feminist scholars. As I have suggested, I think that the source of the paradox is Irigaray's unquestioned assumption that the history of western thought, language, and culture has been defined by an unrelenting repression of différance in the service of a false and dominant Identity. And, hence, that the only response to this situation is, as Margaret Whitford puts it, "to dismantle from within the foundations of western metaphysics."[19]

The idea that all of western thought, language, and culture is founded upon the repression of feminine nonidentity fits all too well into the psychic bent of white, middle-class women whose autonomy and agency have been consistently restricted in exchange for the fantasy of being the all-powerful Woman—who, as Irigaray so insightfully points out, are stuck with the alternatives of being either nothing or everything, with no in-between.

But can the history of western thought really be reduced to a repression of différance? Who is the identitarian thinker here? For in fact, in Irigaray's readings of the texts of western culture, there are many different types of identity being collapsed into one. Platonic idealism, scientific objectivity, the Hegelian concept of the subject and its relation to the universal, the Freudian deep self—all are merely examples of a transcendental concept of identity which is always and only repressive, always based on a logic of the Same against an Other.

Of course, Irigaray's ahistoricism has been criticized. But too often, the critique tends to take the form of a reproach for a failure to detail the specific ways in which the logic of the Same has imposed itself in different times and places. For example, Toril Moi argues that while *Speculum* "shows how some patriarchal discursive strategies have remained constant from Plato to Freud" and that Irigaray "does an important job in trying to expose certain recurrent patriarchal strategies," nevertheless, "*Speculum* is ahistorical . . . in that it implies that this is all there is to say about patriarchal logic. Irigaray signally fails to study the historically changing impact of patriarchal discourses on women."[20] Yet Moi agrees with Irigaray, and with Derrida (and, it should be noted, with de Beauvoir), that "so far femininity has been produced exclusively in relationship to the logic of the Same" [139]. What Moi wants is a study of the different ways in which the patriarchal logic of the Same has been imposed on women throughout history, and of the different effects it has had. I would argue that while Irigaray does not tend to analyze the effects of different discourses on actual women's lives, she does attend very closely to the specificity of the thought of each theorist she studies. She understands and stresses the differences between, for example, Platonic and Hegelian idealism, while nevertheless arguing that the theme of the repression and production of feminine otherness by the masculine logic of the Same runs through each of these discourses. It is hardly fair to berate Irigaray for failing to document the effects of patriarchal discourses on women's lives. In doing so, Moi misconstrues the purpose of a historicist critique of an ahistorical and totalizing theory: the value of such a critique is the capacity to call that theory into question, to show through counter-examples that the theory is not in fact adequate to account for the phenomena it purports to explain. Moi's critique of Irigaray's ahistoricism is not so much a critique as a demand that historical data be added on to the theory, which is never challenged.

Moi goes on to argue that Irigaray's ahistoricism, and her lack of a materialist analysis, forces her into adopting an essentialist definition of woman: "Irigaray's failure to consider the historical and economic specificity of patriarchal power, along with its ideological and material contradictions, forces her into providing exactly the kind of metaphysical definition of woman she declaredly wants to avoid. . . .

Her superb critique of patriarchal thought is partly undercut by her attempt to name the feminine" [148]. Here, Moi claims to side with Derrida:

> But if, as Derrida has argued, we are still living under the reign of metaphysics, it is impossible to produce new concepts untainted by the metaphysics of presence. . . . It follows that any attempt to formulate a general theory of femininity will be metaphysical. This is precisely Irigaray's dilemma: having shown that so far femininity has been produced exclusively in relation to the logic of the Same, she falls for the temptation to produce her own positive theory of femininity. [139]

This is a surprisingly common argument: while Irigaray's (Derridean) deconstruction of phallogocentric discourse is strong and important, her attempt to reconstruct a positive theory of women's identity is misguided, and simply undermines her own very strong deconstructive critique of identity. Interestingly, the gist of this argument is that the purely Derridean part of Irigaray's argument is praiseworthy, but her own contributions are unfortunate. But the argument that it is the "absence of a materialist analysis of power and the lack of historical orientation" [148] in Irigaray's work that forces her to turn away from Derridean deconstruction into an essentialist definition of woman is an odd one. For the same logic of the Same and the same metaphysics of presence that Moi cites as the bases of essentializing claims to a feminine identity underlie, for Derrida, the illusion of objectivity that characterizes materialist and historicist explanations.[21]

In her book *Essentially Speaking,* Diana Fuss argues that Moi and other critics of Irigaray's work have been too quick to use the charge of essentialism to dismiss Irigaray's arguments. More generally, Fuss argues that the meanings of essentialism, and the relationships between essentialism and constructivism, need to be analyzed a little more carefully, given the complexity of questions around identity and difference for feminist, gay and lesbian, and Afro-American politics. This argument is important, but Fuss tends to resolve the issues too quickly with an Irigarayan affirmation of paradox, which results in some rather fuzzy thinking.

Every critique of essentialism, Fuss argues, hides an implicit appeal to essentialism. "Constructionism (the position that differences are constructed, not innate) [and Fuss includes Derrida and Lacan in the class of constructionists] really operates as a more sophisticated form of essentialism."[22] Moreover, she argues that the work of Luce Irigaray encourages us to turn this formulation around: "If essentialism symptomatically inheres in anti-essentialist formulations, is it possible that essentialism may itself be predicated, in turn, on some mode of anti-essentialism?" [55]. Unfortunately, this position seems to amount to a resolution of the difference between essentialism and anti-essentialism into a fundamental unity.

Fuss says that her aim is "to work both sides of the essentialist/ constructionist binarism at once, bringing each term to its interior breaking point." This "bilateral" approach "does not presume, however, that it is possible to speak from a location above or beyond this powerful structuring opposition." Her own position, she says, is that of an anti-essentialist who wants "to preserve (in both senses of the term: to maintain and to embalm) the category of essence" [xiii–xiv]. So, Fuss seems to be arguing that she is an anti-essentialist and that as an anti-essentialist she is really a sophisticated essentialist, but that she really does not presume that it is possible to take sides.

Now, certainly there are paradoxes that human beings are unable to resolve. But the need to expose—indeed to create—irresolvable paradoxes seems to be based not only on a belief that paradoxes are sophisticated but also on the false assumption that resolving any paradox means imposing a false and repressive unity on contradictions.

In her analyses of key poststructuralist theorists, and of issues of identity politics in feminist and gay and lesbian theory and in Afro-American literature, Diana Fuss makes some compelling arguments against the tendency to posit essentialism and constructionism, and identity and difference, as mutually exclusive opposites. In her analysis of Irigaray, she criticizes the ways in which the construction of these false opposites has divided feminists into essentialist and anti-essentialist camps. I am sympathetic with what Fuss is trying to do here. But not once does she question Derrida's and Irigaray's claims, duly repeated in her text, that "femininity has been produced exclusively in relation to the logic of the Same" [56], that "the logic of the gaze" represses "a logic of touch" [60], that "the Symbolic" is "the arm of phallocracy" [60], and that a "predominance of metaphoricity in Western culture" [62] requires "a deconstruction of the metaphor/metonymy binarism operative in Western philosophical discourse" [64]. In short, identity represses difference.

These pronouncements are repeated as if they don't need to be argued for or opened to question, but are simply accepted as the truth. It is the acceptance of these truths which gets Fuss ensnared in what are really false problems and false paradoxes. The central paradox is the one she poses towards the end of her essay on Irigaray: "How do we reconcile the poststructuralist project to displace identity with the feminist project to reclaim it?" [70] And this, after all, is the crux of the problem that is currently dividing feminist theorists.

For Fuss, Irigaray's theory provides a possible solution. The answer lies in Irigaray's replacement of the logic of identity with a metonymic logic which "collapses boundaries" [66] and which rejects the need to claim any identity or likeness between two subjects in order for them to communicate. This is symbolized by the image of the two lips, the significance of which is, for Fuss, summarized in the words "both at once."

> Both at once signifies that a woman is simultaneously singular and double; she is "already two—but not divisible into one(s)," or put another way, she is "neither one nor two." [58]

This "typical Irigarian double gesture," this "both at once" is, for Fuss, the basis of Irigaray's feminist politics: Irigaray proposes, she says, a feminist politics that will work on "two fronts at once—on one side, a 'global' politics that seeks to address the problem of women's universal oppression, and on the other side, a 'local' politics that will address the specificity and complexity of each woman's particular situation" [69]. This proposal strikes me as eminently reasonable, but do we really need to resort to the affirmation of paradox, to mystical formulas of "neither one nor two," or "already two but not divisible into ones," in order to support it? There is really nothing paradoxical, and certainly nothing mystical, about working on both global and local politics—both universal and particular issues—at the same time. The paradox arises only when we assume, as Fuss seems to do, that any claim to universality is necessarily a repression of particularity.

Fuss prefaces her account of Irigaray's "double gesture" with a critique of Irigaray's affirmation of feminist "consciousness raising" as a strategy which aims to expose the experience of oppression as "a condition shared by all women" [68]. Fuss notes that this strategy has been criticized on the grounds that the experiences of white heterosexual middle-class educated women cannot be generalized to all women, and argues that in advocating this model "Irigaray might rightly be accused here of a certain tendency to universalize and to homogenize, to subsume all women under the category of 'Woman'" [68]. But while it is clearly true that the experience of white middle-class heterosexual educated women cannot be generalized to all women, why is this assumed to render impossible the sharing of experience among different women, and in fact to render any attempt to share experience nothing more than a repression of differences?

As for the theoretical problem—"How do we reconcile the poststructuralist project to displace identity with the feminist project to reclaim it?"—Fuss says that for Irigaray, "the solution is again double: women are engaged in the process of both constructing and deconstructing their identities, their essences, simultaneously" [70]. Again, it does not seem to me that criticizing or deconstructing the ways in which women's identities have been constructed necessarily conflicts with attempts to reconstruct our identities. The difficulty arises when we begin from an assumption that "identity" *per se* must be displaced—when we assume, that is, that identity is necessarily repressive of difference. But it is just as possible to argue that identity, like reason, the self, and western philosophy, is not solely the product of a will to unity which represses difference, of a phallic logic which represses the feminine. In the following chapters I attempt to differentiate among repressive and nonrepressive, open and closed, exclusive and inclusive forms of identity, to open a space for reconstructions of identities which are no longer stranded in paradox.

5

From the Subversion of Identity
to the Subversion of Solidarity?

Judith Butler and the Critique of Women's Identity

Judith Butler avoids Luce Irigaray's paradox—the affirmation of a women's identity in the face of a repudiation of identity as a phallogocentric construct—by sticking to a much more consistent deconstruction of identity. For Butler, the subversion of identity must be extended to a subversion of any notion of a women's identity. Butler's critique of gender identity and her theory of gender as performance lead in important directions, but her acceptance of the claim that identity is always a product of a sacrificial logic leads her into new paradoxes.

In her book *Gender Trouble: Feminism and the Subversion of Identity*, Judith Butler offers a compelling political and philosophical analysis of the ways in which fixed gender identities serve to constrain the constitution of subjectivity. To do this, she draws a number of different arguments together. Central to her analysis is the psychoanalytic argument, developed with some ambivalence by Freud and made explicit by Lacan, that gender differences and heterosexual orientation are not simply natural but are rather products of a fixed socio-symbolic order which is fundamentally patriarchal. The psychoanalytic argument is supplemented and criticized by Foucault's argument that gender identities must be understood as the effects of multiple discourses, practices, and institutions, rather than as expres-

112

sions of a single repressive symbolic order. And both of these arguments are supplemented and called into question by feminist analyses of the ways in which the institutions of gender produce sexed identities: in particular, Butler draws on Monique Wittig's critique of the institution of compulsory heterosexuality and on Luce Irigaray's critique of phallogocentrism.

From these theorists Butler draws the important arguments that, first of all, sex and gender identities are not simply natural and prior to social and linguistic influences, but are discursively and culturally constituted; and that, secondly, this constitution is organized in part through regulative institutions which maintain and reproduce specific power relations by enforcing particular performances of gender. In particular, the institutions of phallogocentrism and compulsory heterosexuality operate to define male and female identities through a binary logic: identity is established in terms of opposition to, exclusion of, and desire for the other.

The analysis of the roles of these repressive institutions in the constitution of gender categories is an important one. But Butler places this analysis in the context of a metatheory of identity and of language which effectively undermines any possibility of the subversion of repressive identities. Butler's fundamental claim is that any identity is always and only the product of a system or logic of power/language which generates identities as functions of binary oppositions, and seeks to conceal its own workings by making those identities appear natural. Ironically, by adopting this single, totalizing theory of the logic of identity, Butler herself represses any possibility of *difference* among different forms of identity. It becomes impossible to differentiate between repressive and nonrepressive, exclusive and inclusive, immediate and mediated, metaphysical and socially constructed forms of identity. The identity of the self, the identity of meaning in language, gender identity, women's identity, lesbian identity, feminist identity, identity as uniqueness and as sameness, identity as and identity with, are all understood to be expressions of a single sacrifical logic of identity. In other words, Butler subverts her own call for a subversion of identity by rendering identity so omnipotent and intransigent that the subversion becomes impossible. Thus, it becomes impossible to see the affirmations of existential and political identities which provide a sense of meaning and solidarity to participants in feminist, gay and lesbian, and black struggles for empowerment as anything other than paradoxical affirmations of the identitary logic of domination and exclusion.

In this chapter, I want to argue that, in order to realize Butler's project—to theorize gender as an "effect of institutions, practices, discourses with multiple and diffuse points of origin"[1]—we need to move beyond the assumption that all of those discourses operate according to a single sacrificial and exclusionary logic of identity. We need, first of all, to recognize differences among different types and forms of identity, and secondly, to reformulate and reconstruct identities which can include, rather than exclude, differences.

To develop these claims, I want to begin by looking at what Butler has to say about the problem of women's identity.

> For the most part, feminist theory has taken the category of women to be foundational to any further political claims without realizing that the category effects a political closure on the kinds of experiences articulable as part of a feminist discourse.[2]

In this formulation, Butler is conflating very different types of identity. I think that she's right to call into question any claim to an *immediate* experiential or metaphysical identity among women, and any claim which reifies and naturalizes male and female gender identities. And she's right to criticize any imposition of an identity shared by members of one privileged group upon others—typically, by white middle- or upper-class heterosexual western feminists upon all women—i.e., the imposition of a *false* claim to identity which *represses* differences.

But what exactly is the basis for Butler's claim that "the category of women" necessarily imposes a "closure on the kinds of experiences *articulable* as part of a feminist discourse"? Here, Butler rejects even the position of Gayatri Spivak, who argues that while we need to reject any claims to metaphysical or ontological identity we should retain the "category of women" for strategic purposes, as a political tool. Butler asks:

> But is it the presumption of ontological integrity that needs to be
> dispelled, or does the practical redeployment of the category
> without any ontological commitments also effect a political
> consolidation of its semantic integrity with serious exclusionary
> implications?[3]

What Butler is claiming here is that something called "semantic integrity" necessarily excludes difference and closes off the possibility of articulating different experiences. In other words, language operates to impose false identities that prevent and foreclose the possibility of the emergence of different voices.

As I shall argue, the basis for this claim is the belief that *any* concept of an identity of meaning in language must necessarily be: 1) immediate: a claim to an essential substantive or metaphysical reality prior to the word, and 2) repressive: a fixing or freezing of multiplicity into a unity which excludes and closes off difference and possibility.

Following Irigaray, Derrida, and Foucault, Butler relies on the Nietzschean critique of the "metaphysics of substance" to make her argument that any claim to identity involves an imposition of false unity upon what is in fact multiple and inexpressible, an imposition of order upon what is in fact not at all orderly. Foucault, she argues, draws on the critique of the metaphysics of substance to expose "the postulation of identity as a culturally restricted principle of order and hierarchy, a regulatory fiction."[4]

Butler draws on the same critique to criticize the "substantializing and hierarchizing grammar of nouns" [24] according to which the substantive integrity—the "being"—of the actor implied by the noun is always assumed to precede the actions and attributes which can only be seen to emanate from that being. (In Hegelian terms, identity is assumed to precede negativity.) Butler uses this conception of language as repression to argue that the nouns "man" and "woman" imply the existence of fixed and enduring substantive realities, and thus naturalize and substantialize what are in fact "artificial" and "essentially superfluous" identities [24].

There is an important insight here. Butler wants to argue that "man" and "woman" are not fixed and eternal entities but cultural constructs, effects of technologies of power: there is no natural or transcendental basis for the division of all humanity into two opposed genders. (Why, after all, should the differences between male and female anatomy be more salient than any of a huge variety of physical and other differences among human beings?) The male-female duality is something which is culturally produced and fixed in language, and which thereby obscures the fact that human beings do not in fact fall neatly into two complementary categories. Thus, against the "traditional" feminist argument that sex and gender are two different things, that gender is the social superstructure imposed on a biological foundation, Butler wants to argue that sex is just as much a socio-linguistic construction as gender. But the meaning of "socio-linguistic construction" is what is at issue here.

Butler takes from Monique Wittig the argument that gender identities are constituted and sustained through the institution of compulsory heterosexuality—that is, that we are constituted as male and female through a system that defines male identity in terms of sexual desire for females, and female identity in terms of sexual desire for, or at least, receptivity to, males.[5] But Butler rejects Wittig's materialist argument that the institution of compulsory heterosexuality has emerged primarily out of social, historical, material practices that have developed in interaction with specific conditions, out of the attempts of societies to regulate and institutionalize practices of reproduction. Butler argues that the system of compulsory heterosexuality is just one more expression of the metaphysics of substance which is entrenched in language. And the logic of language itself is seen as the origin or cause of this repressive regime. The central question, for Butler, is "How does language itself produce the fictive construction of 'sex' that supports these various regimes of power?"[6]

Thus, Butler reduces the complexity of the production and emergence of gender identities to a single formula: she moves from the argument that sex and gender are both constituted through discursive practices which are regulated in part by institutions of phallogocentrism and compulsory heterosexuality, to the argument that sex and gender are products of a single, totalizing logic of language

which institutes identities through the production of binary oppositions, and which thereby effects a repression of nonidentity.

Ironically, Butler turns to this metatheory in an attempt to *avoid*
the tendency to invoke a single, totalizing theory to account for gender oppression. She criticizes Luce Irigaray and Monique Wittig for
attempting to identify a single "monolithic cause of gender oppression": phallogocentrism for Irigaray, compulsory heterosexuality for
Wittig.[7] We need, Butler argues, to draw on the strengths of these
theories without accepting their respective designations of a single
cause of gender oppression. Thus, she argues, Wittig's and Irigaray's
theories, along with Foucault's, can all be better understood as different articulations of "the notion that sex appears within hegemonic
language as a *substance,* as, metaphysically speaking, a self-identical
being" [18]. Each of these theorists, she points out, identifies an artificial binary relation which masks a univocal and hegemonic discourse which suppresses subversive multiplicity. Each, then, can be
better understood as a critique of the metaphysics of substance
which is entrenched in language. So, Butler's solution to the problem
of totalizing theories is to resolve these different theories into a single, unified theory at a higher level of abstraction. In other words,
Butler "solves" the problem of totalizing theories by resolving them
into an even more totalizing theory: by erasing the concrete content
and leaving only the pure, abstract form.

Language: Repression, Violation, and Deception

From the argument that sex and gender are both socio-linguistic
constructions, Butler moves to the argument that language always
operates by invoking an "illusion of substance,"[8] and that language,
by imposing identities, represses difference and nonidentity.[9] Thus,
the category of women operates to foreclose the articulation of difference: it "effects a political closure on the kinds of experiences
articulable as part of a feminist discourse."[10]

In *Bodies That Matter,* Butler argues that she has never meant to
claim that this means that the category of women should be thrown
out altogether. Rather, her critique of the category should be under-

stood as "the critique of something useful, the critique of something we cannot do without."[11] The point, for Butler, is that intelligibility always comes at a price. And the price is violation. In the opening pages of Bodies That Matter, Butler defines the category of "sex" as "an ideal construct which is forcibly materialized" through a process of exclusion and repudiation of the other sex [1-3]. With Lacan, she argues that this is the definitive process of subject constitution, and that it "constitutes the very terrain of cultural intelligibility" [6]. The point, she argues, is that "*matter itself is founded through a set of violations*" [29].

Butler is working with a few different models of language here. There is an idealist conception of language as something which produces matter through making it intelligible as such. And a conception of language as a useful and necessary tool for intelligibility. The constant is that intelligibility is violence.

At this point, the meaning of violation, of force and restriction, has become a little blurry. Cultural intelligibility has been reduced to a violation, and there is apparently no way of distinguishing this violation from the violence of compulsory heterosexuality. Nor is there any way of specifying exactly what is being violated.

Ironically, Butler's conception of language as something which operates only according to a logic of exclusion, as something which represses difference, is symptomatic of a continued reliance on a theory of language as representation. The exclusionary logic of language imposes a particular representation of reality and hence can only misrepresent reality because other possible experiences are excluded. (The category of women "effects a political closure on the kinds of experiences articulable. . . .") For Butler, the "reality" which is misrepresented is not just the experience of excluded others who are unable to articulate their difference, but the infinity of possible experience, of *différance* and nonidentity. Language imposes identities upon nonidentity, freezing the multiplicity of possible experience into a false unity which always fails to express that experience and that possibility in its fullness and entirety. Thus, Butler conceives of "identity" as that which stops up and represses multiplicity and nonidentity—a view behind which lurks a rebuke against words like "women" for their failure to express the whole truth, and a rebuke against language for its failure to express everything, for always leaving something out, unexpressed.

Butler's claim that identity categories are the products of a violation, a "linguistic restriction on thought,"[12] echoes the romantic idea that "reason kills," that linguistic concepts trample and destroy the purity of the ineffable, that universals necessarily repress particulars. There is a kernel of truth in this: it *is* impossible to say everything, and labels do restrict us. But there is also a danger: once we define the identity of meaning in language as a form of restriction and exclusion, we are thereby defining our social construction, and our capacity to speak and interact with each other, as a form of violation.

This threatens to render the idea of violation virtually meaningless. Is the violation which enables us to speak and understand each other to be placed on the same level as the violation which produces the female body as lacking, and the homosexual body as "unnatural" and depraved? And does the term "women" only violate, silence, and exclude, or does it also provide a site for the social contestation of meaning, and enable articulations of difference?

Following Nietzsche, Butler moves from the idea that language is a violation to the argument that language is fundamentally *deceptive*. Arguing that the metaphysics of substance underlies the notion of "the psychological person as a substantive thing,"[13] Butler quotes approvingly a passage from a commentary on Nietzsche by Michel Haar, who claims that "all psychological categories (the ego, the individual, the person)" derive from an "*illusion* of substantial identity" which in turn "goes back basically to a *superstition* that *deceives* not only common sense but also philosophers—namely, the *belief* in language, and, more precisely, in the *truth* of grammatical categories." [my italics] It is our "faith in grammar"—in the structure of subject and predicate, wherein being precedes doing—that tricks us into believing in the identity of the self. In fact, however, "the subject, the self, the individual, are just so many false concepts, since they transform into substances fictitious unities having at the start *only* a linguistic reality" [20–21; my italics]. Butler, then, agrees with Haar that language is something that deceives us, that creates false concepts, fictitious unities which we are foolish enough to believe in.

Butler extends this analysis to the linguistic construction of gender identity: she argues that "the unproblematic claim to 'be' a woman and to 'be' heterosexual" is symptomatic of a "metaphysics of gender substances" [21]. Sex or gender "appears within hegemonic language as a *substance,* as, metaphysically speaking, a self-identical being. This appearance is achieved through a performative twist of language and/or discourse that conceals the fact that 'being' a sex or a gender is fundamentally impossible" [18–19]. Once again, language is seen as something which "conceals" a "fact"! But what Butler fails to recognize is that "being" a sex or a gender is impossible only if it is assumed, *a priori,* that "being" necessarily refers to a fixed essence. It is impossible to "be" a woman if we assume that to be a woman is to embody some transcendent and eternal essence of womanhood. It is, however, not impossible to be a woman if we accept that the meanings of "being" and "woman," like all human meanings, are socially and historically mediated, and open to contestation and to change, and can be recognized as such.

To develop this understanding of "being" we can draw on Max Horkheimer's conception of "truth," which is summarized by Thomas McCarthy in support of his critique of relativism:

> Horkheimer argued that the historically conditioned character of a belief is not *per se* incompatible with its being true: only against the backgrounds of traditional ontological-theological conceptions of eternal, unchanging truth could this seem to be the case. But there is no need, he went on, of any absolute guarantee in order to distinguish meaningfully between truth and error. Rather, what is required is a concept of truth consistent with our finitude, with our historicity, with the dependence of thought on changing social conditions. On such a concept failure to measure up to absolute, unconditioned standards would be irrelevant. To regard this failure as leading directly to cognitive relativism is just another version of the "God is dead, everything is permitted" fallacy of disappointed expectations.[14]

It is just such a fallacy of disappointed expectations that Butler falls into when she claims that "being" is impossible, and hence we must regard any claim to identity as illusory and deceptive.

Once we have thoroughly understood the critique of the metaphysics of substance, and begin to explore different models of language and meaning, it becomes possible to recognize that the idea that words like "women" impose a deceptive illusion of substance and repress possible differences is not entirely accurate. As Albrecht Wellmer argues in a discussion of Adorno, "the 'rigidity' of the general concept . . . itself remains in a certain sense a rationalistic fiction. Wittgenstein pointed out that, as a rule, the grammar of our language shows us that words can be used in many and various ways, without our always being able to hit upon a 'fundamental,' 'authentic' or 'primary' meaning of words."[15] For Wittgenstein, words could be better understood on the model of a rope that consists of a multiplicity of individual fibres: thus, the meanings of words can be better understood in terms of a multiplicity of interrelated usages. Once this model of language is combined with an historical model, it becomes possible to understand meanings as mediated through complex interrelations of different social practices in different contexts, through different discourses and institutions, which invest these concepts with multiple layers of meanings. Thus, the concept of "women" already *includes* multiple and often contradictory meanings, and is already open to shifts and changes in meaning.

For Butler, if identity "includes" difference, it is only as the repressed other which returns to haunt the concept. But this implies a defensive rigidity in the nature of concepts which is only sometimes there, and which surely cannot exhaust our understanding of language. Like Foucault, Butler criticizes Lacan's model of language as a one-dimensional symbolic order and argues for an understanding of culture in terms of multiple discourses, only to redescribe these discourses in Lacanian terms: language is psychologized as a defensive structure which operates through repression and deception.

The insight into the repressive and deceptive elements of language, brilliantly expressed in the work of Nietzsche, and developed by Lacan, Foucault, and Butler, has been important. But we need to move beyond the repetition of this insight to recognize differences among types of violation, and to formulate concepts of meaning and identity which are more capacious, more inclusive of difference, and more open to change. Thus, I want to argue, we will be better able to avoid reducing all language, and hence our social being, to a form of violence.

Identity and Agency: Performative Paradoxes

Against the assumption that sexes and selves are prediscursive substances, Butler draws on theories of masquerade and mimesis to develop a theory of gendered identity as performance. But Butler's analysis of the nature of self-identity and agency in terms of performativity is confusing: she seems to oscillate between the argument that subject identities are produced through monotonous repetitions of the logic of language (relieved only by random variations which accidentally produce change, but which never emerge from the logic of sacrifice), and the argument that we can subvert our identities through spontaneous acts. Butler dismisses any suggestion that she treats language as a metasubject, or that she romanticizes a subject outside the law. But because she provides no account of a process of mediation between norms and acts, it's difficult to see how she avoids either of these claims. To account for this mediation, we need to be able to differentiate between the concepts of immediate and substantive identity, and of the prediscursive subject (which Butler rightly criticizes), and concepts of existential identity, moral and ethical identity, reflection, and intentionality, which I think we need to hold on to.

a) Existential Identity: Experience as Mediation

Butler's belief that any claim to identity is always a deceptive claim to an immediate, essential, or metaphysical identity discounts any possibility of a *mediated* identity. Thus, she asserts, quoting Nietzsche, that "there is no 'being' behind doing, effecting, becoming; 'the doer' is merely a fiction added to the deed—the deed is everything."[16]

To this she adds: "There is no gender identity behind the expressions of gender; that identity is performatively constituted by the very 'expressions' that are said to be its results" [25]. The fact that gender is "performatively constituted" means that it is "a stylized repetition of acts. The effect of gender is produced through the stylization of the body and, hence, must be understood as the mundane way in which bodily gestures, movements, and styles of various kinds constitute the illusion of an abiding gendered self" [140].

Butler is making the point that the idea of a subject which precedes its constitution is fallacious and deceptive. But she moves from this point to the assumption that if there is no transcendental *a priori* subject, no fixed essence of being, no immediate identity that precedes everything, then the ideas of subject, being, and identity are merely deceptive illusions. The doer is merely a fiction added to the deed. Butler thus sets up a false opposition: either there is a transcendental being which precedes doing, or there is only doing, only performance and its repetition. The fiction of identity needs to be deconstructed into the series of discrete practices which it really *is*.

While I would agree with the argument that the gendered self is constituted through practices, I see no reason to assume that this means that the idea of an "abiding gendered self" is an "illusion"—unless "abiding gendered self" is taken to mean "fixed and predetermined essence." Butler is assuming that any concept of a continuous self-identity is a deceptive illusion of substance. But a sense of self and a sense of gender which is experienced as meaningful and continuous is not necessarily based on an illusion of substance. I can quite consciously believe that I am made, not born, a woman, and I can experience my gendered self as subject to change and diffusion, as ambiguous and complex, layered and conflicted, restrictive and enabling, shaped through identifications with and desires for others of various genders, while still experiencing myself in a meaningful way as a woman. This may seem to be an obvious point; the point is that it cannot be accommodated within the terms of Butler's theory. For Butler, the category of experience necessarily reintroduces the *verboten* concept of the prediscursive subject. But the absence of a category of experience pushes her into a difficult position. On one hand, she wants to argue that gender *is* only practice, only a series of acts: the deed is everything. At the same time she wants to argue that "gender is also a norm," a regulatory ideal, a law, which "acts [not actors] seek to approximate" [141]. And there is no mediation between the acts and the ideal. Such a position denies any capacity for reflection, and would seem to provide no basis for *resistance* to gender categories: the only source Butler can provide for the "possibilities of gender transformation" is the "occasional discontinuity," the "failure to repeat" [141] which accidentally exposes the illusion of gender—but exposes it to whom?

b) Moral and Ethical Identity: Accountability

Butler's attempt to use Nietzsche's critique of the doer behind the deed in order to desubstantialize gender identities opens up a second problem. What Butler doesn't mention is that Nietzsche's assertion that "there is no 'being' behind doing" is made in the context of a critique of the ideal of freedom and accountability, and a defense of essentialism. Nietzsche is arguing that we are deluded when we believe in a subject who is able to act with reference to ethical ideals, and who can therefore be held accountable for choices and actions, for in fact, actions are simply expressions of the actor's essence or nature. Thus, Nietzsche is able to defend the domination of the strong over the weak with the argument that it is in the nature of the strong to dominate and in the nature of the weak to be dominated. The concept of ethics, and the belief in a "neutral independent 'subject'" capable of acting in accordance with moral principles, is a creation of the weak, an expression of "the vengeful cunning of impotence" which makes of weakness a freely chosen virtue, "just as if the weakness of the weak—that is to say, their *essence,* their effects, their sole ineluctable, irremovable reality—were a voluntary achievement willed, chosen, a *deed,* a *meritorious* act."[17]

I don't want to suggest that Butler accepts this argument uncritically. But clearly, Nietzsche's critique of the idea of the doer behind the deed doesn't provide much of a basis for a denaturalization of gender identities, for it takes us right back into the realm of essence and nature. What it does provide is a model of spontaneous action, pure performance, which allows us to evade the restrictiveness of ethical or moral identity—of any capacity to account for oneself to oneself and to others. When Butler argues that we need to subvert identities which are "self-identical, persisting through time as the same," in favor of identities which "come into being and dissolve," which are contingent and "without obedience to a formative telos of definitional closure"[18] is she looking for a sort of immediacy, a spontaneity which will allow us to act without having to commit to any enduring sense of self, without having to take responsibility for our actions, for any continuity in our relations to others, in our principles and ideals? I don't think this is something Butler would seriously want to advocate. But is it possible to differentiate, within the terms of Butler's theory, between the repressive identity which should be subverted, and a sense of ethical and moral identity which we might want to affirm?

c) Agency: Reflection and Intentionality

Butler's attempt to relate her theory of identity to some sort of emancipatory politics necessarily opens up the problem of agency. In the concluding chapter of *Gender Trouble,* Butler attempts to specify a concept of agency which could be consistent with her theory. Right from the start, she states that agency must not be understood as a "capacity for reflexive mediation" [143]. Such a concept, she argues, necessarily appeals to an assumption of a "prediscursive 'I'" [143]. The idea of reflexive mediation is necessarily based on the epistemological model of an opposition of subject and object: the subject or prediscursive "I" confronts an object or prediscursive reality. We need, Butler argues, to "shift from an *epistemological* account of identity to one which locates the problematic within practices of *signification*" [144]. Thus, "the question of *agency* is reformulated as a question of how signification and resignification work" [144].

The attempt to understand agency in terms of signifying *practice* is, I think, a positive step. The problem lies in Butler's understanding of this practice—that is, in her account of "how signification and resignification work." For Butler, "to understand identity as a *practice,* and as a signifying practice, is to understand culturally intelligible subjects as the resulting effects of a rule-bound discourse that inserts itself in the pervasive and mundane signifying acts of linguistic life" [145]. But this does not mean, she asserts, that subjects are *determined.* "As a process," she argues, "signification harbors within itself what the epistemological discourse refers to as 'agency.' The rules that govern intelligible identity, i.e., that enable and restrict the intelligible assertion of an 'I' ... operate through *repetition*.... The subject is not *determined* by the rules through which it is generated because signification is *not a founding act, but rather a regulated process of repetition* that both conceals itself and enforces its rules precisely through the production of substantializing effects" [145]. It is in this understanding of signifying practice as a repetition of the rules of the institutions of power/language that Butler locates the possibility of agency. "Agency," she argues, "is to be located within the possibility of a variation on that repetition" [145]. The injunctions of the Law produce "necessary failures, a variety of incoherent configurations that in their multiplicity exceed and defy the injunction" [145]. Agency, then, for Butler, consists of accidental "variations on repetition," produced by failures to repeat the letter of the law.

At this point, Butler jumps to a discussion of subversive repetition, of parodic performances which can serve to expose and thereby subvert the deceptive workings of the systems of power. But how do we move from variations on repetition, which are understood as accidental failures to repeat, to practices of parody, subversion, and resistance, without resorting to a concept of the reflexive mediation of a knowing, critical subject? For while variation and failure probably do not require critical reflection, parody does. Somebody, at some level—and it may only be at the level of the unconscious—has to get the joke.

In her discussion of the film *Paris Is Burning,* in *Bodies That Matter,* Butler seems to acknowledge this. She notes that, contrary to what many readers of *Gender Trouble* understood, there is no necessary relation between subversion and parodic performances like drag. Drag performances have a complex relation to gender norms: they can denaturalize and subvert them, and they can reidealize them. Typically, they do both together. Moreover, once we recognize that all gender is a form of drag—is an imitative repetition of a norm—we need to be able to differentiate between subversive and non-subversive forms of drag, unless we want to say that gender is automatically its own subversion. For Butler, the decisive criterion which turns performance into subversion is *reflection,* along with *resistance:* "drag is subversive to the extent that it *reflects* on the imitative structure by which hegemonic gender is itself produced and *disputes* heterosexuality's claim on naturalness and originality" [125; my italics].

Still, Butler won't go so far as to suggest that not only the performance but subjects might be doing the reflecting. She stresses that when she talks about parodic performances, she is not invoking a notion of a subject who thinks or acts intentionally. "Performativity must be understood not as a singular or deliberate 'act,' but, rather, as the reiterative and citational practice by which discourse produces the effects that it names" [2].

What's lost here is any recognition of the perspectives of the participants in these performances, and hence, any meaningful differentiation among unreflective, deliberate, dogmatic, defensive, anxious, ironic, playful, and parodic performances of gender, and any understanding of the ways in which these interact and conflict in specific performances and particular subjects. What's lost then, is any meaningful concept of agency, and any meaningful concept of subversion.

For Butler, to recognize the role of subjective reflection and intention in performances, of a doer who does the deed, is necessarily to invoke the transcendental subject, the prediscursive "I," the "subject before the law." But in fact there is no need to invoke the specter of the prediscursive "I" in order to grant the capacity of critical reflection to human subjects. There is no need to jump from the critique of the epistemological model of a transcendental subject in opposition to objects to a rejection of any concept of subjective mediation.

The alternative is a recognition that subjects, while they do not originate, do *participate* in the ongoing process of the constitution of subjectivity. For of course we are constituted as subjects, but from the time we begin to be constituted, we also participate in our own constitution, through our spontaneous acts and responses to others, through the development of our capacities for reflection, deliberation, and intention, through our constant attempts to make meaning, to understand ourselves and others, to express ourselves to others, to act in accordance with ideals, to account for our failures and our incoherences. Any useful model of the constitution of subject identities has to be able to account for these processes. But once substantive identity, existential identity, ethical and moral identity, and the capacities for reflection and intention are all subsumed under the single concept of the "subject before the law," it becomes impossible to account for the ways in which subjects participate in their own constitution, and in social and political struggles for change.

From the Subversion of Identity to the Subversion of Solidarity?

I have argued that, because Butler sees language as a force of deception and repression, restriction and exclusion, she is unable to move beyond a conception of the *social* as purely restrictive, and leaves no room for any kind of positive development in the social, discursive constitution of identities.

The conception of language and the social as a violation, as the imposition of *order* on heterogeneity, is what unites Butler's *metaphysical* critique of identity as the repression of nonidentity, as the illusion of being which is the repression of doing, and specific *political* critiques of the imposition of repressive identities upon differences. The metaphysical critique, because it reduces all forms of identity to the same thing, just waters down the political one. There is no basis for differentiation between repressive and non-repressive forms of identity. As Nancy Fraser writes in a critique of Foucault:

> The problem is that Foucault calls too many different sorts of things power and simply leaves it at that. Granted, all cultural practices involve constraints—but these constraints are of a variety of different kinds and thus demand a variety of different normative responses. Granted, there can be no social practices without power—but it doesn't follow that all forms of power are normatively equivalent nor that any social practices are as good as any other. . . . Clearly, what Foucault needs, and needs desperately, are normative criteria for distinguishing acceptable from unacceptable forms of power.[19]

What Butler needs, I would argue, are normative criteria for distinguishing acceptable from unacceptable forms of identity. This is a crucial distinction, because without it, it becomes impossible to grant the importance of affirming *political* identities, and identifications, without lapsing into paradox. It is important to be able to see that it is possible to come out as a lesbian, to identify with women, and to affirm solidarity with feminists, without necessarily repressing difference and nonidentity.

Because her argument rests on the critique of all forms of identity as repressive, Butler reduces the idea of an essential Woman, the socio-linguistic category of women, and the ideal of feminist solidarity, all to the same thing.

As I have argued, Butler conflates the "category of women" with the idea of an essential Woman: it is impossible to be a woman because "being" implies a transcendental essence. But the socio-linguistic category of women, rather than invoking the deceptive illusion of an immediate identity (according to a representational model of language) can instead be understood as a socially mediated form of identity which is inclusive of differences, and which is open to change.

Butler shifts again from her critique of a metaphysical *identity of women* to a rejection of the ideal of *feminist solidarity*. While she can accept, she says, the value of coalitional politics which bring together different interest groups to work on specific goals, there must be no attempt "to assert an ideal form for coalitional structures *in advance*," or to insist "in advance on coalitional 'unity' as a goal."[20] This barred "in advance" signifies, once again, the rejection of the imposition of any immediate or transcendental identity upon the coalition as an agent, any claim to a collective "being" that would precede or restrict the "doing" of individual or group members. For Butler, this translates into an assumption that the ideal of solidarity is a repressive one. "The insistence in advance on coalitional 'unity' as a goal assumes that solidarity, whatever its price, is a prerequisite for social action" [14]. And she asks, rhetorically, "Does 'unity' set up an exclusionary norm of solidarity at the level of identity that rules out the possibility of a set of actions which disrupt the very borders of identity concepts ... ?" [15].

Solidarity, then, is rejected as a basis of feminist politics, because it *excludes* the possibility of subversions or disruptions of the group identity, and, presumably, of disruptions of group actions aimed at the achievement of agreed-upon goals. In other words, a coalitional activist group should refrain from affirming any solidarity or common purpose, because it might thereby thwart its own subversion. An interesting notion, in the abstract, but it's difficult to imagine how such a group could actually get anything done. Or why it would want to.

Butler claims that this policy of "no commitments" allows for the spontaneous emergence and dissolution of group identities in the service of achieving particular, specific goals. But this evades the issues of group solidarity, the need for a sense of shared meaning and purpose, and the importance of a capacity for commitment to a future and a consciousness of a past. And it denies the possibility of developing group identities which could include and facilitate differences, which could accommodate change without disintegration, which could sustain enduring commitments to ideals and identifications with others.

Butler is making the false assumption that commitment and solidarity necessarily exclude the possibility of conflict and disruption. Either we have a restrictive and repressive totalizing group identity based on false assumptions of substantive unity which effectively exclude the possibility of change, creativity, questioning, and difference; or we have freedom from restrictions, spontaneous self-creation, and dissolution. But this, once again, is a false opposition between identity and difference. For of course it is possible to affirm solidarity and allow for conflict and difference. In fact, without an ideal of identity and a commitment to solidarity there will be no conflict. What would produce conflict among people whose guiding principle for political action is "do your own thing"?

The point is that by imposing her own *a priori*, "in advance" rule that there must be no commitment to a feminist solidarity which might restrict our freedom, Butler is approaching the problem from the wrong end. Rather than beginning from the transcendental claim that identity represses difference, we need to begin with the question of how we can do politics. For it's one thing to claim that doing must precede being, but another, in practice, for a group to decide what to do, and which action to take. This, of course, raises the question of collective and individual agency. And Butler argues that too many feminists have wrongly assumed that there must be a "metaphysical locus of agency" [25]—an individual human subject, a collective identity—at the origin of any political action. But the argument Butler anticipates is not the argument I want to make. Rather than join Butler on the terrain of disputes about ontology and origins, I want to approach the question from the other end—from the standpoint of the goals of our actions, and the normative ideals which guide those actions.

Butler argues that there is no need to posit a normative ideal of individual or collective identity as a basis for feminist politics. It is quite enough to define our politics in terms of our immediate goals and strategies. But it is not very difficult to show that it is impossible to define our goals without appealing to the normative ideals of individual autonomy and collective solidarity. We need only list some very basic feminist goals.

Feminists are in fact surprisingly united in agreement on many basic political positions: there is little controversy as to the importance of rights to abortion and reproductive freedom, freedom of sexual orientation, equal pay and equitable conditions and relations of work, universal access to childcare, autonomy and solidarity in our personal relationships, and genuine and meaningful participation and representation in political and public spheres. There is also fundamental agreement as to the need for the abolition of all forms of sex, race, and class oppression and exploitation, and hence for the abolition of oppressive and exploitative economic, political, social, familial, and cultural structures. In all of these positions we are appealing, necessarily, to the normative ideals of the integrity and autonomy of the individual, and of the equal rights of all individuals to freedom of choice, thought, and action. At the same time, we are appealing to an ideal of the collective good, of a society where all individuals and social groups have basic rights to self-determination, freedom, and happiness, however these may be defined. Moreover, we are affirming, as feminists, a solidarity in our collective commitment to these goals, as well as a collective capacity to interpret and articulate our collective needs and values in order to establish these goals. Given this unavoidable and perhaps embarrassing consensus in practice, how are we to argue consistently that we can define our goals without reference to the norms of individual autonomy and collective identity? And how are we to argue that the identity (or the autonomy) of the individual, and the collective identity or solidarity of feminists (or of women), are oppressive concepts? One way of dealing with this situation, as we have already seen, is simply to affirm paradox, and learn to live with it. After all, life is complex and full of contradictions. So we have to fight for a woman's right to choose on one hand, and deny the validity of the concepts of rights, choice, and women, on the other. This option is becoming, for me, less and less sustainable.

The problem, I think, lies not in the disjuncture between theory and practice, but within the theory itself. Ultimately, Butler's attempt to eliminate the paradox between the deconstruction and affirmation of identity by consistently deconstructing it has simply produced another paradox. And the paradox is an unnecessary one, for it is produced by the false assumption that identity is necessarily repressive of difference. Rather than equating identity with domination on one hand while we continue to affirm it on the other, we need to reformulate our conceptions of identity. We need conceptions of identity which are not essentialist, not metaphysical, and not repressive. Thus, it becomes possible to formulate self-identity and autonomy not simply in terms of repression, but in terms of a capacity to participate in a social world, to interpret and articulate needs and desires, to act with reference to values and ideals, even given our states of ambivalence and confusion. And our collective identity as feminists can be formulated in terms of a collective capacity to interpret and articulate collective needs, to set collective goals, through a continual process of dialogue based on a commitment to the inclusion of all voices. This, of course, depends upon an ability to understand language as a medium of shared understanding and dialogue, of the articulation of difference, and not only as a force of deception and oppression. We need to understand language, then, as the medium of a social identity which is not simply repressive.

A model of feminist solidarity as something which can *include* difference and conflict is suggested by bell hooks. hooks has argued that feminists need to shift from an affirmation of mutual "support," which would correspond to Butler's conception of immediate and repressive identity, to an ideal of solidarity, which would correspond to a conception of mediated and non-repressive identity. The idea of support, hooks argues, has corresponded to a shallow notion of sisterhood as a sort of direct identification based on shared victimization, which demands an avoidance of conflict and a suspension of critical judgment. The illusion of undivided unity has inevitably been shattered with the emergence of divisions and hostilities. "The fierce negative disagreements that have taken place in feminist circles have led many feminist activists to shun group or individual interaction where there is likely to be disagreement which leads to confrontation. Safety and support have been redefined to mean hanging out in groups where the participants are alike and share similar values."[21] In other words, the response to the unavoidable recognition of diversity and division has frequently been an avoidance of conflict through an affirmation of the impossibility of solidarity, and a retreat back into support and safety, in the name of an irreducible nonidentity. Thus, hooks traces the affirmation of nonidentity back to an ideal of undivided identity, an ideal which is ultimately unsustainable, and which always leads to failure. Rather than avoiding confrontation through avoiding participation in a collectivity, she argues, we need to shift from an ideal of undivided unity to a form of identity which will not be shattered by confrontation. We need to affirm an ideal of solidarity: a sustained, ongoing commitment to shared values, which will allow for confrontation without complete destruction. The shift from an ideal of support to an ideal of solidarity is, I think, the political dimension of a theoretical shift from an ideal of immediate identity, which turns out to be repressive, to an ideal of mediated identity, which has the potential to include, rather than exclude, difference and heterogeneity. hooks concludes her discussion with an affirmation of feminist solidarity which is certainly idealistic:

> Women do not need to eradicate difference to feel solidarity. We
> do not need to share common oppression to fight equally to end

oppression. We do not need anti-male sentiments to bond us together, so great is the wealth of experience, culture, and ideas we have to share with one another. We can be sisters united by shared interests and beliefs, united in our appreciation for diversity, united in our struggle to end sexist oppression, united in political solidarity.[22]

Ideals can be discounted as unrealistic and illusory; but they can also give us something to strive for.

6

'Resistance Must Finally Be Articulated in a Voice Which Can Be Heard'

Jacqueline Rose and the Paradox of Identity

For Jacqueline Rose, the deconstruction and subversion of identity can only be one side of a viable political theory. For ideals of individual identity, collective identity, and the identity of meaning in language continue to be essential to political struggles. Rose is acutely sensitive to the ambiguities and complexities involved in the attempt to maintain a tension between these two theoretical directions.

In her book, *Sexuality in the Field of Vision,* Rose argues that there is an essential tension in the engagement between feminism and psychoanalysis. On the one hand, psychoanalysis provides a theory of how patriarchy is internalized and reproduced through individual psyches—how, then, women actively participate in the perpetuation of their own oppression. The unconscious is understood as the locus of mediation of socio-historical practices and institutions which have become sedimented and rigidified into psychic structures. (This understanding of the unconscious as a product of human practice—and as mediating between socio-historical and individual practice—is, I think, preferable to a too-simple understanding of psychoanalytic theory as a psychologism or a biological determinism.) In this reading, psychoanalysis is understood to be complementary to Marxism, providing an account of the modes of ideological reproduction of the transhistorical system of patriarchy, through an analysis of the organization of sexuality in terms of sex roles, complementary to Marx's account of the historically specific modes of economic production, which focusses on the organization of labor in terms of class divisions.[1] What emerges from this engagement of feminism with psychoanalysis is a theory and description of how patriarchy is incorporated into women's very *self-identities*.

But, as Rose points out, the use of psychoanalysis as a theory of women's internalization of patriarchal culture is only half the story. For the functionalist account of an *identity between* a transhistorical patriarchal culture and individual identities provides, as has so often been pointed out, no basis for social, political, and individual change.[2] Thus, on the other hand, psychoanalysis is taken up by feminists precisely because it does *not* simply provide a functionalist and deterministic theory of ideology—a theory of the identity between patriarchal culture and individual identities. On the contrary, Rose argues that the use of psychoanalysis as only a theory of women's internalization of patriarchal culture betrays the very concept specific to psychoanalysis: the concept of the unconscious. Following Lacan, Rose argues that the fundamental insight of psychoanalysis is the understanding of the unconscious as that which undermines or calls into question the identity of the subject, and of sexual or gender identity—and hence an identity between a social order and individual subjects.

> What distinguishes psychoanalysis from sociological accounts of gender (hence for me the fundamental impasse of Nancy Chodorow's work) is that whereas for the latter, the internalisation of norms is assumed roughly to work, the basic premise and indeed starting-point of psychoanalysis is that it does not. The unconscious constantly reveals the "failure" of identity. Because there is no continuity of psychic life, so there is no stability of sexual identity, no position for women (or for men) which is ever simply achieved.[3]

In other words, for Rose, psychoanalysis is not only, as it is for Chodorow, a theory of self and gender identity, established through identification with social roles. Psychoanalysis is just as much a theory of *nonidentity*—of the nonidentity of the subject, and of women with the feminine roles in a patriarchal culture. Thus, "psychoanalysis becomes one of the few places in our culture where it is recognized as more than a fact of individual pathology that most women do not painlessly slip into their roles as women, if indeed they do at all" [91]. And thus, according to Rose, "Feminism's affinity with psychoanalysis rests above all, I would argue, with this recognition that there is a resistance to identity at the very heart of psychic life" [91]. And it is this resistance to identity which, for Rose, is the basis of the possibility of social and political change—of resistance to the patriarchal order and to the feminine roles which support it.

In her valorization of the "resistance to identity," Rose shares ground with Irigaray and Derridean feminists. The difference, however, is crucial: while on one hand Rose insists that the source of social and political change can only be the "resistance to identity at the very heart of psychic life," on the other hand she insists equally strongly, echoing Julia Kristeva, that this "resistance must finally be articulated in a voice which can be heard."[4] In other words, social and political change is impossible without an *acceptance of identity:* of the symbolic order of language, which serves as the only medium we have of shared understanding, or social identity; and of "the subject's very ability to hold itself together in speech" [148]—the minimum condition for the capacity of the subject to realize and articulate a coherent ethical position. For Rose, then, the resistance to identity requires the acceptance of identity, and therefore it is necessary to maintain a constant tension between these two moments.

Following Lacan, Rose sees language primarily as a medium of social and subject identity. In Rose's work, the Lacanian focus on the development of the subject through assimilation into the socio-symbolic order—into, that is, an intersubjective sphere of meaning—is turned to a focus on the subject as agent of social and political change, who, not only as subject to but also as participant in a given social order, requires a capacity to recognize, and to produce in speech, some sort of intersubjective identity of meaning. Thus, the simple resistance to identity, the attempt to simply evade or subvert identity, the celebration of différance as a constant deferral of identity, the rejection of any concept of the coherence of the subject and of social identity loses the tension between identity and nonidentity—the tension (or conflict) which is essential for social and political change.

The maintenance of this tension—between identity and resistance to identity, identity and nonidentity, identity and negativity—is the central focus of Rose's theory. And it is the maintenance of this tension which Rose identifies as the key to the work of Julia Kristeva.

Thus, in her incisive analysis of Kristeva's work, Rose argues that "Kristeva's challenge to language and identity can perhaps be recognised as another version of a more familiar political question: how to effect a political transformation when the terms of that transformation are given by the very order which a revolutionary practice seeks to change."[5] Kristeva recognizes that while the norms of language and of self and sexual identity must be criticized, a wholesale rejection of these norms amounts to the rejection of the possibility of change—indeed, of survival.

If we are to criticize the symbolic order of *language,* we have to do so without renouncing our capacity to speak to each other. We are faced, then with the question of "how to challenge the very form of available self-definition without losing the possibility of speech" [158].

Similarly, if we are to criticize the identity of the *subject,* we have to do so without advocating the fragmentation of self, which, as many feminists have pointed out, is a rather dubious ideal for women who are struggling for some measure of autonomy. Here, Rose says that Kristeva's basic insight is that "identity is necessary but only ever partial and therefore carries with it a dual risk"—on one side, "the wreck of all identity"; on the other, "a self-blinding allegiance to psychic norms. To hold onto both sides of this dynamic is, Kristeva argues, almost impossible, although one is in fact always implicated in both" [150].

And finally there is the problem of *women's* identity, and of feminist politics. Rose points out that much of Kristeva's work is directed toward the analysis and critique of "the way in which the limits of language and its dissolution are constantly thought of in terms of sexual difference, the way that cultures define and secure their parameters by relegating the woman to their outer edge" [156]—i.e., the construction of patriarchal culture through a sacrificial logic which designates femininity as "otherness," nonidentity and negativity. At the same time, however, Kristeva consistently returns to the project of recasting *for* women the problem of identity [160].

And while she rejects any claim to an essential identity of women, Kristeva does argue that the place of women in history and culture (in interaction with their bodily specificity: the capacity for maternity) gives women a unique capacity to recognize the necessity of an ethics based on both acceptance of and resistance to norms of self and social identity, as the basis of feminist politics.

> Against the offered and familiar alternatives of bureaucracy and madness, it is women for Kristeva who know the necessity of, and demand, a place on the historical stage, while also calling the bluff of a psychic and sexual order of things which they pass through and across: *'traverser'*, a word central to Kristeva's writing, implies that you go *through* certainly, but also *out*. [158]

Feminist politics, then, must take account of the need to maintain the tension of identity: "No politics without identity, but no identity which takes itself at its word" [157].

Given the difficulty of maintaining this tension between identity and nonidentity, on so many levels, "we should not be surprised," Rose contends, "nor too comfortably critical or dismissive," [151] when Kristeva sometimes tips over to one side or the other—to a disturbing affirmation of the patriarchal symbolic order and its laws of identity, on one side, and to an equally disturbing affirmation of the dissolution of identities, on the other. To a rejection of any basis for feminist solidarity on the grounds that any claim to an identity of women must be rejected, on the one hand, and to a quasi-mystical affirmation of an essential femininity on the other. These failures— and they are failures—in Kristeva's work should be understood in the context of the central thrust of her theory, which is the attempt to theorize identity in light of the critique of identity, to maintain the tension between identity and nonidentity.

Rose's analysis of Kristeva's work in terms of this central tension is, as far as it goes, accurate. But too often the abstractions of identity and nonidentity obscure differences among types of identity, and different conceptions of language and self-identity.

For instance, when Rose argues against Derrida that social and political change requires an acceptance of the symbolic order of language, she is appealing to a conception of language as the means of articulating one's position "in a voice which can be heard" [147], "on *this* side of meaning or sense" [146], and as "the very form of available self-definition" [158]. In other words, she is appealing to a conception of language as a medium of self-expression and mutual understanding—and, therefore, as a medium of participation in a social world, without which any critique or resistance would be impossible.

But when she argues that the identity represented by the symbolic order of language must constantly be resisted, she is equating language with the metaphysical law of identity, and the transhistorical law of patriarchy, and equating the learning of language with an acceptance and internalization of structures of domination. Thus, we are constantly confronted by the "turgid resistance of common-sense language to all forms of conflict and political change" [88].

When she argues that self-identity must be accepted, she is speaking of self-identity as "the capacity to hold oneself together in speech" [148]. Some form of psychic "integration," Rose argues, "was always seen by Kristeva as the pre-condition of any effectivity in the social. . . . Psychosis—we can be thankful—was never offered as a revolutionary ideal" [147]. Like language, self-identity is understood in terms of a subject's capacity for participation in a social world—the capacity to recognize and maintain some sort of coherence of the self, which, not incidentally, is the precondition of any commitment to an ethical or political position.

This is very different from the self-identity which must be resisted: the identity which is merely an identity *with,* or conformity to, the norms of patriarchal culture;[6] or the identity of the "bourgeois individual" based on internalization of norms and requiring a defensive self-mastery, a repression or denial (or appropriation) of nonidentity and difference—of, that is, any source of resistance to a patriarchal culture.[7]

Thus, when Rose argues that social and political change requires an *acceptance of identity,* she is at least implicitly appealing to a form of social and self-identity defined as a capacity for some sort of shared understanding, and an openness to nonidentity, difference, criticism, and change. But when she argues that *identity must always be resisted,* she is referring to a form of identity which closes off and represses nonidentity.

Thus, the central paradox that Rose identifies in Kristeva's work, "how to effect a political transformation when the terms of that transformation are given by the very order which a revolutionary practice seeks to change" [148], is perhaps not a paradox at all. For, if the terms of political transformation are the possibility of shared understanding and a capacity for criticism, these must be differentiated from, and not identified with, the terms of a repressive, patriarchal order. If self-identity is defined, on one hand, as conformity to a social role in a patriarchal order, then it makes no sense to argue that self-identity can also be the capacity to articulate resistance. And if the symbolic order of language is thoroughly patriarchal, and completely repressive of difference, then it cannot also be a medium for mutual understanding. The paradox emerges only when the repressive and non-repressive forms of self-identity and language are collapsed together into a single, repressive form of identity which is, alas, necessary for survival.

Thus, Rose ultimately shares Derrida's evaluation of identity as fundamentally repressive. The difference is that Rose argues that if we want to avoid total chaos, identity must nevertheless be accepted. Rose falls into an oscillation between two terms of a paradox: between a rejection of identity as fundamentally repressive, and a stoical acceptance of identity as the only means we have of escaping psychosis and aphasia.[8]

But the paradox is not inevitable. Rather, Rose is locked into this paradox because, in her theory, self-identity, language, gender roles, and patriarchy are so tightly locked together. Self-identity is seen as subjection to a symbolic order of language which is structured in terms of a phallic law, and sexual identity and sexual difference are determined by that law, except insofar as the law necessarily fails. Once these different terms are collapsed together, we are left with the very reductive identity which Rose herself wants to criticize: a functionalist identity between patriarchal culture and individual identities. To which we can add a Lévi-Straussian structuralist identity of social roles with an unchangeable symbolic order, and a Lacanian identity of the symbolic order with patriarchy. Thus, Rose collapses the complexity of the concepts of self-identity and language, collapses the tensions between identity and nonidentity, into a reading of every form of identity as a capitulation to the law—a capitulation that, in the event, must be accepted. (Yet always resisted.) But, once any emancipatory potential of self-identity and language is given up, the insistence on the need for identity is rendered merely conformist.

Rose's paradox emerges out of a tendency to theorize the identity of the self as a form of repression—which, nevertheless, must be grudgingly accepted for survival, for the avoidance of psychosis. Rose doesn't adequately theorize the positive or neutral dimensions of the identity of the self, which are implicit in her theory. And this is because she is committed to a theory of psychic nonidentity as the source of resistance to an identitarian, one-dimensional society.

Thus, Rose argues that "the politics of Lacanian psychoanalysis" depend upon an insistence upon the *incoherence of the self*. "From the 1930s, Lacan saw his intervention as a return to the concepts of psychic division, splitting of the ego, and an endless (he called it 'insistent') pressure of the unconscious against any individual's pretension to a smooth and coherent psychic and sexual identity" [93]. This position was taken in explicit opposition to the development of ego psychology in America, which is seen as an uncritical practice aimed at resolving contradictions and resistances in subjects and therefore rendering them happy conformists to bourgeois individualism.[9] Against the ego psychologists, Lacan insists that "psychoanalysis does not offer an account of a developing ego which is 'not *necessarily* coherent,' but of an ego which is 'necessarily *not* coherent,' that is, which is always and persistently divided against itself" [94]. In other words, Lacan considers the incoherence or fragmentation of the self not as a problem to be solved, but as the normal state of human beings. Rather than calling for a resolution of nonidentity into identity, for an appropriation or repression of difference within the self in the name of an ideal simple identity, Lacan criticizes the ideal of identity as a phallic phantasy and insists that the subject is necessarily nonidentical, necessarily "incoherent." And it is this *nonidentity* of the subject which is taken up as a "Lacanian politics" by Althusserian structuralist Marxists and feminists as the source of resistance to the patriarchal Law of Identity which demands the spurious "unity of the culture and the psychic unity of subjects" [142]. Or, as Rose puts it, "the force of the unconscious in Lacan's interpretation of Freud was felt to undermine the mystifications of a bourgeois culture proclaiming its identity, and that of its subjects, to the world" [94].

Rose recognizes that, for feminists, the attempt to base a politics on the incoherence of the self is, to put it mildly, problematic. "Feminists could legitimately object that the notion of psychic fragmentation was of little immediate political advantage to women struggling for the first time to find a voice, and trying to bring together the dissociated components of their life into a political programme" [94]. But because she does not theorize a form of self-identity different from the "bourgeois individualism" based on the repression of difference, and different from the narcissistic identity based on simple conformity to a one-dimensional culture, Rose ends up calling for an oscillation between resistance to, and stoical acceptance of, a repressive, conformist form of self-identity which is, unfortunately, unavoidable. Self-identity is understood, once again, as identity with the patriarchal law of identity, which, because it underlies the symbolic order of language, must be accepted if we are to speak, yet must continually be resisted if we are to change.

In her introduction to Lacan's work on feminine sexuality, Rose writes that Lacan's theory underwent a shift from an early concept of language as intersubjective mediation to a later concept of language as that which upholds a fantasy of the possibility of intersubjective relationship—a fantasy of intersubjective unity, which suppresses the reality of difference or nonidentity among and within subjects. (This nonidentity, Rose maintains, is an effect of the unconscious.)[10] Thus, whereas in the early theory the developmental transition from imaginary to symbolic is a shift from a fantasy of the unity and omnipotence of the self to a recognition of differentiation among subjects as participants in an intersubjective sphere mediated by language, in the later work the symbolic is seen merely to repeat the fantasy of unity.

> In the earlier texts, the unity was assigned to the imaginary, the symbolic was at least potentially its break. In the later texts, Lacan located the fantasy of "sameness" within language and the sexual relation at one and the same time.

> Thus there is no longer imaginary "unity" and then symbolic difference or exchange, but rather an indictment of the symbolic for the imaginary unity which its most persistent myths continue to promote. [46–47]

According to Rose, then, Lacan gave up a delusory faith in the possibility of intersubjectivity for a recognition of its impossibility—gave up the fantasy of a social unity of differentiated and nonidentical subjects for a recognition of the truth: that any form of unity is necessarily repressive, and any ideal of relationship a fantasy covering over the reality of lack.

Thus, for Rose, the development of a self-identity through entrance into the symbolic order of language is nothing more than an acceptance of a fantasy of identity based on conformity to a delusion of intersubjective relationship and understanding. But, as I have argued, this view of things clashes with Rose's claim that we can, after all, speak to each other, and with her insistence that our capacity to do so is essential to any struggle for social and political change.

Rose's assumption that a paradoxical tension must be preserved between the acceptance and rejection of identity leaves her oscillating between abstract negation and stoical acceptance of a form of identity which is understood to be repressive but necessary, and inescapable. The alternative to this oscillation is, as Rose's theory already implies, a differentiation between open and closed, repressive and nonrepressive forms of identity.

7

Toward a Theory of Self and Social Identity

Julia Kristeva

Interpretations of Julia Kristeva's work seem to fall into a series of diametrically opposed positions. Kristeva has been taken up as a theorist of negativity, of the dissolution of identities,[1] and on the other hand she has been criticized as a defender of the Lacanian phallus, of the need to maintain the identity of the given patriarchal socio-symbolic order against the encroachments of negativity.[2] She has been criticized as an essentialist, as a defender of libidinal drives and of the maternal space of the semiotic chora outside language,[3] and as a structuralist, as a defender of a linguistic determinism which excludes human practice.[4] She has been criticized for her idealization of maternity and for her rejection of any claim to an essential women's identity. She has been called anti-political because she rejects any concept of individual or collective agency, and bourgeois because she is too focussed on agency at the expense of *différance*.

There is, I think, some truth to each of these critiques, and a good reason for the oppositions: Kristeva's work is characterized by a series of ambivalences, rooted in a fundamental ambivalence between a sacrificial model of identity and a theory of identity as something that can include difference and heterogeneity, and openness to change. In this chapter, I want to draw out the second dimension in

Kristeva's work, to develop a model of self-identity as a capacity for participation in a social world.

It's not without some misapprehension that I've chosen to emphasize Kristeva's theory to suggest some positive directions for feminist theories of identity. Kristeva's politics are dubious at best; in comparison to theorists like Judith Butler, Kristeva seems like a remote figure, outside of the problems and issues that face us now. I want to argue that Kristeva's work is, nevertheless, important because of the stress she places on the existential and ethical dimensions of affirming and living an identity of self, and because she theorizes the development of this self, through a reanalysis of psychoanalytic concepts, in the context of a theory of language as the basis of a social identity which is not purely repressive.

Against structuralist and poststructuralist theories of language as a totalizing and unchangeable system, Kristeva argues for an understanding of language in terms of a dialectic between structure and practice, such that the structure is produced through and always open to change by human practice. This opens the way to a theory of the formation of self-identity as the development of a capacity for social symbolic interaction, rather than as an acceptance of repression. Thus, Kristeva's theory provides a basis for differentiating between sacrificial and nonsacrificial, repressive and nonrepressive aspects of identity.

"Women's Time": Toward a Non-sacrificial Model of Identity

In her early essay on feminism, "Women's Time," Kristeva identifies two opposed directions of European feminism: on one hand, the demand for equality—for inclusion within social and economic and political structures on an equal basis with men—and on the other hand, a refusal of the given "socio-symbolic order," on the grounds that it is based on a sacrificial logic—specifically, on the sacrifice of women.[5] Kristeva affirms the unquestionable importance of the concrete political goals of the "universalist" stream of the women's movement, and asserts that the effects of this movement will be no less than revolutionary.[6] She affirms also the critique of the given socio-symbolic order and the attempt to generate alternatives to it.

But she is critical of the one-sidedness of both positions, which she understands in terms of theories of identity. The former represents, for Kristeva, a "logic of identification ... with the logical and onto-logical values of a rationality dominant in the nation state" [19] and "the idea of a necessary identification between the two sexes as the only and unique means for liberating the 'second sex'" [20]. And the latter amounts to a refusal of identification which tends to be based on an affirmation of "irreducible difference" [20]—an insistence on the nonidentity between men and women, and a corresponding appeal to women's "irreducible identity" which is "exploded, plural, fluid, in a certain way nonidentical" [19].

Kristeva devotes most of the essay to an analysis of the second, more recently developed position. "The new generation of women," she writes, "is showing that its major concern has become the socio-symbolic contract as a sacrificial contract" [25]. Kristeva acknowl-edges the difficulty, if not impossibility, for women, of identifying with a socio-symbolic order which is predicated on the sacrifice of women. But while she supports the critique and analysis of the sacri-ficial logic which underpins the "given socio-symbolic order" and supports the attempt by women to articulate and analyze their own desires, their own histories and experiences, Kristeva warns that "attacks against Language and Sign" [32] are frequently so totalizing as to be self-destructive. The "protests against the constraints of the sociosymbolic contract," she argues, constitute a threat not only to patriarchal, oppressive social forms, but to "the very principle of sociality" [33]. At this point, the critique can be read in two ways: either Kristeva is arguing that we have to accept patriarchy and the sacrifice of women as the necessary conditions of any socio-symbolic order; or, she is arguing that we have to make a distinction between the necessary conditions of a social community, and of language, and the pathological conditions of domination. As I shall show, Kristeva's line of argument leads to the latter conclusion.

Kristeva warns against the dangers of a Woman-identified femi-nism (and she clearly distinguishes "Woman" from women) which, against the given socio-symbolic order, upholds as an alternative a fantasy of a "female society" which "is then constituted as a sort of alter ego of the official society, in which all real or fantasized possibilities for *jouissance* take refuge. Against the socio-symbolic contract, both sacrifical and frustrating, this countersociety is imagined as harmonious, without prohibitions, free and fulfilling ... an a-topia, a place outside the law" [27]. For Kristeva, this fantasy is simply a repetition of one of the central myths of patriarchal culture: the myth of the archaic mother.

> If the archetype of the belief in a good and pure substance, that of utopias, is the belief in the omnipotence of an archaic, full, total, englobing mother with no frustration, no separation, with no break-producing symbolism (with no castration, in other words), then it becomes evident that we will never be able to defuse the violences mobilized through the counterinvestment necessary to carrying out this phantasm, unless one challenges precisely this myth of the archaic mother. [29]

Here, as elsewhere in her work, Kristeva argues that the fantasy of complete gratification in the "archaic mother" is itself a central fantasy of patriarchy. Thus, its adoption by women as a basis of emancipation, as an alternative to a patriarchal order, will always backfire, because the archaic mother represents in our cultural imaginary not only gratification and pleasure, but a power against which we are helpless, and against which we must struggle to defend ourselves. Women must differentiate themselves from this mythic Mother-Woman—and this, she argues, is the only way to make sense of Lacan's "scandalous sentence" that "There is no such thing as Woman." "Indeed," Kristeva argues, "she does *not* exist with a capital 'W,' possessor of some mythical unity—a supreme power, on which is based the terror of power and terrorism as the desire for power" [30].

Against the utopia/dystopia of a countersociety "outside the law," Kristeva offers a different ideal. She envisions a society in which the sacrificial basis of social relations and institutions is replaced by an *"interiorization of the founding separation of the sociosymbolic contract,* as an introduction of its cutting edge into the very interior of every identity whether subjective, sexual, ideological" [34]. A non-patriarchal, non-dominating social order *not* based on the sacrifice of women, or of any social group or individual by another, would have to be based on a form of self-identity, and of social identity, characterized by an *acceptance* of a "founding separation." For Kristeva, this acceptance begins with a social and individual recognition and acceptance of violence.

> In this sense and from a viewpoint undoubtedly too Hegelian, modern feminism has been but a moment in the interminable process of coming to consciousness about the implacable violence (separation, castration, etc.) which constitutes any symbolic contract. [28]

This can be read as a too-Hegelian (and too-Freudian and too-structuralist) assumption of a fundamental opposition between primary pleasure and language/sociality—a fundamental opposition which can be resolved only through the acceptance of some form of repression/domination. It can be read, then, as a rationalization of domination, of the internalization of the law, and the mastery of difference, particularity, pleasure, and desire—and the repudiation of connection with the mother—as the conditions of civilization.

This is not, however, what Kristeva means. She is arguing that the domination which has been exposed by feminism, the struggle to the death between man and woman, between the mother goddess and the patriarchal law, is a stage we can move beyond. Our recognition of this struggle must lead not to a reconciliation with an order of domination, but rather to an eradication of domination. This requires that

> the struggle, the implacable difference, the violence be conceived in the very place where it operates with the maximum intransigence, in other words, in personal and sexual identity itself, so as to make it disintegrate in its very nucleus. [34]

The "interiorization of the founding separation of the sociosymbolic contract" means that

> the habitual and increasingly explicit attempt to fabricate a scapegoat victim as foundress of a society or a countersociety may be replaced by the analysis of the potentialities of *victim/executioner* which characterize each identity, each subject, each sex. [34]

I want to argue that Kristeva is, in effect, calling for a *differentiation* between the violence of separation, which is unavoidable, and the violence of domination, which can perhaps be overcome. The interiorization of the founding separation means that separation must be accepted as a subjective experience: the experience of pain and loss in the process of differentiating self from other, of recognizing the other's separateness, and in the process recognizing one's own partiality, one's own limitations and responsibilities, must be accepted as an inevitable part of the process of becoming an individual in a social world. But the violence of this founding separation and of the aggressions and desires it involves must be clearly distinguished from, and accepted in order to achieve the end of, the violence of domination of one group by another, one person by another, or the defensive repudiation of parts of the self.

Unlike Chodorow, Irigaray, and Benjamin, all of whom collapse separation into domination, all of whom ultimately implicate separation from the mother and the development of a separate self as the basis of male domination, Kristeva wants to differentiate between an experience of separation which is painful, difficult, and psychically violent, and the violence of domination, which is a very different thing.

The crucial point is that the interiorization of the founding separation means the development of a different form of identity: an identity founded not on a defensive opposition to the other, but on an acceptance of internal differentiation—an acceptance of the otherness within the self. This development in the subjective experience of identity corresponds to a development in other forms of identity: gender identities and the identities of social collectivities need to be reconceptualized through a reflexive and affective acceptance of internal differentiation, of the existence of the other within. This entails an identification with the (internally differentiated) difference of others.[7]

For Kristeva, this process can only be achieved through analysis—through a development in our understanding of the sacrificial logic, and of the need to replace it with a logic of inclusion.

If Kristeva sees the acceptance of separation as the acceptance of violence and pain as necessary parts of the development of the self, she wants also to reject the portrayal of the development of self-identity as an acceptance of "necessary unhappiness"—as the repression of pleasure, of nonidentity, which is necessary for individuation, for rationality, and hence for civilization.[8] Here and throughout her work, Kristeva stresses that the development of self-identity, far from requiring the repression of pleasure, in fact is a *pleasurable* process. The pleasure of differentiation, the pleasure of signification, the pleasure of identification and interaction with others, the pleasure of learning to participate in a social world, are all thematized by Kristeva as essential to the formation of self-identity. The process of becoming an individuated member of a society must be seen, she argues, not only in terms of loss and lack, but as "the possibility for *jouissance,* for various productions, for a life made up of both challenges and differences" [35].

This emphasis on the pleasure of self-development emerges, I want to argue, from an emphasis on the sociality of the self. The development of self-identity need not be seen as the development of a lonely, isolated self who lives forever fighting against the slide back into primal pleasure—fighting against, that is, the thing he most desires—in order to preserve himself. Rather, it can be seen as the development of a capacity for *participation* in a social world. Unlike Benjamin, Kristeva sees the development of a "separate self" not as a move from intersubjective relation into isolation, but as a move from a sociality based solely on primary drives and affective bonds into a capacity for social relations mediated through symbolic interaction and based on a full conscious acceptance of one's separateness, of the differences within oneself, and of the differences of others. Unlike Irigaray, she sees the development of self-identity not as the sacrifice of nonidentity or particularity or difference in order to achieve conformity to a given socio-symbolic order, but as the capacity for *realization* and *expression* of nonidentity—of the realization and expression of one's own uniqueness and differences through acquisition of the capacity for signification, and hence for symbolic interaction.

For Kristeva, the understanding of self-development as a pleasurable process, of the development of a separate self as a capacity for participation, and of social and self-identity as a capacity for realization and expression of nonidentity, depends on a demystification of social identity, of the "sociosymbolic order" and of language.

We need, she argues:

> to demystify the identity of the symbolic bond itself, to demystify, therefore, the community of language as a universal and unifying tool, one which totalizes and equalizes. In order to bring out—along with the *singularity* of each person, and, even more, along with the multiplicity of every person's possible identifications ... *the relativity of his/her symbolic as well as biological existence,* according to the variation in his/her specific symbolic capacities" [35].

In other words, we need to criticize the concept of language as a necessarily totalizing force, and reject the belief that the universality maintained through language—social identity, maintained through social identifications—necessarily represses particularity, difference or singularity. The "community of language," the "symbolic bond," is a universal which *can* allow for both the singularity and the complexity of individuals.

In differentiating between a social order based on the sacrifice of women, and a social order based on the acceptance of separation, difference, and nonidentity—in differentiating between the break or separation necessary for any symbolic order and the sacrifice of woman/body/pleasure which is specific to patriarchy—Kristeva provides a basis for *differentiating* between the structure of language and of socio-symbolic order *per se* and the historical structures and institutions of patriarchal domination. Rather than reducing all socio-symbolic order to patriarchal forms, and thereby allowing no way out but to abolish sociality altogether, Kristeva is able to leave open the possibility that "the social order" can be *changed.*

For Kristeva, feminism is and will be a central force for such change. Ideally, "having started with the idea of difference, feminism will be able to break free of its belief in Woman, Her power, Her writing, so as to channel this demand for difference into each and every element of the female whole, and, finally, to bring out the singularity of each woman, and beyond this, her multiplicities, her plural languages" [33]. In other words, Kristeva wants feminism to hold onto the emphasis on difference, but to shift that emphasis from the claim to an irreducible feminine identity (which merely reaffirms the tired old essentialist concept of Woman) to an affirmation of the differences among women, of the specificity and singularity of each woman—a singularity which can encompass nonidentity and complexity.

This "third attitude" of feminism is not meant to *replace* the projects of seeking full social and political equality with men, and of attempting to theorize and analyze women's difference or specificity. The "third generation … does not exclude—quite to the contrary— the *parallel* existence of all three in the same historical time, or even that they be interwoven one into the other" [33]. What it does is to introduce a theoretical basis for the acceptance and valuation of nonidentity and difference within the feminist community, to offer a vision of an ideal social whole which is open to differences without dissolving into them, through a model of a coherent yet open self-identity for women.

In the following sections, I want to show how this model of self-identity is grounded in Kristeva's theory of language as a dialectic between structure and the practice of subjects.

Language as a Dialectical Interaction of Structure and Practice

In her earliest work, Kristeva is primarily engaged with analyses of language, and with the critique and reformulation of linguistic theories. She criticizes the structuralist understanding of language solely in terms of structure or system or code, and argues instead for a theory of language as a *discursive practice of subjects*. Thus, Kristeva's "poststructuralism" is unlike that of Derrida and Butler, who see the subject as nothing more than a reflection or function of the law of language, and who therefore want to move beyond the subject, into the analysis of transcendental laws; and it is unlike that of Lacan, and of Rose, who, while they want to reintroduce the subject as a necessary construct, persist in regarding the subject as only a function of the law, and who therefore end up caught in an oscillation between the two poles of an ineradicable paradox. Kristeva, whose theories of language and society are influenced by the discourse theorist Mikhail Bakhtin and the sociologist Lucien Goldmann, and whose psychoanalytic theory, while certainly influenced by Lacan, is closer to that of Freud and of the analyst André Green, argues for the reintroduction of the subject, the body and history into analyses of language—for, that is, an understanding of language in terms of human discourse.

While on one side Kristeva challenges the concept of language as a fixed, unchanging structure, on the other side, she rejects the concept of a subject as a "Cartesian subject," as generator or originator of language. In "The System and the Speaking Subject," Kristeva stresses that a theory of language as the practice of subjects must not be simply the "rehabilitation of the Cartesian conception of language as an *act* carried out by a *subject*."[9] The revival of a subject-centred understanding of language "will not get beyond the reduction ... of signifying *practices* to their systematic aspect" [27]. The point, Kristeva argues, is not only to identify "the systematic constraint within each signifying practice" but to move beyond that to specify "just what, within the practice, falls outside the system and characterizes the specificity of the practice as such" [26–27]. Kristeva argues that "the practice of subjects" must be analyzed in terms of its historical and cultural specificity, and "subjects" must be understood as subjects of "heterogeneous processes." The subject must be understood not as a "*transcendental ego,* cut off from its body, its unconscious and also its history" [28]. The subject reintroduced into linguistic analysis must be "the speaking subject as subject of a heterogeneous process" [30]—must be understood, that is, "in connection with that externality, which may be social, natural, or unconscious," [27] subject to "forces extraneous to the logic of the systematic"—on one side, to "bio-physiological processes" and on the other, to "social constraints (family structures, modes of production, etc.)" [28].

At the same time, Kristeva stresses that the study of language as the practice of subjects must focus not only on what is "extraneous to the logic of the systematic." The focus must be on the *dialectical interaction* of the practice with a system or structure. The practice of speaking subjects cannot be analyzed without an understanding of the linguistic structure or code which must be learned by every subject who learns a language—of "the symbolic and/or social *thesis* (in Husserl's sense of the word) indispensable to every practice" [27]. The point is not to reject the analysis of linguistic structures for an analysis of practices, but to analyze the ways in which practice and structure interact: to analyze the practice of subjects in terms of a necessary interaction with a structure, and to analyze the structure as a production of subjects. In particular, Kristeva focuses on the intrasubjective processes underlying subjects' engagement with, acquisition of, production of, and transformation of a structure.

Signifying practice is understood by Kristeva as "the acceptance of a symbolic law together with the transgression of that law for the purpose of renovating it" [29]. In other words, the acceptance (or learning) of the system or structure of a language (and through language, of a society) is an essential component of the signifying practice of subjects. But equally essential are the "transgressions" which continually produce changes in the system or structure. For Kristeva, the structure of language is an open structure, open to constant renewal and constant change through the discursive practice of subjects. Unlike Rose, for whom the acceptance and transgression of the structure of language is a constant oscillation between two incompatible positions—an oscillation which leaves the structure untouched and intact—Kristeva sees acceptance and transgression as two moments in a dialectical process of constant change and renewal. Kristeva's structure is a structure produced through, and open to change through, human practice.

This is a conception of language quite different from the structuralist understanding of language purely in terms of structure or code. And, therefore, it is quite different from the poststructuralist positions of Derrida, Irigaray, and Butler: rather than providing a *critique* of the structuralist conception of language as a code, these theorists offer only an abstract negation. They analyze the laws underlying the system, and demonstrate the system's production of identities through the exclusion and repression of nonidentity. But they fail to question the structuralist position that the system of language is fixed, eternal, and unchanging. Derrida and Butler argue that there can be no escape from the logic of exclusion, and Irigaray calls for a body language outside the law.

Kristeva's understanding of language in terms of a dialectical interaction between system and practice provides a basis for a critique of the understanding of language as a manifestation of an abstract law of identity, upheld through the repression of nonidentity. Kristeva's model allows for an understanding of the structure of language as an identity which does not exclude but rather includes, does not repress but rather expresses nonidentity, understood as the practice of subjects. This opens up an understanding of "transgression," and of negativity, not as a constant subversion of the ultimately unchangeable system or law, but as the constant change and the constant renewal of structure and system.

Language as the Practice of "the Subject of a Heterogeneous Process": Psychoanalysis and Plurality

In her doctoral dissertation in linguistics, Kristeva argued that a theory of language as the discursive practice of subjects is necessary for an understanding of *differences* among languages, discourses, and "signifying systems." This understanding of differences is opened up with the the psychoanalytic understanding of the subject.

In her dissertation, published later as *Language—The Unknown,* Kristeva argues that the rehabilitation of the "Cartesian subject" as generator of language (here Kristeva is referring to Chomsky's generative grammar) merely produces a homology between the structuralist concept of language as a unified system and the unified subject as generator of that system, and thereby closes off any analysis of the *plurality* of discourses and languages across cultures and through history. Generative grammar "studies neither *la langue* in its diversity nor discourse in its multiple functions. It demonstrates instead the coherence of the logical subject-predicate system," and simply describes the linguistic structure corresponding to the Cartesian psychological structure.[10] "But," Kristeva asks, "is that the only structure? Should the enormous variability of linguistic functioning be subordinated to this one structure?" Such an approach,

she argues, renders impossible any recognition of "the *plurality* of signifying systems recorded in other languages and discourses" [260].

Against this conception of language as a unified structure produced by unified subjects, Kristeva argues that an understanding of
the plurality and specificity of languages and of different language
structures is opened up through recourse to a psychoanalytic understanding of the subject as "a subject who destroys and reconstructs
himself in and through the signifier," [261]—a subject who "makes
and unmakes himself" [265] in and through language. Such a conception of language in terms of the practice of subjects in the process
of self-making (and thus, in the process of making meaning) opens
up "the theory, in the plural, of the signs and modes of signification
in history" [261].

Against the linguistic understanding of language as a closed system of signifiers, psychoanalysis is based on the understanding that
language does not exist outside its *realization* in the *discourse* of
subjects [274], and moreover, that "the subject and meaning are ...
produced in *discursive work,*" [275] always in relation to others and
their discourses. Kristeva argues that the "Cartesian postulate, which
underlies the procedure of modern linguistics ... was shaken up by
the Freudian discovery of the unconscious and its logic. From then
on, it became difficult to talk about a subject without following the
various configurations revealed by the different relations between
subjects and their discourse. The subject *is* not; he makes and
unmakes himself in a complex topology where the other and his
discourse are included. One cannot possibly talk about the *meaning*
of a discourse without taking this topology into account" [274–75].

Kristeva sees the project of psychoanalysis as a hermeneutic analysis of the discourse of subjects, through which it is possible to derive
an explanatory science of the modes of operation of the "discursive
work" underlying the signifying practice of the subject. By analyzing
the general processes or laws of this discursive work (such as
condensation, displacement, inversion, double meaning), Freud was
able to provide the means for understanding discourses or signifying
systems which are "types of languages" (for example, dreams, myths,
idioms, jokes, totems, and taboos), as well as different discourses
within a language [273]. "This amounts to saying that the psycho-

analytic intervention prevents the metaphysical gesture of identifying various language practices with One *Langue*, One discourse, One syntax, and that it encourages the search for differences in languages, in discourses, in the plural, or rather of signifying systems constructed in what was taken for *La langue* [273]."

The psychoanalytic understanding of language as a practice of subjects opens up an understanding of *meaning* which brings together the universality of meaning essential for social communication with the plurality of modes of signification, and with the specificity of meaning for a particular subject. "The production of meaning is . . . an actual production that transverses the surface of the *uttered* discourse, and that engenders in the *enunciation*—a new stratum opened up in the analysis of language—a particular meaning with a particular subject" [275]. The subject produces herself through her discourse, through a practice of engagement with symbolic systems which allow the realization/expression/production of meaning, and which thereby allow the realization/production of a subject as a singular, unique individual. If the subject is produced through language, she is not simply a reflection or function of language; for language and meanings are themselves "productions," produced only through human practice.

The Thetic

The interaction and engagement of the practice of the subject with the structure of language is understood in terms of what Kristeva calls "the thetic." Linguistically, the thetic refers to the act of naming,[11] of the grammatical identification and specification of subject and object, as preconditions of propositionality—i.e., of stating a thesis [43]. This corresponds to the subjective process of the development of self-identity: of the identification of the self as a self through identification with, and recognition of separateness from, objects/others, and one's own image. Kristeva locates the beginnings of this process at an early stage of development. Even a child's first "holophrastic enunciations," which include a gesture, the object, and vocal emission, are already thetic insofar as they identify and separate an object from the subject, and attribute to it "a semiotic fragment,

which thereby becomes a signifier." Such enunciations thus constitute "an *attribution,* which is to say, a positing of identity or difference," which "represents the nucleus of judgment or proposition"
[43]. Through this process of attribution/identification/separation of
self and objects, the symbolic system of language emerges. "This
image and objects must first be posited in a space that becomes
symbolic because it connects the two separated positions, recording
them or redistributing them in an open combinatorial system" [43].
The symbolic, then, is understood as the means of reconnecting or
mediating self and its objects, and creating meaning.

For the subject, Kristeva argues, this "thetic moment" entails a
"break in the signifying process": a shift from pre-representational,
drive-governed bodily processes (what Kristeva calls "the semiotic")
to "the realm of signification, which is always that of a proposition
or judgment, in other words, a realm of *positions*" [43]. This is a
developmental shift, but it is also one that is continually repeated in
the production of discourse. It is a shift from a practice or process
which is "meaningless" to a practice governed by investment in a
symbolic system. This shift from making sounds to making meanings—to signifying—corresponds to a shift from doing or acting to
taking a position as an agent or actor.

For Kristeva, the concept of "the thetic" serves to bring together
an analysis of linguistic structure with an analysis of the practice of
subjects, through a focus on the intrasubjective processes of language acquisition and production. It serves, moreover, as a basis for
understanding the identity of the subject, developed through a
process of identification with a linguistic structure, as an essential
dimension of signifying practice. It is impossible, Kristeva argues, to
understand the practice of subjects without an understanding of the
production of identities in a symbolic system. This understanding of
identity as a product of signifying practice is linked to an understanding of signifying practice as a "productive negativity."

Productive Negativity: Kristeva's Critique of Derrida

Against the Derridean identification of negativity with *différance,*
with the abstract play of the signifier which resists identity, Kristeva,

following Hegel more closely, identifies negativity with both the negation and the production of identity. Kristeva understands negativity as the fourth term of Hegel's dialectic, as the mediation of pure abstractions: "Negativity constitutes the logical impetus beneath the thesis of negation and that of the negation of negation, but is identical to neither since it is, instead, the logical functioning of the movement that produces the theses."[12] It is "the liquefying and dissolving agent that does not destroy but rather reactivates new organizations and, in that sense, affirms." And it is the "transition" which constitutes both "necessary connection" and the emergence of distinctions [109].

Unlike her French colleagues, Kristeva draws her reading of Hegel not from Kojève, but, presumably as a function of her Bulgarian education, from Lenin. Thus, while she avoids the one-sidedness of the Kojèvian interpretation of negativity as the resistance to any form of identity, she falls prey to, and inexplicably seems to accept, Lenin's metaphysics, according to which negativity is "the objective principle of all physical and spiritual life" [110]; "the logic of matter" [112]; "the very movement of heterogeneous matter" [113].

However, Kristeva reinvests this abstract "negativity" with a concrete content: Kristeva argues that Hegel's concept of negativity is concretized and given its material content through the understanding of language in terms of the signifying practice of subjects. She bases her own model of the analytical method of "semanalysis" on this revised concept of negativity.

> Thus intent on revealing the negativity which Hegel had seen at work beneath all rationality but which, by a masterly stroke, he subordinated to absolute knowledge, *semanalysis* can be thought of as the direct successor of the dialectical method; but the dialectic it continues will be one which will at last be genuinely materialist since it recognizes the *materiality—the heterogeneity—* of that negativity whose concrete base Hegel was unable to see and which mechanistic Marxists have reduced to a merely economic externality.[13]

Kristeva understands negativity as the "heterogeneity" of the practice—material, bodily, and social—which underlies signification, and the positing of self-identity.

This is the essence of Kristeva's critique of Derrida: first, Derrida's concept of negativity is an abstract concept, with no grounding in the practice of subjects; second, Derrida sees negativity only as a force of resistance to identity, rather than as a force of production of identities that are open to change. In *Revolution in Poetic Language* Kristeva acknowledges that Derrida's "grammatology" is "the most radical of all the various procedures that have tried, after Hegel, to push dialectical negativity further and elsewhere."[14] But because Derrida analyzes language as a transcendental structure outside of the practice of subjects, he can understand the symbolic order only as an abstract law of identity which represses an equally abstract nonidentity, or pure negativity. Derrida attempts to rescue and affirm the movement of pure negativity, of an endless *différance*, which endlessly defers the violence of repressive identity and which operates only to transgress, subvert, and dissolve identities. The irony is that because he remains in the realm of the abstract opposition of identity and nonidentity, positing an abstract nonidentity against an equally abstract identity, Derrida neglects the "heterogeneity" which his concept of *différance* is supposed to rescuscitate.

For Kristeva, heterogeneity is better understood as the concrete practice of embodied, speaking subjects embedded in specific discursive structures, in specific historical and social contexts. Only once heterogeneity is concretized as a practice of embodied speaking subjects is it possible to understand the moment of identity not as a stopping up of negativity, but as the moment of the subject's engagement with language and with social meanings, an engagement which allows the realization/expression of "heterogeneity." Only then can the moment of identification, which Kristeva calls the thetic moment, be understood in terms of the need of a subject to affirm an identity, to identify herself in relation to objects and others in a social world. And only then can taking up and affirming an identity be understood as a prerequisite to taking ethical positions.

In its relentless resistance to and subversion of identity, Derrida's "trace," Kristeva argues, "dissolves every thesis—material, natural, social, substantial, and logical—in order to free itself from any dependence on the *Logos*" [143]. There are no differences. Every thesis is subsumed under the category of Identity and rejected. "The trace marks *anteriority* to every entity and thus to every position" [143]. Thus, "in its desire to bar the thetic, ... the grammatological deluge of meaning gives up on the subject and must remain ignorant of [the subject's] functioning as social practice" [142].

The rejection of the thetic moment is a rejection of the thetic *break* which intervenes to cut short the movement and play of *différance*, the break of separation/identification which is essential to the subject's capacity to identify objects in the world, to recognize others as separate selves, and to recognize and affirm one's own identity as a self. This break is essential to the subject's capacity to take up, or identify *with*, an *ethical* position with respect to a situation which the subject confronts in the world. The break or separation which produces identity is essential, then, to the capacity for criticism, for resistance, for "negativity" as *contradiction* within and against a social order. In the concept of *différance*, Kristeva writes, "negativity has become positivized and drained of its potential for producing breaks. It holds itself back and appears as a delaying *[retardement]*, it defers and thus becomes merely positive and affirmative" [141]. Thus "*différance* neutralizes productive negativity" [142], maintaining a stasis of "non-contradiction" which preserves a "neutral peace" [140], avoiding the violence of the break, of identity, of ethics, of resistance. Social structures and the problems they pose for subjects are held at a distance, where they can remain abstract and untouchable. "Neutral in the face of all positions, theses, and structures, grammatology is, as a consequence, equally restrained when they break, burst or rupture: demonstrating disinterestedness toward (symbolic and/or social) structure, grammatology remains silent when faced with its destruction or renewal" [142].

Beyond the Phallus: Violence and Pleasure in Language

Kristeva reads Derrida's concept of *différance* in psychoanalytic terms, as "the formation of the symbolic function preceding the mirror stage" [143]. In holding to the movement of negativity, in deferring or dissolving every identity, Derrida is attempting to remain in the "semiotic chora," which is Kristeva's rendering of the developmental stage prior to the differentiation of the self as a separate identity. "If in this way the trace dissolves every thesis—material, natural, social, substantial, and logical—in order to free itself from any dependence on the *Logos,* it can do so because it grasps the formation of the symbolic function preceding the mirror stage and believes it can remain there, even while aiming toward that stage" [143]. "The trace that includes its effacement, and writing that inscribes only while under protection and by delaying—both can be thought of as metaphors for a movement that retreats before the thetic but, sheltered by it, unfolds only within the stases of the semiotic *chora*" [141–42].

Here, the relation between Kristeva's critique of Derrida's radical anti-essentialism and her critique of essentialist Woman-identified feminism in "Women's Time" becomes apparent. In her critique of Derrida, as in "Women's Time," Kristeva is arguing for the recognition and acceptance of a "violence" which is essential to the development of self-identity, to the recognition of others as subjects, and to the attribution of an identity to objects—and hence, to the capacity to take an ethical position with respect to states of affairs in the world. The refusal of this recognition and acceptance, Kristeva argues, leaves us trapped in a dream of pure *différance,* not much different from the dream of return to the "archaic mother," to a space before the law, with no separation, no identity, and, therefore, no differences.

At this point, Derrida would argue that Kristeva's position is merely a restatement of Lacan's: that Kristeva is insisting upon a tragic/stoic conception of a subject who must accept castration, or the lack of the phallus. As I have argued, the implication of Kristeva's argument is that the refusal to accept an identity as a subject within the socio-symbolic order is based in a failure to differentiate between the violence of separation/identification—of the thetic break which introduces identity and difference into *différance*—and the violence of domination, of phallogocentrism. Unlike Freud and Lacan who tend to align the acceptance of the violence of separation essential for identity with the acceptance of the violence of civilization or of necessary repression and unavoidable domination, Kristeva argues that the acceptance of the violence of identity is a prerequisite to *resisting* the "violence of civilization," resisting repression, resisting domination. The differentiation between these forms of violence requires a move beyond the abstract negation of the order of language and identity, to a differentiation between the repressive and emancipatory dimensions of symbolically mediated interaction.

While Derrida argues that self-identity is a phallogocentric fiction, and while Lacan argues that (divided) self-identity requires the acceptance of the lack of the phallus, Kristeva is at least sometimes able to shift her focus away from Lacan's and Derrida's metaphoric phalluses. Most of Kristeva's work can be seen as an attempt to understand the "signifying practice" of subjects in terms other than the terms of phallocentrism, of submission to the law of identity. Against Lacan, Kristeva wants to understand the constitution of subjectivity through language not primarily as a castration, a renunciation of the phallus, but as the development of a *capacity* for social interaction. To do this, she turns to an exploration of the processes of language acquisition and production, through empirical studies of prelinguistic vocalizations in infants, and through a reconsideration of Freud's concepts of the oral and anal drives. The aim is to reconceptualize the processes of differentiation and identification in the development of the capacity for signification.

Central to this work is a critique of the psychoanalytic assumption that the acquisition of language (and with language, of social norms) entails a renunciation or repression of pleasure. "Freud sets up an opposition ... between the symbolic function and *Einbeziehung—* unification, incorporation—which refers to orality and pleasure" [149]. In other words, Freud holds to a central tenet of romanticism, that all desire is for unity, for wholeness, for a return to a stage of nondifferentiation/mastery, and that socialization entails a sacrifice of the pleasure principle for the reality principle.

> The symbolic function is thereby dissociated from all pleasure, made to oppose it, and is set up as the paternal place, the place of the superego. According to this view, the only way to react against the consequences of repression imposed by the compulsion of the pleasure principle is to renounce pleasure through symbolization by setting up the sign through the absence of the object, which is expelled and forever lost. . . . What this interpre-

tation seems to rule out is the pleasure underlying the symbolic function. [149]

Kristeva argues that the positing of the identity of the self, through engagement with the socio-symbolic order in the act of linguistic signification, is better understood as "a separation which is not a lack but a discharge, and which . . . arouses pleasure" [151].

The "pleasure in separation" is analyzed at some length in Kristeva's work. Referred to variously as rejection, expulsion, expenditure and abjection and extensively theorized in the *The Powers of Horror: An Essay on Abjection,* it seems to have its basis in Freud's anal and death drives. The concept of productive negativity reappears here, understood as an aggressive, and violent, destruction of unity—but it is a destruction which opens up the way to differentiation. For Kristeva, the concept of "abjection" provides a way of bringing together an analysis of violence, of aggression, understood as a normal—and pleasurable—part of human development, with an analysis of human sociality. For, while abjection *can* contribute to a system of domination, it is also seen as a root of language and of social interaction.

If language acquisition and the separation of self are theorized in terms of an anal drive to expel and reject, in terms of the "pleasure in separation," they are theorized also in terms of an oral drive to incorporate, to devour, which is associated with the "pleasure in identification" with an other.

On what ground, within what material does *having* switch over to *being?*—While seeking an answer to that question it appeared to me that incorporating and introjecting orality's function is the essential substratum of what constitutes man's being, namely *language.* When the object that I incorporate is the speech of the other—precisely a non-object, a pattern, a model—I bind myself to him in a primary fusion, communion, unification. An identification. For me to have been capable of such a process, my libido had to be restrained; my thirst to devour had to be deferred and displaced to a level one may well call "psychic," provided one adds that if there is repression it is quite primal, and that it lets one hold on to the joys of chewing, swallowing, nourishing oneself ... with words. In being able to receive the other's words, to assimilate, repeat and reproduce them, I become like him: One. A subject of enunciation. Through psychic osmosis/identification. Through love.[15]

The point here is not to claim that fundamental drives are at the origin of self and language, but to attempt to theorize ways in which psychosomatic pleasure, aggression, and affect are not excluded from or repressed by, but are included within and in fact realized through, the processes of language acquisition and self-development.

While there is often a disturbingly metaphysical quality to Kristeva's explorations of bodily drives, her attempt to incorporate an understanding of human pleasure and violence into an understanding of language and self-identity seems to me far more productive than Judith Butler's argument that in order to "cure ourselves of the illusion of a true body beyond the law" we need to turn to a vision of the world in which "the law" determines all—until we emerge into a world in which nothing is determined. "If subversion is possible," writes Butler, "it will be a subversion from within the terms of the law, through the possibilities that emerge when the law turns against itself and spawns unexpected permutations of itself. The culturally constructed body will then be liberated, neither to its 'natural' past, nor to its original pleasures, but to an open future of cultural possibilities."[16]

Butler is of course right to object to an appeal to a prediscursive "body beyond the law" as a source or goal of emancipation. But if libidinal revolution is admittedly inadequate as a basis of emancipatory change, surely there must be an alternative to just waiting for the law to turn against itself. And if the vision of a return to original pleasures is inadequate as a goal of emancipation, surely the vision of a totally open future for bodies—for bodies with no nature, no past, and apparently no memory of pleasure or of suffering—is equally unrealistic, and perhaps even more disturbing.

What I want to argue is that Kristeva moves beyond the opposition between law and body in her attempt to analyze language acquisition and the development of self-identity as processes which include, and produce, bodily pleasure. Kristeva understands language and identity not in terms of a law which produces bodies and subjects but in terms of a dialectical interaction between a structure of language and a practice of subjects—a practice which includes psychosomatic processes. The difference is that Kristeva's theory includes the dimension of *motivation*. She argues that the body, as a site of drives and desires, aggression and pleasure, has to be included in any theory of motivation for change.

Self-development and language acquisition are pleasurable not only insofar as they include bodily drives but also insofar as they are inherently *social*. Kristeva's introduction of a "pleasure in sociality" into the development of self-identity goes beyond Jessica Benjamin's, both because her conception of the motivation for and process of this development is considerably expanded, and because she sees sociality as a *goal* of the development of self-identity.

It will be recalled that Benjamin, in her attempt to understand the development of self-identity as an inherently social process, stresses the importance of a theory of a positive motivation for self-identity, and she does so by theorizing the development of self-identity as a process of identification with another subject.[17] Kristeva similarly locates the pleasure in and motivation for the development of self-identity in identification. But Kristeva locates the pleasure in the development of self-identity not only in identification with a particular other but also in the development of a capacity to signify, which is understood to be a precondition of symbolic interaction. This pleasure in signification is connected to some sort of primary desire for sociality on a larger scale, a desire to be part of a larger world, which is initially represented by the parents.

Benjamin's stress on the role of a positive motivation for the development of self-identity, while important, is limited insofar as the *goal* of self-identity remains the achievement of a negative freedom: a separate and isolated autonomy, which inevitably clashes with the capacity for mutual recognition. For Kristeva, the goal or meaning of the development of self-identity is not isolation; rather, the achievement of self-identity is seen as the achievement of a capacity for symbolic interaction with others—and hence, a capacity for participation in a larger social world, beyond immediate relations between parent and child.

I shall return to these arguments in the last section of this chapter.

Toward a Non-repressive Theory of the Subject:
Poetry and Mastery, Semiotic and Symbolic

In theorizing language acquisition and production in terms of bodily and social pleasure, Kristeva is rejecting the psychoanalytic truism that language acquisition and socialization—the learning of linguistic and social norms—is a process of repression. Against Lacan's conception of language as a phallocentric monologue, Kristeva follows Mikhail Bakhtin in focussing on the multiple levels of meaning and multiple influences incorporated in language. (The difference is that Kristeva focusses on the role of intrasubjective processes involved in language acquisition and production rather than on intersubjective dialogue *per se.*)

Just as Bakhtin's work encompasses both: 1) the analysis of the *inherent* dialogism of language and 2) the *differentiation* between monological and dialogical forms of discourse, so Kristeva both: 1) analyzes language acquisition as a process which is *inherently* "heterogeneous"—which necessarily includes, rather than repressing, bodily and social pleasure—and 2) *differentiates* between repressive and non-repressive forms of language.

Again, against Lacan, who argues that poetic language is a product of repression, Kristeva differentiates between poetic language, which is a non-repressive form, and mastering language, which is a repressive, defensive form of linguistic practice. Kristeva describes the "mastering" modality in a manner analogous to Irigaray's analysis of phallogocentric language. It will be recalled that Irigaray describes the economy of language as a "hom(m)osexual economy" of relations among men, mediated by the designation of woman as object of exchange, based on a denial of relationship with women, and therefore a denial of difference. In a similar fashion, Kristeva describes the modality of mastery as "the reconstitution of a *homosexual phratry* that will forever pursue, tirelessly and interminably, the murder of the One, the Father, in order to impose *one* logic, *one* ethics, *one* signified."[18] Like Irigaray, Kristeva uses the term "hom(m)osexual" to describe an order of language which excludes otherness—in psychoanalytic terms, an order/modality of language based on the boy's repression of relationship to the mother, and hence to feminine otherness. In both cases, the use of the term "homosexual" to refer to a pathological condition—the system of male domination based on a repudiation of women—is offensive and unnecessary. What both Irigaray and Kristeva are describing is a system of male identification which is organized around a defensive repudiation, exclusion, and domination of women. As both theorists should know, this needs to be clearly differentiated from forms of homoerotic desire and identification which are *not* based on repudiation, exclusion, and domination. Or, to shift to the terms of the sacrificial logic, homosexual identifications are based on exclusion only to the same extent as heterosexual identifications. Given the institutions of compulsory heterosexuality and male dominance, heterosexual desire and "sublimated" or defensively desexualized male identifications are reinforced by systematic repudiations of both homoerotic desire and male identifications with women. Both Irigaray and Kristeva argue that to enter into these institutions, girls have to repress the erotic relationship to the mother's body—to feminine otherness—just as boys have to repress identification with it.

But unlike Irigaray, Kristeva argues that phallogocentric mastery is not the only modality available in language. Kristeva describes the poetic modality as "*oralization:* a reunion with the mother's body, which is no longer viewed as an engendering, hollow and vaginated, expelling and rejecting body, but rather as a vocalic one—throat, voice, and breasts: music, rhythm, prosody paragrams...." [153]. This description of the alternative to mastering discourse in terms of a reconnection to the mother's body is in some ways similar to Irigaray's. The difference is that Kristeva does not consistently equate symbolic language, or socio-symbolic order, with mastery and repression. She does not call for an escape from symbolic language into a language emergent from the body—an escape from universals into particulars. Nor does she call for an escape from identity into multiplicity or connection. Kristeva presents two different modes of signification, based on two different modes of unification, or identity formation: one defensive and exclusive, and one based on reunification with, and inclusion and acceptance of, embodiment and connection.

While Kristeva tends to privilege poetic language (and particularly avant-garde literature written by men) as the sites where emancipation can take place,[19] the concepts of the poetic and mastering modalities of language are included within a much broader theory of alternative paths for self-formation and linguistic practice. A subject, Kristeva argues, can constitute her/himself either through mastery, through a defensive identification with the law of exclusive identity, or through a "constant return" to and expression of the nonidentity which underlies identity. Thus, self-identity can be developed either through an acceptance or through a denial of nonidentity.

This differentiation between repressive and non-repressive forms of identity and of symbolic ordering casts a different light on Kristeva's theory of the relation between the two signifying modalities which she refers to as the semiotic and the symbolic. The theory of the relation between the symbolic and the semiotic is typically read as a theory of the repression of bodily drives by language. Thus Elizabeth Grosz describes Kristeva's theory as follows:

> The symbolic organises the libidinal drives according to a phallic sexual economy, a normative and generative linguistic structure (including grammar, logic, syntax, and access to the shifter "I", which gives the subject access to appropriating discourse as its own, as referring to itself), and a subjective and social identity. These various identities—sexual, linguistic, subjective—are provisional and threaten to dissolve when the thetic is challenged and the semiotic transgresses its boundaries. These are moments of breakdown of identity (psychosis), meaning and coherence (poetry) and sexual identity (perversion, fetishism), instances privileged by Kristeva. Each demonstrates the usually repressed semiotic contributions to the symbolic by providing the semiotic with expression.[20]

Grosz goes on to say that the symbolic is an organizing system which "functions by hierarchical subsumption, using relations of logical and grammatical convention, and the distinctions between meta-and object-language to cohere and integrate the signifying elements provided by the semiotic. It is the sacrificial order, whose 'cost' is the repression of the semiotic and the pre-oedipal" [48–49].

According to this reading, the symbolic and semiotic are posited as a duality: the symbolic represents the phallic law of identity which represses the semiotic, and this law can be subverted only in moments of crisis when the semiotic breaks through, transgressing the law by dissolving identities.

Kristeva herself is to blame for the conflation of the symbolic with patriarchal domination and of the semiotic with the subversive potential of feminine otherness. In her analyses of the ways in which the symbolic and semiotic orders *have* been gendered in patriarchal societies, she often fails to disentangle the orders of language from their gendered associations, and from relations of domination and subordination. Given this conflation, her call for the necessary inter-relationship between the symbolic and the semiotic comes off as an apology for the necessity of heterosexual union, and an acceptance of the domination of patriarchal law.

But for Kristeva the symbolic is not simply identified with paternity, mastery, and repression. While Kristeva does frequently identify the symbolic order with the patriarchal law, she also, as I have shown, commonly conceives of the symbolic order in neutral and non-gendered terms, not as a form of domination, but as the form or structure of language which facilitates mutual understanding or social identity; not as a necessary repression, but as the means of realization/expression of a singular self-identity.

Nor is the semiotic simply equated with libidinal drives. The semiotic is understood as a "pre-sign functioning" specific to "psychosomatic" processes which develop in the earliest relationship to the mother, and which are therefore influenced by both "biological" and social dimensions. Kristeva argues that these processes have their own specific form of ordering, which is not subsumable to linguistic forms, and which can give rise to other signifying systems, but that they must also be conceived as part of the larger process of linguistic signification.[21]

Thus Grosz is wrong to claim that psychosis and poetry are "moments of breakdown of identity" which demonstrate the "usually repressed contributions to the symbolic by providing the semiotic with expression" [48]. Kristeva clearly differentiates between psychosis, which is a pathological breakdown of identity, and which, because it abolishes form, renders coherent expression impossible, and poetry, which is a capacity to give a coherent form and meaning, and hence expression, to what is "nonidentical" and "heterogeneous."

This is why it makes no sense to complain that for Kristeva the semiotic is invariably subordinate to an intransigent symbolic, and that there is no possibility for the liberation of the semiotic in Kristeva's system. Thus, Judith Butler writes that in addition to the problem of locating the basis of emancipation in primary drives:

> A second problem emerges when Kristeva argues that this libidi-
> nal source of subversion cannot be maintained within the terms
> of culture, that its sustained presence within culture leads to
> psychosis and to the breakdown of cultural life itself. Kristeva
> thus alternately posits and denies the semiotic as an emancipa-
> tory ideal. Though she tells us that it is a dimension of language
> regularly repressed, she also concedes that it is a kind of lan-
> guage which never can be consistently maintained.[22]

As I have argued, Kristeva never claims that the sustained presence of the semiotic in culture leads to psychosis; in fact, she argues that the semiotic is always "present" in culture, and she cites ideal forms of perception, subjectivity, language, and art as those which manage to express rather than repress the semiotic. It is not the sustained presence of the semiotic but the failure to engage with the symbolic (and hence an incapacity to express the semiotic) which, for Kristeva, leads to psychosis and to the breakdown of cultural life.[23]

Thus, it makes no sense to call for the liberation of the semiotic from the symbolic. Such a demand could only be made on the assumption that political change requires a pure negation or aboli-tion of the symbolic. Kristeva's theory of the relation of semiotic to symbolic is precisely a critique of the call to escape from the sym-bolic order into another space—into the body or anywhere else. If the semiotic has an emancipatory force, it is not as an escape from or destruction of an unchangeable symbolic order, but as a constant reintroduction of heterogeneity into linguistic and social structures— a constant remembering and reassertion of difference, which pro-duces conflict and change.

Toward a Psychoanalytic Theory of Women's Self-Identity
From Archaic Mother to Subject in Process

I want now to return to the problem with which I opened my discussion of Kristeva, in the analysis of "Women's Time": the problem of self-identity for women. In "Women's Time," Kristeva insists that there can be no society without a "socio-symbolic contract," and that that requires a "founding separation, some sort of "break-producing symbolism." But she argues that this symbolism need not be the sacrifice of the Woman/Mother. We need, Kristeva argues, to move away from our preoccupation with—either defense against or celebration of—the archaic mother. We need, then, a different basis for social community, and for self-identity.

Kristeva argues that the fantasy of complete gratification in an "archaic, full, total, englobing mother with no frustration, no separation"[24] is itself a product of a patriarchal order, and is essential to the preservation of that order. Thus, rather than refusing the father and turning to mother (or, in other terms, refusing identity within the symbolic order and turning to nonidentity within a semiotic order), we need to expose the ways in which the order of patriarchy is dependent upon the dream of gratification with the mother. We need to show how the mystique of motherhood serves to appease and contain both men's and women's desires for immediacy, for pleasure. We need to show, also, how the construction of the mother as the all-powerful, all-enveloping womb, as a place of utter peace—and, therefore, death—serves to warn the subject against any attempt at escape from identity and identification with a patriarchal order.

In her essays on the problem of identity for women, Kristeva analyzes the cultural images of motherhood, or "the maternal," as something sacred—and hence, as something both idealized and dreaded. And she attempts to analyze the role such cultural images play in the development of self-identity for women. In a society in which, as Kristeva puts it, "the *consecrated* (religious or secular) representation of femininity is absorbed by motherhood,"[25] and in which, empirically, the earliest relationship of most children is with mothers, the development of women's self-identities through differentiation from and identification with real mothers is a crucial problem for feminism.

In her essay "Stabat Mater," Kristeva analyzes the ways in which the cult of the Virgin Mary served to uphold individual women's investment in a self-identity as archaic mother. In "The Pain of Sorrow in the Modern World: The Works of Marguerite Duras," Kristeva shows how this image endures in modernity and postmodernity, serving to offer women an immediate identity which provides a substitute for the achievement of a more complex self-identity as a "subject in process." Through an analysis of these essays on the problem of women's identities, and of the essay "Freud and Love: Treatment and Its Discontents" on the problem of self-development in childhood, I attempt to draw out a model of self-development in which the recognition of and identification with the subjectivity of the mother, as a participant in a social world, plays a central role.

In "Stabat Mater," Kristeva traces the idealization of the mother through the medieval and modern cult of the Virgin Mary, which culminates in the cultural idealization of maternity in the nineteenth and twentieth centuries. According to Kristeva, the cult of the Virgin served to appease—and to foreclose—the cultural desire for return to the mother, while ensuring both men's and women's identification with the patriarchal social order. This is because the Virgin represents the semiotic order—the order of psychosomatic drives and pre- and extra-linguistic expression, which is associated with the mother—and reconciles this with a patriarchal symbolic order, under God the Father.

Kristeva defines the dominant cultural meaning of "the maternal" as

> the ambivalent principle that is bound to the species, on the one hand, and on the other stems from an identity catastrophe that causes the Name to topple over into the unnameable that one imagines as femininity, non-language or body.[26]

According to this representation, motherhood exists on the borderline between nature and culture, body and language. It is not a real mother and not even the fantasy of the archaic mother but rather a fantasy of *relationship* to the mother—the fantasied relationship of primary narcissism—which is idealized in our "consecrated" representations of motherhood [161]. These representations enshrine a memory/fantasy of immediate fusion, pure gratification—a dream of wholeness, prior to the separation of language from body, and hence prior to—and outside of—"the law." Yet, the real mother also serves to mediate for the child, between body and language, "nature" and "culture." Thus, the relationship of "primary narcissism" exists on the borderline between identity and nonidentity, Name and unnameable. The mother's role as mediator, then, is colored by a fantasy of not only "primal fusion," but also its loss. And it is perhaps this borderline condition (and not simply a lack of identity, prior to the Law) which, "remembered," is projected onto the mother as identity catastrophe.

Kristeva argues that the cult of the Virgin Mary served to absorb the economy of "the maternal"—of primary narcissism—into the social order, under the Law of the Father. In other terms, it served to absorb the pagan belief in the mother goddess into Catholicism. Kristeva argues that by taking up the myth of the mother goddess, thereby preserving the maternal order within the jurisdiction of the paternal one, Catholicism was able to maintain "a certain balance between the two sexes" [167]:

> [T]he representation of virgin motherhood appears to crown the efforts of a society to reconcile the social remnants of matrilinearism and the unconscious needs of primary narcissism on the one hand, and on the other the requirements of a new society based on exchange and before long on increased production, which require the contribution of the superego and rely on the symbolic paternal agency. [181–82]

Thus, the Virgin served—in the words of a Church Father—as "a 'bond,' a 'middle,' or an 'interval'" [163] between the unnameable and the Name. It is through the idealization of the Virgin Mother, who incorporates the dream logic of the semiotic and the heterogeneity of the drives into a representation which supports and upholds a patricentric social order, that Christianity is able to "account for" what lies "outside" of that order, without opening the way for subversion.

> Starting with the high Christly sublimation for which it yearns and occasionally exceeds, and extending to the extra-linguistic regions of the unnameable, the Virgin Mother occupied the

tremendous territory hither and yon of the parenthesis of language. She adds to the Christian trinity and to the Word that
delineates their coherence the heterogeneity they salvage.
[174–75]

This heterogeneity is represented in the figure of the Virgin by
the milk and tears which, Kristeva says, became the privileged signs
of the Mater Dolorosa. Milk and tears: oral absorption, fusion,
and the moment of its loss. Symbols of a pre-symbolic, a non-lin-
guistic relationship.

> Even though orality—threshold of infantile regression—is dis-
> played in the area of the breast, while the spasm at the slipping
> away of eroticism is translated into tears, this should not conceal
> what milk and tears have in common: they are the metaphors of
> non-speech, of a "semiotics" that linguistic communication does
> not account for. The Mother and her attributes, evoking sorrow-
> ful humanity, thus become representatives of a "return of the
> repressed" in monotheism. They re-establish what is non-verbal
> and show up as the receptacle of a signifying disposition that is
> closer to so-called primary processes. [174]

While satisfying the desire for the mother and the heterogeneous
order she represents, the cult of the Virgin also takes care of both
man's and woman's desires for self-identification. Man is able to
erect him-self in triumph over death, through the support of a
dreamed/remembered mother's love, now appropriated as his own.

> Man overcomes the unthinkable of death by postulating maternal
> love in its place—in the place and stead of death and thought.
> [176]

As for women's desires for self-identification, the Virgin was "able
to attract women's wishes for identification as well as the very
precise interposition of those who assumed to keep watch over the
symbolic and social order" [180]. Kristeva argues that the identification of a woman with the Virgin is a way—and "not among the less
effective" ways—of dealing with (by both enacting and constraining)
"feminine paranoia" [180]. Here, it must be noted that paranoia is a
condition produced by the repression of homoerotic desire for the

same-sex parent.[27] Thus, feminine paranoia is an effect of the repression of a woman's desire for her mother—and, by extension, for other women. And therefore feminine paranoia is the product of a social order which demands that the female child give up her desire for her mother and turn to her father—give up her desire for other women and turn to men. The effect is a "paranoid" denial of any relationship.

For the required "turn to men" too can be circumvented through identification with the Virgin. Through this identification, a woman is able to effect a denial of the other sex (of man) and establish her unique relation with (albeit in subordination to) God. "*I* do not conceive with *you* but with *Him*" [180]. She is thus able to satisfy her "paranoid" desire for power—while stifling it by "putting it on its knees before the child-god" [180]. Identification with the Virgin "obstructs the desire for murder or devoration" and allows women to assume "the paranoid fantasy of being excluded from time and death" [180–81]. Most importantly, identification with the Virgin facilitates "repudiation of the other woman (which doubtless amounts basically to a repudiation of the woman's mother) by suggesting the image of A Unique Woman" [181]. This uniqueness, however, is attained only through "an exacerbated masochism.... A bonus, however: the promised *jouissance*" [181].

The self-identities granted by the Virgin to both men and women are illusions, caught in the realm of the imaginary. The unitary identity, whole and undivided, is a fantasy; one cannot have nor can one be the dreamed-of Mother. In the case of women, Kristeva argues that this identification with the Unique Woman, in repudiation of "the other woman," prevents women from developing singular identities as complex subjects in relation to other complex subjects. "The war between mother and daughter," Kristeva notes, was "masterfully but too quickly settled by promoting Mary as universal and particular, but never singular—as 'alone of her sex'" [180].[28] Thus:

A woman will only have the choice to live her life either *hyperabstractly* ("immediately universal," Hegel said) in order thus to earn divine grace and homologation with symbolic order; or merely *different,* other, fallen ("immediately particular," Hegel said). But she will not be able to accede to the complexity of being divided, of heterogeneity, of the catastrophic-fold-of "being" ("never singular," Hegel said). [173]

If we want to move beyond the illusory identity as Unique Woman, to become what Kristeva calls "subjects in process"—subjects who can recognize ourselves as individuals through recognizing and accepting our complexity—we need to move beyond our fixation on the archaic mother.

For the loss of the Virgin Mother has not liberated us from the fixation. In "The Pain of Sorrow in the Modern World: The Works of Marguerite Duras," Kristeva uses an analysis of the characters in Duras's novels as the framework for an analysis of the problematic status of identification, and in particular, of women's identification with their mothers, in the postmodern age of the breakdown of identity. Whereas the subject described in "Stabat Mater" was entrapped in identification, through the Virgin, with the law, the contemporary subject is left with no God and no Virgin to unify law and desire, language and body. A space opens up—a hole where the whole of the subject's identity was. A hole between language and body, now untraversable. The false, fixed identity with the Virgin, under the law, has given way not to a freedom of difference, an open identity in process, but to a new trap of emptiness.

For Kristeva, Duras's heroines are "borderline" cases, trapped in melancholy, unable to mourn the loss of their mothers. It's not that they live in illusion. They have learned the language and the terms of the patriarchal socio-symbolic order all too well. But there is, understandably, no libidinal or amorous investment in that order; this has "remained in the emptiness of maternal fusion and/or maternal absence."[29] Thus, the desire of these women is void of illusion. They desire completion, but they have been forced, in a world abandoned by God, by the Virgin, to acknowledge that they can never have it. So they live an unendable sadness, a disillusion which is just (to borrow a phrase from Luce Irigaray) as illusory.[30]

Duras's sad women are walking memories of the hole left by their abandonment. Focussed always inward, they keep the mother's absence in their bodies like a wound. Unable to invest in a We beyond the fantasied relation to mother—and therefore unable to accept division, fragmentation, absence—Duras's sad women remain fixated on the emptiness created by the mother's separation.

> This sorrow, expressing an impossible pleasure, is the agonizing sign of frigidity. Holding back a passion that cannot flow, this sorrow is, more profoundly, the prison of an impossible mourning for an ancient love made up wholly of sensation and auto-sensation; it is inalienable, inseparable, and, for that very reason, unnameable. . . . Indeed, at the source of this sorrow, there exists an unassumable abandonment.[31]

So these daughters remain at the stage of autoerotic immediacy with their fantasied mothers. Instead of identification there is a "reduplication" of/with the mother.

> (Re)duplication is a blocked repetition. Whereas repetition extends in time, reduplication is outside of time, a reverberation in space, a game of mirrors with no perspective, no duration. For a while, a double can freeze the instability of the same, give it temporary identity, but eventually it explores the abyss of the same, probing those unsuspected and unplumbable depths. The double is the unconscious depth of the same, that which threatens it, can engulf it. [147]

Caught in the unnameable space of reduplication, preceding, never achieving, identity, Duras's heroines are caught in a choked passion for the other woman—a passion which is endlessly thwarted. But the mother is as much feared and hated as loved; the hatred and the fear are inextricable from the love, knotted up in the ambivalence of intense desire. And Duras's mothers are all mad women, desired-hated, inaccessible.

> Out of fear of maternal madness, the novelist eliminates the mother, separating from her with a violence no less murderous than that of the mother who beats her prostituted daughter. Destroy, the daughter-narrator seems to say in *The Lover*, but in erasing the figure of the mother, she actually takes her place, substituting herself for maternal madness. She does not kill the mother so much as extend her presence into the negative hallucination of an always loving identification. [146]

Reduplication, then, serves as the "negative hallucination" of an unachieved identification, casting the daughter, like the mother, into the space of the "inaccessible woman."

"The mythification of the inaccessible feminine in Duras," Kristeva argues, "contains a certain truth about the female experience of a *jouissance* of sorrow" [147]. Duras's daughters still live the myth of the Unique Woman, alone in her sadness. Borderline cases, they reduplicate their mothers' borderline status as lack of identity—pure lack, pure sorrow. The truth of division is revealed as pure, beautiful tragedy once more.

Through her analyses of the cult of the Virgin and of Duras's female characters, Kristeva is describing the identification with a fantasied Mother which provides a false sense of shelter in a patriarchal culture, and which inhibits any engagement with the social world which could lead to change. If we want to get beyond this empty identity, she argues, we need to open a discourse of motherhood which is not based on a desire to repudiate, nor on a desire to merge with, "the other woman." We need, then, to open the possibility of relation to "the other woman"—beginning with our mothers, recognized as singular subjects, located in their specificity, their difference from the archaic mother. And from ourselves. Thus, the relation to the mother must be reformulated if we want to reformulate identity. For only once we can recognize our mothers' difference and complexity can we recognize our own.

In "Freud and Love: Treatment and Its Discontents," Kristeva argues that the subjectivity of the "subject in process" requires an identification through or with the "divided mother." But it is not entirely clear how the mother's division is to be constituted. On one hand, she is apparently arguing, with Freud and Lacan, that the child must accept the mother's castration, and must move from a state of non-differentiation with the mother to a tenuous and always divided identity based on the internalization of the symbolic law of the father—an identity which is always predicated on the lack of the phallus. On the other hand, Kristeva is holding out the possibility of identification with a mother who is divided but not lacking.

The acceptance of the mother's division means that the child must accept that s/he is not the sole object of the mother's desire—that the mother desires something else besides the child. Following Freud, Kristeva refers to that "something else" as the "imaginary father of individual prehistory." And Kristeva argues that it is this image that introduces an early model of identity for the child. The idea of an "imaginary father" as the model of self-identity is, of course, problematic. And Kristeva sometimes does seem to be saying that what the mother wants—and what the child identifies with—is the phallus. Hence, the accession to the symbolic order entails acceptance of the mother's lack. This is quite compatible with the original Freudian-Lacanian position: the child originally identifies with the object of the mother's desire—with the phallus she lacks; but in order to accede to the symbolic order, the child must accept the impossibility of being, or having, the phallus for her, and so must accept and identify with her lack or division.

> Let me now point out that the most archaic unity that we thus retrieve—an identity so autonomous that it calls forth displacements—is that of the phallus desired by the mother. . . . The imaginary father would thus be the indication that the mother is not complete but that she wants. . . .[32]

So here we are back at the phallus. And if phallus there must be, it had better be the father's. "The archaic inscription of the father seems to me a way of modifying the fantasy of a phallic mother playing at the phallus game all by herself" [259].

Here, it seems that Kristeva has reaffirmed the absolute dichotomy between father and mother: the symbolic order belongs to the father, is inherently phallic, and the mother has no place in it except through her dissembling artifice of masquerade as the phallus. We are warned, once again, against identification with "a phallic mother playing at the phallus game all by herself." As if there were no other game to play.

However, in other places Kristeva argues explicitly that the "imaginary father" is simply a metaphor for the "third term"—something which intervenes in the child's fantasy of unity with the mother, to introduce the dimension of sociality by facilitating the child's recognition of the mother as a subject.

> Nobody knows what the "good-enough mother" is. I wouldn't try to explain what that is, but I would try to suggest that maybe the good enough mother is the mother who has something else to love besides her child, it could be her work, her husband, her lovers, etc. If for a mother the child is the meaning of her life, it's too heavy. She has to have another meaning in her life. And this other meaning in her life is what Freud refers to as the father of prehistory.[33]

What for Freud was "the father of prehistory," then, is for Kristeva whatever the mother desires, whatever gives her life meaning. The point is that the child has to learn to recognize that the mother desires something else besides the child. But more than this, in coming to recognize the mother's desire, the child gets her first image of self-identity: the mother's identity begins to be grasped through a very rudimentary recognition of what gives her life meaning. The child's own development of a sense of self-identity has one of its roots in an ability to share in the mother's desire for the world beyond the child. It is not that the child shares the same object with the mother; rather, the child identifies with the mother's desire, and thus has the first glimmerings of recognition of what an identity means: of a self-identity rooted in desire, in the world, and in meaning. This shared desire, this rudimentary sense of meaning, of investment in the world, is, Kristeva suggests, "some sort of archaic occurrence of the symbolic,"[34] which precedes internalization.

This elementary grasp of the symbolic depends upon the mother's relation to—and positioning within—a social world which is not entirely patriarchal, but which is composed of competing discourses, institutions, and practices. Thus, the mother does not exist outside the socio-symbolic order, as its support. It is the mother's position within a social world which provides the child with a mode of investment in that world. The mother's relation to the symbolic provides a means of reconciling differentiation and identification for the child: the child is able to identify as a self by identifying with the mother's investment in the socio-symbolic order. Thus, the child begins to develop a sense of self-identity through taking a first step toward a capacity for participation in a social world. Because the mother's relation to the symbolic is thereby reconciled with her relation to the child, the mother is able to serve as a model of a subject "unified in division." Divided between her relation to the child and her investment in the social world (but not pulled apart and fragmented by this division), the mother serves as a model of a subject who can sustain her identity in division.

This opens up the possibility of a form of self-identity not based on the repudiation of the mother, nor on an identity with a Unique inaccessible Woman, nor on an identificatory merging with the mother, nor on an identity as a separate isolated self. The differentiation of self is a process which entails a recognition of and identification with the mother's investment in the world, and which facilitates the capacity to participate in a social world. That capacity is essential to the ability to understand that world—and essential to the ability to change it.

Conclusion

I have been arguing that a reformulation and reconstruction of concepts of the self which could include difference, connection, and heterogeneity is one of the most important tasks facing contemporary feminist theorists. We need new models of identity, of individuation, of agency, and of autonomy, which will take account of the important critiques of these concepts which have been generated by feminist theorists. At this point I want to sketch a model of self-identity which can address some of the concerns of both relational feminism, which argues that the ideal of self-identity too often conceals a defense against connection with others, and postmodern and poststructuralist feminism, which argues that the concept of self-identity can be understood only in terms of the system of meaning which produces it: a system predicated on a logic of exclusion of nonidentity or difference. My attempt to try to clarify a normative ideal of self-identity comes out of a conviction that we need to uphold a commitment to women's struggles for identity and autonomy, in the context of feminist critiques of defensive, atomistic individualism and critiques of the concept of the disembedded subject as the free and unfettered author of his destiny. We need to make a space for an understanding of self-identity and autonomy which will not clash with our conviction that individuals must be understood as embedded, embodied, localized, constituted, fragmented, and subject to systems of power, oppression, and exploitation. We need, still, to understand ourselves clearly as actors capable of learning, of changing, of making the world, and ourselves, better.

It is important that I begin by saying what a defensible ideal of self-identity is not. It is not some sort of essentialist ontology, not an idealist conception of an original, pre-given authentic self. It is not an alienated individualism severed from connections and solidarities, severed from collective struggles, immune to systems of power and oppression. It is not an attempt to repress or deny the embodiment, fragmentation, dividedness, and multiplicity of human selves, or the constitution of subjects in and through language and power.

The concept of self-identity that I want to defend can be defined as the capacity to experience oneself as an active and relatively coherent participant in a social world. Essential to self-identity, then, is "the ability of a person to relate to him or herself and to be able to relate to others in a meaningful way, to act and react self-consciously."[1] This emphasis on a capacity for *meaningful* interaction with self and others takes us in two directions, for it introduces both reflexivity and intersubjectivity as essential components of self-identity. Reflexivity, for the meanings of my relationships to myself and to others come down to me: I am the one faced with the question of who I am and who I want to be. I am the one who must invest my existence with meaning for me. Intersubjectivity, because this meaning can be generated only through my participation in social meanings, which are intersubjectively constituted. The very concept of a self, of an I, of a me, is something which is constructed only through intersubjective interactions, which take place always in contexts of shared meanings. Similarly, my identity as this specific individual is constructed through my participation in communities, institutions, and systems of meaning, which organize my interactions with, and through which I interpret my interactions with, the world, my self, and others. My identity is produced through a complex process through which I am identified, and identify myself, in terms of intersubjective contexts of meaning.

The capacity, and the responsibility, to problematize and define one's own meaning (one's own identity) is both the burden and the privilege of modern subjects. No longer defined by a fixed position in a social system, I am (relatively) free (or, at the least, I aspire to a normative ideal of freedom) to determine, through my practices, who I am and who I am going to be. The flip side of this freedom is the burden of self-definition: every action, every decision becomes self-defining; every action, every position is open to question.[2] This freedom and this responsibility are absolutely inescapable in our daily lives. At the same time, along with the increasing need for self-definition goes an increasing production and differentiation of identity-attributes: of possible roles and values, attachments and affiliations, beliefs and commitments, needs and desires, styles and modes of expression. And we are exposed to more and more frameworks for reflection on and demystification of the constitutive influences which shape our identities (such as family and relationship dynamics, unconscious processes, collective identities, economic, social, and linguistic systems, systems of power and oppression . . .).

Central to self-identity, then, is the capacity to sustain and in some sense reconcile multiple and often conflicting identities, and to understand, criticize, and reconcile multiple and often conflicting interpretations of those identities. Not to mention the capacity to live with and somehow reconcile all of the ambiguity and complexity of our lives that does not (and never will) readily lend itself to this identity work.

Ideally, these reconciliations are achieved not through the imposition of an identity which excludes or represses difference and nonidentity (the concern of postmodernists), but through a capacity to reflexively and practically accept, live with, and make sense of differences and complexity. And this capacity is based not on a denial of connections with others (the concern of relational theorists), but on a cognitive and affective acceptance of intersubjectivity and autonomy, of dependence on and independence from others, which underlies a capacity to recognize when my meaning differs from others' meaning, and when my identity is bound up with the identity of a particular or general We.

This is, of course, an enormously demanding project, the difficulty of which is increased as various identities are recognized as being tied up with systems of oppression, and with communities and institutions which define themselves through exclusions. This is acutely expressed by Gloria Anzaldúa, who writes of her ongoing attempts to make some sense out of the conflicts among her various identities as a Catholic-raised, lesbian, Chicana, (Mexican, Anglo-American): "I have so internalized the borderland conflict that sometimes I feel like one cancels out the other and we are zero, nothing, no one."[3]

The experience of lack of self is the familiar dark side of a culture characterized by increasing pressure for self-identity under conditions of increasing fragmentation. But the other side of this pressure and this fragmentation is a freedom of conscious self-determination, and a capacity for analysis: Anzaldúa describes her conscious choice to live her life as a lesbian, and describes her struggle for self-analysis and self-making as a "path of knowledge" which opens up a process of analysis and critique of social and cultural institutions governing race, class, gender, and sexuality.

Essential to an individual's capacity to problematize and define her own identity are cognitive and practical capacities for self-knowledge, self-realization, and self-direction,[4] which involve cognitive capacities for learning, for critique, and for organization, and practical capacities for expression, engagement, commitment, and flexibility. I want to argue that the development of self-identity requires the learning of social and linguistic norms, through which the expression or realization of one's specificity, and the development of a capacity for the critique of norms, becomes possible. (I also want to say that it is through these practices of expression and critique that social and linguistic norms change, and are kept open and diverse.) The development of self-identity requires the cognitive capacity to reflect on who I am and what matters to me, and to organize diverse identitities, and identity-attributes, into some sort of meaningful narrative or constellation. It also requires the practical, existential capacity to discover and define and *commit* to what matters to me, to my meaning, while remaining flexible and open to change. To some extent, all of this depends on an ability to resolve particular differences and conflicts into more general meanings.

This notion of self-identity as a capacity to *resolve* differences and conflicts has not been popular among feminist theorists. Iris Young, for example, argues that "any individual subject is a play of differences that cannot be comprehended" and that the struggle for self-identity (and the struggle for reciprocal recognition with others) is necessarily based on a logic of identity which *necessarily* denies differences.[5] For Young, identity and difference are mutually exclusive; thus, she argues for an ideal of "unassimilated otherness."[6] Similarly, as I have argued, Luce Irigaray, Diana Fuss, and Jessica Benjamin all claim that the attempt to resolve contradictions is an act of domination, and that it is better to leave contradictions and paradoxes unresolved. All of these theorists make these arguments in the name of a model of the self as an open process of constant change.

I want to argue that the struggle to resolve conflicts through an openness to difference is essential to the practice of change, and to the generation of new meaning. Surely it is impossible to understand the developments in the self-understanding of feminists, and of the feminist movement, without acknowledging the role played by individual and collective struggles to understand differences and resolve conflicts. To take just one example, the "Sex Wars" debates were provoked by some women's struggles to explore sexuality, pleasure, violence, and desire past the boundaries set by anti-porn feminism. At the individual level, the struggle of a particular woman to make sense of the relationships between her fantasies and her feminist values requires a struggle to reconceptualize the relationship between her feminist values and her experiences of pleasure and desire. In the process, both the understanding of feminism and the understanding of desire—and, in turn, her own self-understanding—undergo change: a change which could not have happened if she had simply accepted paradox and had made no attempt to resolve it; if, that is, she had not taken either her desires or her commitment to feminist values seriously enough to attempt to resolve the apparent conflict between them. Surely it is such individual and collective struggles to resolve conflicts which have fueled the opening up of feminist discourses about pleasure and desire, and have radically changed the landscape of feminist theory and practice. This does not mean that we ever get to a point where we all agree. It means that we see the problem of identifying feminist values as an important one—important enough to struggle over.

I want to argue, then, that the struggle to make meaning through an attempt to *resolve* apparent contradictions is essential to the ongoing constitution of self-identity. Since it is impossible to make meaning in abstraction from the practical activity of making meaning for and with other people, the development of self-identity is possible only through the development of a capacity for mutual understanding, within intersubjective relationships. But this means that we have to be able to conceptually abstract from the relationships themselves to the intersubjective *meanings* which mediate relationships.

To put this another way, the problem of the *identity of the self* is bound up with the problem of *identity of meaning,* and with the problem of *identification with, or relationship to, others.* It seems to me that attempts by feminist theorists to formulate a positive conception of self-identity often founder because one or the other of these elements has been left out. Relational theories like Nancy Chodorow's focus on the relationship between self-identity and identification with others, but leave out any consideration of identity of meaning. Thus, they see the identity of the self and identity with others as either locked in eternal opposition, or merged into one, because they lack any concept of mediation through identity of meaning in language. On the other hand, poststructuralist theories tend to focus on the structural homology between the identity of the self and the identity of meaning in language, but leave out any conception of mediation through social relations with others. Thus, they see the identity of the self and the identity of meaning in language as being locked together in a logic or structure of totalizing repressive identity. The effect is that each is unable to abstract, either from concrete relationships or from the system of language, to a concept of the individual as a participant in the intersubjective constitution of meaning, and hence in the social contestation of meanings.

I think it is crucially important that feminist theorists reconsider a common tendency to see abstraction as the enemy. For example, Judith Butler argues that we need to reject any conception of agency as a capacity for reflexive mediation, because such a conception falsely "separates [the] subject from its cultural predicates." It abstracts from the subject's color, sexuality, ethnicity, class, and the "illimitable et cetera," and abstracts from the process of signification, or the linguistic constitution of the subject. Furthermore, she argues that any claim to a capacity for reflection upholds a false "epistemological" conception of a subject who is separated from and opposed to its object/other.[7] This argument is surprisingly similar to the arguments of relational theorists like Evelyn Fox Keller, Susan Bordo, Sandra Harding, and others who criticize a characteristically masculine emphasis on abstraction, which is associated with the separation of subject and object, the denial of connections to others, and the domination of the other/object. What is common in these otherwise disparate arguments is an association of abstraction and separation with domination or repression.

While there is much to be learned from feminist critiques of the abstraction of the individual from the intersubjective relationships and the contexts of power, language, and meaning which constitute us, there is also a danger here of sliding into absurdity: once we get to the point where we reject any abstraction of the individual from contexts, and reject any postulation of the individual's capacity for reflection on contexts, we effectively deny any capacity of agents to criticize and change those contexts. In rejecting abstraction, feminist theorists forget that the capacity to abstract from particular relationships, from linguistic systems and social norms, is essential to a capacity to *criticize* those relationships, systems, and norms. The challenge, then, is not to reject abstraction for embeddedness, but to theorize a capacity for abstraction, for detachment, for critique, which is not opposed to but continuous with, and in fact constitutive of, participation.[8]

Notes

Notes to Introduction

1. Simone de Beauvoir, *The Second Sex,* trans. H.M. Parshley (Harmondsworth: Penguin: 1972), 17.

Notes to Chapter 1

1. It should be noted here that Virginia Woolf's analysis, in *A Room of One's Own,* of woman's position as other to man's self, actually predates de Beauvoir's. (*A Room of One's Own* was published in 1929; *Le Deuxième Sexe,* in 1949.) However, it was de Beauvoir who related the insight to central concepts in modern philosophy, and who developed it into an extensive and exhaustive analysis of women's situation.

2. Simone de Beauvoir, *The Second Sex,* trans. H.M. Parshley (Harmondsworth: Penguin, 1972), 16–17.

3. De Beauvoir, *The Second Sex,* 17; quoted from Claude Lévi-Strauss, *The Elementary Structures of Kinship.*

4. It should be noted that *The Second Sex* and *The Elementary Structures of Kinship* were both published in 1949, before the dispute between phenomenology and structuralism had developed. Lévi-Strauss's structuralist method was intended to be an explicit critique of the "philosophy of consciousness," but de Beauvoir's smooth and unproblematic elision of the two positions attests to their compatibility: both are concerned with specifying fundamental, transhistorical structures or elements of human consciousness.

5. De Beauvoir, *The Second Sex,* 17.

6. Alexandre Kojève, *Introduction to the Reading of Hegel: Lectures on the Phenomenology of Spirit,* trans. James H. Nichols, Jr., ed. Allan Bloom (New York: Basic Books, 1969), 209.

191

7. Vincent Descombes, *Modern French Philosophy*, trans. L. Scott-Fox and J.M. Harding (Cambridge: Cambridge University Press, 1980), 32–33. I am indebted to Descombes for his analysis of the significance of Kojève's concept of negativity for existentialist philosophy.

8. Kojève, *Introduction to the Reading of Hegel*, 215.

9. Charles Taylor, *Hegel* (Cambridge: Cambridge University Press, 1975), 148. For Hegel, this understanding is possible only within a conception of knowledge that transcends the subject-object dualism of representational knowledge—i.e., the conception of knowledge as a representation of the object by the subject. And for Hegel, the dualism of representational knowledge can be transcended only by an idealist conception of knowledge as the appearance or manifestation of Spirit. But if we understand Spirit as human intersubjectivity, it is possible to draw from Hegel's theory a materialist analysis of knowledge as an intersubjective product of embodied human beings.

10. G.W.F Hegel, *Phenomenology of Spirit*, trans. A.V. Miller (Oxford: Oxford University Press, 1977), 113.

11. Hegel, *Phenomenology*, 115.

12. Taylor, *Hegel*, 157.

13. Hegel, *Phenomenology*, 120.

14. See, for example, the critiques of de Beauvoir in Jean Grimshaw, *Philosophy and Feminist Thinking* (Minneapolis: University of Minnesota Press, 1986); Genevieve Lloyd, *The Man of Reason: "Male" and "Female" in Western Philosophy* (Minneapolis: University of Minnesota Press, 1984); and Mary O'Brien, *The Politics of Reproduction* (Boston: Routledge and Kegan Paul, 1981).

15. As I shall show in subsequent chapters, this argument is a common thread in the otherwise divergent perspectives represented by the Lacanian/Derridean theory of Luce Irigaray and the object-relations theory of Nancy Chodorow and Jessica Benjamin.

16. Peter Dews, *Logics of Disintegration: Post-Structuralist Thought and the Claims of Critical Theory* (London: Verso, 1987), 10.

17. Derrida's debt to Kojève is implied by Vincent Descombes in *Modern French Philosophy*.

18. Jacques Derrida, *Writing and Difference*, trans. Alan Bass (Chicago: University of Chicago Press, 1978), 248.

19. Hegel, *Phenomenology*, 21.

20. Derrida relates this to Saussure's theory that the meaning of every linguistic term is the effect of its difference from others. This is the basis of Derrida's theory of différance: the idea of a difference which precedes and produces an identity which must always be deferred.

21. Jacques Derrida, *Positions*, trans. Alan Bass (Chicago: University of Chicago Press, 1981), 44.

22. Derrida, *Positions*, 101.

23. Derrida, *Writing and Difference*, 196.

24. Derrida, *Writing and Difference*, 196.

25. Derrida, *Writing and Difference*, 229.

26. Derrida, *Writing and Difference*, 197.

27. Derrida criticizes Levinas for doing this. See "Violence and Metaphysics: An Essay on the Thought of Emmanuel Levinas," in *Writing and Difference*.

28. Kojève, *Introduction to the Reading of Hegel*, 216.

29. Hegel, *Phenomenology*, 9.

30. Jessica Benjamin, *The Bonds of Love: Psychoanalysis, Feminism, and the Problem of Domination* (New York: Pantheon Books, 1988), 7.

31. Like Derrida, Benjamin contrasts the maintenance of tension with the resolution into a "closed system of opposites" which is definitive of domination. See Benjamin, *The Bonds of Love*, 62, 67.

32. In chapter three, I discuss Benjamin's model of the self as paradox in more detail through an analysis of the relation of Benjamin's work to Adorno's and Chodorow's psychoanalytic theories.

33. Benjamin makes this argument with reference to object-relations theorists, who argue that psychic states are the products of human interaction rather than innate drives. It should be noted, however, that Freud distinguished his concept of the drive from the concept of natural instinct, arguing that drives are historically produced and that the unconscious, far from being a reservoir of fixed biological instincts, is the locus of mediation between society and individual.

34. Here, I am drawing from Charles Taylor's conception of "expression" as an essential dimension of the modern concept of self-identity. See Taylor, *Hegel*, esp. chapter one: "Aims of a New Epoch." Through practice, I produce or realize a self-identity which I recognize as my own and invest with meaning. And, by clarifying this identity and this meaning, I am able to guide my practices. This self-identity thus becomes a realization and expression of my own meaning. And this practice of realization and expression is definitive of the modern necessity/capacity for self-identity, self-determination, and the creation of one's own meaning. But once it is recognized that the practices of self-production are intersubjective practices, and that the meanings attributed to those practices, and hence to the self, are intersubjective meanings, then the development of self-identity is recognized as a process of learning and producing social meanings; in other words, one comes to realize and "express" one's identity (or nonidentity) through the acquisition and production of social identity.

Notes to Chapter 2

1. Alison M. Jaggar, *Feminist Politics and Human Nature* (Totowa, N.J.: Rowman and Allenheld, 1983), 131.

2. Important exceptions are Rosalind Petchesky, *Abortion and Woman's Choice: The State, Sexuality and Reproductive Freedom* (New York: Longman, 1984) and Diana Meyers, *Self, Society and Personal Choice* (New York: Columbia University

Press, 1989). Of particular relevance in this context is Meyers's article "The Subversion of Women's Agency in Psychoanalytic Feminism: Chodorow, Flax, Kristeva," in Nancy Fraser and Sandra Lee Bartky, eds., *Revaluing French Feminism* (Bloomington: Indiana University Press, 1992).

3. See, for example, Susan Bordo, *The Flight to Objectivity: Essays on Cartesianism and Culture* (Albany, N.Y.: SUNY Press, 1987); Jane Flax, "Political Philosophy and the Patriarchal Unconscious: A Psychoanalytic Perspective on Epistemology and Metaphysics," in M. Hintikka and S. Harding, eds., *Discovering Reality* (Dordrecht: Reidel, 1983); Carol Gilligan, *In a Different Voice* (Cambridge, Mass.: Harvard University Press, 1982); Sandra Harding, "Is Gender a Variable in Conceptions of Rationality? A Survey of the Issues," *Dialectica* 36, 2–3 (1982); Nancy Hartsock, "The Feminist Standpoint: Developing the Ground for a Specifically Feminist Historical Materialism," in Hintikka and Harding, eds. *Discovering Reality;* Evelyn Fox Keller, *Reflections on Gender and Science* (New Haven: Yale University Press, 1985).

4. See, for example, Jean Grimshaw, *Philosophy and Feminist Thinking* (Minneapolis: University of Minnesota Press, 1986); Iris Marion Young, "Is Male Gender Identity the Cause of Male Domination?" in *Throwing Like a Girl and Other Essays in Feminist Philosophy and Social Theory* (Bloomington: Indiana University Press, 1990).

5. See Jacqueline Rose, *Sexuality in the Field of Vision* (London: Verso, 1986) and Patricia Elliot, *From Mastery to Analysis* (Ithaca: Cornell University Press, 1991).

6. Simone de Beauvoir, *The Second Sex,* trans. H.M. Parshley (Harmondsworth: Penguin, 1972), 29.

7. Put this way, the critique sounds remarkably Kantian. Relational feminists would not approve.

8. Carol Gilligan, "Remapping the Moral Domain: New Images of Self in Relationship," in Carol Gilligan, Janie Victoria Ward, and Jill McLean Taylor, eds., *Mapping the Moral Domain* (Cambridge, Mass.: Harvard University Press, 1988), 4.

9. Owen Flanagan and Kathryn Jackson have pointed out that Gilligan continually shifts among three different positions, arguing at different times that the two ethics are fundamentally incompatible, that they are complementary, and that they should be integrated into a unity. See Flanagan and Jackson, "Justice, Care, and Gender: The Kohlberg-Gilligan Debate Revisited," *Ethics* 97 (April 1987), 628.

10. Nancy Chodorow, *The Reproduction of Mothering: Psychoanalysis and the Sociology of Gender* (Berkeley: University of California Press, 1978), 7.

11. Jacqueline Rose, "Femininity and Its Discontents," in *Sexuality in the Field of Vision,* 90.

12. Sigmund Freud, "Three Essays on the Theory of Sexuality," *Pelican Freud Library,* vol. 7, trans. and ed. James Strachey (Harmondsworth: Penguin Books), 57.

13. See Freud, "Three Essays," 52–60.

14. Freud, "An Outline of Psychoanalysis," *Standard Edition,* vol. XXIII, 188.

15. Freud, "Femininity," *Pelican Freud Library,* vol. 2, 152–53.

16. See Juliet Mitchell, *Psychoanalysis and Feminism* (New York: Vintage, 1974); Gad Horowitz, *Repression: Basic and Surplus Repression in Psychoanalytic Theory* (Toronto: University of Toronto Press, 1977); and Jane Gallop, *The Daughter's Seduction* (Ithaca: Cornell University Press, 1982) for excellent and extensive analyses of the ways in which Freudian theory undermines assumptions of the naturalness, normalcy, and fixity of masculine and feminine gender roles and of heterosexuality.

17. Chodorow, *The Reproduction of Mothering,* 3.

18. Nancy Chodorow, "Introduction" to *Feminism and Psychoanalytic Theory* (New Haven: Yale University Press, 1989), 6.

19. Chodorow thus answers the argument made by Young in "Is Male Gender Identity the Cause of Male Domination?" 36–61, revised from Joyce Trebilcot, ed., *Mothering: Essays in Feminist Theory* (Totowa, N.J.: Rowman and Allenheld, 1984), 129–46. Young argues that male dominance cannot adequately be explained as a function of gender identity, produced by mothering, but must be understood to be a product of social, economic, and political institutions.

20. Linda J. Nicholson, *Gender and History: The Limits of Social Theory in the Age of the Family* (New York: Columbia University Press, 1986), 86. See also Young, "Is Male Gender Identity the Cause of Male Domination?"

21. Chodorow, *The Reproduction of Mothering,* 67.

22. It should be noted that Lacanians will argue that the concept of frustration was never used by Freud. (Most Freudians disagree.) They will not, however, contest the significance of separation, and certainly there is no controversy as to the legitimacy of the concept of repression.

23. In his theory of the "primal horde" (see, for example, *Moses and Monotheism*), Freud speculates that early humans dealt with their guilt at the wish to murder the dreaded powerful father by internalizing his domination to form the superego, and by setting up a patriarchal God, to reinstate the Law of the Father. For a very interesting reading of this theory as a *critique* of patriarchy, see Horowitz, *Repression,* 119–23.

24. Chodorow, "Gender, Relation, and Difference in Psychoanalytic Perspective," in *Feminism and Psychoanalytic Theory,* 105.

25. Chodorow, "Toward a Relational Individualism," in *Feminism and Psychoanalytic Theory,* 156, 158.

26. Chodorow, "Gender, Relation, and Difference in Psychoanalytic Perspective," 106.

27. Bordo, *The Flight to Objectivity,* 6.

28. See references on page 77.

29. Jaggar, *Feminist Politics and Human Nature,* 375.

30. Grimshaw, *Philosophy and Feminist Thinking,* 182. See also Marilyn Frye, *The Politics of Reality* (Trumansburg, N.Y.: The Crossing Press, 1983), 75.

31. Jacqueline Rose, "Introduction—II" to Juliet Mitchell and Jacqueline Rose, eds., *Feminine Sexuality: Jacques Lacan and the École Freudienne* (New York: W.W. Norton, 1985), 38.

Notes to Chapter 3

1. Jessica Benjamin, *The Bonds of Love: Psychoanalysis, Feminism, and the Problem of Domination* (New York: Pantheon, 1988), 191.

2. I shall elaborate on these three arguments in the discussion of Benjamin's *The Bonds of Love.*

3. Jessica Benjamin, "The End of Internalization: Adorno's Social Psychology," *Telos* 32 (1977), 56.

4. Benjamin addresses this problem in *The Bonds of Love,* where she stresses the importance of the child's reciprocal recognition of its parents—in particular, the mother—as separate subjects. But, as I shall show, because her concept of recognition remains limited to a concept of benign love, the integration of the child's recognition of the parents into her theory produces a concept of the self as an eternal paradox.

5. These ideas are developed by Jürgen Habermas. See in particular Habermas's discussion of the work of G. H. Mead in *The Theory of Communicative Action,* v. 2, trans. Thomas McCarthy (Boston: Beacon Press, 1987).

6. This emphasis on the primacy of identification is characteristic of contemporary object-relations and self psychology, which depart from Freudian theory in stressing the primacy of the narcissistic desire to *be* a self over the libidinal drive to *have* an object. Thus, whereas for Freud both male and female children begin life actively seeking satisfaction from as-yet-undifferentiated objects, and develop gender identity only through internalizing social roles, for Chodorow and Benjamin gender identity is established through direct identification with the same-sex parent. Thus, girls form their gender identity through maintaining the primary identification with the mother, and boys form theirs through disidentifying from the mother and, only secondarily, identifying with the father.

7. Benjamin argues that in the development of the male self, the balance between "mutual recognition and proud assertion" is upset. "Male identity, as Nancy Chodorow points out, emphasizes only one side of the balance of differentiation—difference over sharing, separation over connection, boundaries over communion, self-sufficiency over dependency" [76]. As this example indicates, the terms of Benjamin's paradox are defined rather broadly.

8. Benjamin notes that it is only in modern western middle-class families that the care of children is the exclusive responsibility of "one lone mother" and acknowledges that this theory may thus only apply to such families [75].

9. Benjamin's investment in this model of self-development emerges from her experience as an analyst: the most common problems identified by contemporary analysts are not oedipal but narcissistic disorders—not problems with the superego but affective disorders of the self, characterized by a lack of affective investment.

Whether this shift of emphasis from the problem of internalization (which is arguably a problem of cognition) to the problem of identification (a problem of affect) reflects a change in the patient population or simply a change in the emphasis of analytic theory is open to question.

10. Jürgen Habermas, "Moral Consciousness and Communicative Action," in *Moral Consciousness and Communicative Action,* trans. Christian Lenhardt (Cambridge, Mass.: MIT Press, 1990), 154.

11. Note that Benjamin has shifted here from the more common critique of internalization as a subsumption of the self by the other, through the acceptance of authority, to an understanding of internalization as a consumption of the other by the self, through what is typically understood as *identificatory* incorporation.

12. G.H. Mead, *On Social Psychology,* ed. Anselm Strauss (Chicago: University of Chicago Press, 1964), 228.

Notes to Chapter 4

1. See, for example, Linda Alcoff's intelligent discussion in "Cultural Feminism versus Poststructuralism: The Identity Crisis in Feminist Theory," *Signs* 13, 3 (1988). I share Alcoff's conviction that we need to move beyond these two opposed positions, but I think that we need to begin by questioning the terms of their opposition.

2. Thus, my position is opposed to that of Iris Marion Young, who argues that both the ideal of the individual and the ideal of community are symptoms of identitarian thought which privileges unity over difference. My argument is that the reduction of the ideals of individuality and community to instances of Adorno's "logic of identity" and Derrida's "metaphysics of presence" represents a simple equation of any form of identity with domination. See Young, "The Ideal of Community and the Politics of Difference," in Linda Nicholson, ed., *Feminism/Postmodernism* (New York: Routledge, 1990), 300–23.

3. Irigaray draws as much on Nietzsche, Levinas, and Lacan as on Derrida for her critique of the violence of identity. I am focussing here on the relation of her theory to Derrida's analysis of the abstract logic of identity as a phallogocentric logic which represses the movement of différance.

4. In the essay "Différance," Derrida argues that with his use, in the Jena *Logic,* of the unusual expression *"differente Beziehung,"* Hegel refers to a "differentiating relation" which is exactly what Derrida means by "différance." See "Différance" (1968), *Margins of Philosophy,* trans. Alan Bass (Chicago: University of Chicago Press, 1982), 13–14.

5. Luce Irigaray, *Speculum of the Other Woman,* trans. Gillian C. Gill (Ithaca: Cornell University Press, 1985), 221.

6. See Alice Jardine, *Gynesis,* 178–207; Jacqueline Rose, *Sexuality in the Field of Vision* (London: Verso, 1986); 21; Gayatri Spivak, "Love Me, Love My Ombre, Elle," *Diacritics* Winter (1984), 22–29; Diana Fuss, *Essentially Speaking: Feminism, Nature and Difference* (New York: Routledge, 1989), 13–14.

7. Luce Irigaray, *This Sex Which Is Not One,* trans. Catherine Porter (Ithaca: Cornell University Press, 1985), 24.

8. This argument, which I made in my paper "Speaking Otherwise: Reading Through Luce Irigaray" (unpublished, 1986), is made by Diana Fuss in *Essentially Speaking,* 62.

9. Irigaray, *This Sex Which Is Not One,* 193.

10. Jacques Lacan, "The Agency of the Letter in the Unconscious," *Ecrits,* trans. Alan Sheridan (New York: W.W. Norton, 1977), 158.

11. Lacan, "The Signification of the Phallus," *Ecrits,* 290.

12. Jacqueline Rose, "Introduction—II" to Juliet Mitchell and Jacqueline Rose, eds., *Feminine Sexuality: Jacques Lacan and the École Freudienne* (New York: W.W. Norton, 1985), 55.

13. Irigaray, *This Sex Which Is Not One,* 31.

14. Irigaray, *This Sex Which Is Not One,* 26.

15. Irigaray, *Speculum,* 236.

16. Irigaray, *This Sex Which Is Not One,* 209.

17. Irigaray, *Speculum,* 232.

18. Irigaray, *This Sex Which Is Not One,* 215.

19. Margaret Whitford, "Rereading Irigaray," in Teresa Brennan, ed., *Between Feminism and Psychoanalysis,* 108.

20. Toril Moi, *Sexual/Textual Politics,* 148.

21. Foucault got around this paradox by insisting that his analyses of historical data were only interpretations of interpretations. Moi follows Derrida on a (paradoxical) crossing over into the realm of facts for the purposes of illustrating the theory.

22. Fuss, *Essentially Speaking,* xii.

Notes to Chapter 5

1. Judith Butler, *Gender Trouble: Feminism and the Subversion of Identity* (New York: Routledge, 1990), xi.

2. Judith Butler, "Gender Trouble, Feminist Theory, and Psychoanalytic Discourse," in Linda Nicholson, ed., *Feminism/Postmodernism* (New York: Routledge, 1990), 325.

3. Butler, "Gender Trouble, Feminist Theory, and Psychoanalytic Discourse," 325.

4. Butler, *Gender Trouble,* 24.

5. It should not be forgotten that the development of the concept of compulsory heterosexuality to deconstruct gender identities coincided with a development in the opposite direction: the Radicalesbians and Adrienne Rich argued that the institution of compulsory heterosexuality serves to violate the identity of women-iden-

tified women, and called for a reaffirmation of that identity. See Radicalesbians, "The Woman-Identified Woman," in Anne Koedt, Ellen Levine, and Anita Rapone, eds., *Radical Feminism* (New York: Times Books, 1973); Adrienne Rich, "Compulsory Heterosexuality and Lesbian Existence," *Signs* 5, 4 (1980).

6. Butler, *Gender Trouble,* xi.

7. Butler, *Gender Trouble,* 18.

8. Butler, *Gender Trouble,* 29.

9. In *Gender Trouble,* Butler argues that she is not talking about repression, for, following Foucault, she rejects the "repressive hypothesis"—the claim that there is some pure substance which can be emancipated once power is lifted. On the contrary, she argues, following Foucault, that "sexuality is always situated within matrices of power" [97], that "to be sexed . . . is to be subjected to a set of social regulations, to have the law that directs those regulations reside both as the formative principle of one's sex, gender, pleasures, and desires and as the hermeneutic principle of self-interpretation" [96]. This of course would be accepted as a definition of repression by any Lacanian. In arguing that Butler (following Foucault) conceives of language as a form of repression, I am arguing that she understands language in terms of a repression of nonidentity by identity. That nonidentity often does come to be associated with some sort of repressed substance is a problem Butler shares with Foucault, and with Derrida.

In fact, in the very place where she repeats Foucault's critique of the repressive hypothesis, Butler defines the system of power/language as a repression of plurality. Following Foucault, she argues: "The object of repression is not *the desire* it takes to be its ostensible object, but the multiple configurations of power itself, the very plurality of which would displace the seeming universality and necessity of the juridical or repressive law" [75].

(In *Bodies That Matter: On the Discursive Limits of "Sex"* {New York: Routledge, 1993], Butler acknowledges that repression can be a useful concept.)

10. Butler, "Gender Trouble, Feminist Theory, and Psychoanalytic Discourse," 325.

11. Butler, *Bodies That Matter,* 29.

12. Butler, *Gender Trouble,* 8.

13. Butler, *Gender Trouble,* 20.

14. Thomas McCarthy, "Contra Relativism: A Thought Experiment," in Michael Krausz, ed., *Relativism: Interpretation and Confrontation* (Notre Dame: University of Notre Dame Press, 1989), 258.

15. Albrecht Wellmer, *The Persistence of Modernity,* trans. David Midgley (Cambridge, Mass.: MIT Press, 1991), 71.

16. Butler, *Gender Trouble,* 25.

17. Friedrich Nietzsche, *The Genealogy of Morals,* trans. Walter Kaufman (New York: Random House, 1967), 46.

18. Butler, *Gender Trouble,* 16.

19. Nancy Fraser, "Foucault on Modern Power: Empirical Insights and Normative Confusions," in *Unruly Practices: Power, Discourse, and Gender in Contemporary Social Theory* (Minneapolis: University of Minnesota Press, 1989), 31–33.

20. Butler, *Gender Trouble*, 14.

21. bell hooks, *Feminist Theory: From Margin to Center* (Boston: South End Press, 1984), 63.

22. hooks, *Feminist Theory*, 65. hooks's argument is echoed by Lisa Kahaleole Chang Hall, who quotes a comment made by one frustrated participant after weeks of infighting in a group that called itself Sisters in Solidarity: "'Sisters in Solidarity,' shit. Y'all are gonna end up 'Bitches in Solitude.'" Hall argues that "[i]dentity politics at its best is about making connections between people and groups not normally perceived as related.... There's no possibility of solidarity when people assume that identities are singular and fixed, self-evident and mutually exclusive." Lisa Kahaleole Chang Hall, "Bitches in Solitude: Identity Politics and Lesbian Community," in Arlene Stein, ed., *Sisters, Sexperts, Queers; Beyond the Lesbian Nation* (New York: Plume, 1993), 220–21.

Notes to Chapter 6

1. See Juliet Mitchell, *Psychoanalysis and Feminism* (New York: Vintage Books, 1975), xx; and Jacqueline Rose, "Feminism and Its Discontents," in *Sexuality in the Field of Vision* (London: Verso, 1986), 90.

2. Rose, "Femininity and Its Discontents," 89–94.

3. Rose, "Femininity and Its Discontents," 90.

4. Jacqueline Rose, "Julia Kristeva—Take Two," in *Sexuality in the Field of Vision,* 147.

5. Rose, "Julia Kristeva—Take Two," 148.

6. This version of identity could be seen as, in psychoanalytic terms, narcissistic identity; in Hegelian terms, immediate or unmediated identity.

7. For many critics of psychoanalysis, this would correspond to oedipal identity; psychoanalysts would describe this form of self-identity as paranoia. Hegel would call it negative supersession.

8. Rose's position is thus aligned not only with Lacan's but also with Adorno's stoic/tragic model of the self, against Derrida's and Butler's sceptical model. I am arguing, however, that both models are based on a misconstrual of identity as repression.

9. This is the same argument that was made by Adorno and the early Frankfurt School theorists.

10. Jacqueline Rose, "Introduction—II" to Juliet Mitchell and Jacqueline Rose, eds., *Feminine Sexuality: Jacques Lacan and the École Freudienne* (New York: W. W. Norton, 1982), 46.

Notes to Chapter 7

1. See, for example, Drucilla Cornell and Adam Thurschwell, "Feminism, Negativity and Intersubjectivity," in Seyla Benhabib and Drucilla Cornell, eds., *Feminism*

as Critique (Minneapolis: University of Minnesota Press, 1987) and Diana Coole, "Beyond Equality and Difference: Julia Kristeva and the Politics of Negativity," in *Denken der Geschlechter differenz,* ed. Herta Nagl-Docekal and Herlinde Pauer-Studer (Vienna: Wiener Frauenverlag, 1990).

2. See, for example, Judith Butler, *Gender Trouble: Feminism and the Subversion of Identity* (New York: Routledge, 1990); Elizabeth Grosz, *Sexual Subversions: Three French Feminists* (Sydney: Allen and Unwin, 1989); Eleanor H. Kuykendall, "Questions for Julia Kristeva's Ethics of Linguistics," in *The Thinking Muse: Feminism and Modern French Philosophy,* ed. Jeffner Allen and Iris Marion Young (Bloomington:Indiana University Press, 1989).

3. See Jacqueline Rose, "Julia Kristeva—Take Two" in *Sexuality in the Field of Vision* (London: Verso, 1986); Kaja Silverman, *The Acoustic Mirror: The Female Voice in Psychoanalysis and Cinema* (Bloomington: Indiana University Press, 1988); Butler, *Gender Trouble.*

4. See Nancy Fraser, "The Uses and Abuses of French Discourse Theories for Feminist Politics," in Nancy Fraser and Sandra Lee Bartky, eds. *Revaluing French Feminism: Critical Essays on Difference, Agency and Culture* (Bloomington: Indiana University Press, 1992).

5. Kristeva takes the concept of sacrifice as a basis of social cohesion from the work of René Girard. See Girard, *Violence and the Sacred,* trans. Patrick Gregory (Baltimore: Johns Hopkins University Press, 1977).

6. Julia Kristeva, "Women's Time," *Signs* 7, 1 (1981), 19.

7. Kristeva makes this argument again in her book *Strangers to Ourselves.* Very simply, she argues that we need to recognize and accept difference within ourselves in order to accept the difference of others.

8. This is the story of the development of self-identity told by Freud in *Civilization and its Discontents,* and by Adorno and Horkheimer in *Dialectic of Enlightenment.*

9. Julia Kristeva, "The System and the Speaking Subject," in Toril Moi, ed., *The Kristeva Reader* (Oxford: Basil Blackwell, 1986), 27.

10. Julia Kristeva, *Language—The Unknown: An Initiation into Linguistics,* trans. Anne M. Menke (New York: Columbia University Press, 1989), 260.

11. Julia Kristeva, *Revolution in Poetic Language,* trans. Margaret Waller (New York: Columbia University Press, 1984), 32.

12. Kristeva, *Revolution in Poetic Language,* 109.

13. Kristeva, "The System and the Speaking Subject," 31.

14. Kristeva, *Revolution in Poetic Language,* 140.

15. Julia Kristeva, "Freud and Love," in *The Kristeva Reader,* 244.

16. Judith Butler, "The Body Politics of Julia Kristeva," *Gender Trouble,* 93.

17. See chapter three, page 85.

18. Kristeva, *Revolution in Poetic Language,* 153.

19. See, for example, Fraser, "The Uses and Abuses of French Discourse Theories for Feminist Politics," 187.

20. Grosz, *Sexual Subversions*, 48.

21. Kristeva, *Revolution in Poetic Language*, 40–41.

22. Butler, *Gender Trouble*, 80.

23. Similarly, Butler's claim that Kristeva equates female homosexuality with psychosis is based on the assumption that Kristeva's description of the semiotic bond between mother and daughter is to be taken as a model of adult lesbian relationships. But for Kristeva, the experience of the "return to the mother's body" is similar for men; the difference is that *in a patriarchal society* men have access to the symbolic order as a means of expressing this "return" in a way that women do not.

24. Kristeva, "Women's Time," 29.

25. Julia Kristeva, "Stabat Mater," in *The Kristeva Reader*, 161.

26. Kristeva, "Stabat Mater," 161–62.

27. See, for example, Freud's essays "On the Mechanisms of Paranoia" (*Pelican Freud Library*, vol. 9, 196–219) and "A Case of Paranoia Running Counter to the Psychoanalytic Theory of the Disease" (*Pelican Freud Library*, vol. 10, trans. and ed. James Strachey [Harmondsworth: Penguin Books], 145–58).

28. Kristeva is referring here to Marina Warner's book *Alone of All Her Sex: The Myth and Cult of the Virgin Mary* (New York: Knopf, 1976), which was a primary source for "Stabat Mater."

29. Julie Kristeva, "Freud and Love: Treatment and its Discontents," in *The Kristeva Reader*, 266.

30. Luce Irigaray, *Speculum of the Other Woman*, trans. Gillian C. Gill (Ithaca: Cornell University Press, 1985), 145.

31. Kristeva, "The Pain of Sorrow in the Modern World: The Works of Marguerite Duras," trans. Katharine A. Jensen, *PMLA* 102, 2 (March 1987), 145.

32. Kristeva, "Freud and Love: Treatment and Its Discontents," 256.

33. Kristeva is referring to Winnicott's notion of the "good enough mother." "Julia Kristeva in conversation with Rosalind Coward," in *Desire*, ed. Lisa Appignanesi, ICA Documents, 1984, p. 23.

34. "Julia Kristeva in conversation with Rosalind Coward," 23.

Notes to Conclusion

1. Rainer Forst, "How (Not) to Speak about Identity: The Concept of the Person in *A Theory of Justice*," in *Philosophy and Social Criticism* 18, 3/4 (1992), 294.

2. Here I want to point out that the line between crucial existential choices and trivial preferences, dispositions, and inclinations is in practice increasingly blurred. Even "preferences in automobiles and sweaters" (Habermas) are more and more subject to what Charles Taylor calls "strong evaluations." See Jürgen Habermas, "On the Pragmatic, the Ethical, and the Moral Employments of Practical Reason," in *Justification and Application: Remarks on Discourse Ethics*, trans. Ciaran Cronin (Cambridge, Mass.: MIT Press, 1993), 4; and Charles Taylor, "What Is Human

Agency?" in *Human Agency and Language* (Cambridge: Cambridge University Press, 1985), 15ff.

3. Gloria Anzaldúa, *Borderlands/La Frontera* (San Francisco: Spinsters/Aunt Lute, 1987), 63.

4. This is a variation on Diana Meyers's categories of self-discovery, self-definition, and self-direction. See Meyers, *Self, Society, and Personal Choice* (New York: Columbia University Press, 1989).

5. Iris Young, "The Ideal of Community and the Politics of Difference," in Linda Nicholson, ed., *Feminism/Postmodernism* (New York: Routledge, 1990), 310–11.

6. Young, "The Ideal of Community," 301.

7. Butler, *Gender Trouble: Feminism and the Subversion of Identity* (New York: Routledge, 1990), 143–44.

8. I develop this argument through an analysis of the theories of Jürgen Habermas and Julia Kristeva in "Toward a Model of Self-Identity: Habermas and Kristeva," in Johanna Meehan, ed., *Feminists Read Habermas: Gendering the Subject of Discourse* (New York: Routledge, 1995).

Bibliography

Adorno, Theodor W. "Subject and Object." In *The Essential Frankfurt School Reader*. Ed. Andrew Arato and Eike Gebhardt. New York: Urizen Books, 1978.

——. "Sociology and Psychology." *New Left Review* 46/47 (Dec. 1967/Jan. 1968), 67–80, 79–90.

Alcoff, Linda. "Cultural Feminism versus Poststructuralism: The Identity Crisis in Feminist Theory." *Signs* 13, 3 (1988), 405–36.

Anzaldúa, Gloria. *Borderlands/La Frontera*. San Francisco: Spinsters/Aunt Lute, 1987.

Benhabib, Seyla. *Situating the Self: Gender, Community and Postmodernism in Contemporary Ethics*. New York: Routledge, 1992.

—— and Drucilla Cornell, eds. *Feminism as Critique: On the Politics of Gender*. Minneapolis: University of Minnesota Press, 1987.

Benjamin, Jessica. *The Bonds of Love: Psychoanalysis, Feminism, and the Problem of Domination*. New York: Pantheon Books, 1988.

——. "Authority and the Family Revisited: Or, A World without Fathers?" *New German Critique* 13 (Winter 1978).

——. "The End of Internalization: Adorno's Social Psychology." *Telos* 32 (Summer 1977).

——. "The Oedipal Riddle: Authority, Autonomy, and the New Narcissism." In *The Problem of Authority in America*. Ed. John P. Diggins and Mark E. Kann. Philadelphia: Temple University Press, 1981.

Bordo, Susan. *The Flight to Objectivity: Essays on Cartesianism and Culture*. Albany: State University of New York Press, 1987.

Brennan, Teresa, ed. *Between Feminism and Psychoanalysis*. London: Routledge, 1989.

Butler, Judith. *Gender Trouble: Feminism and the Subversion of Identity*. New York: Routledge, 1990.

———. "Gender Trouble, Feminist Theory, and Psychoanalytic Discourse." In *Feminism/Postmodernism*. Ed. Linda J. Nicholson. New York: Routledge, 1990.

———. *Bodies That Matter: On the Discursive Limits of "Sex."* New York: Routledge, 1993.

Chodorow, Nancy. *The Reproduction of Mothering: Psychoanalysis and the Sociology of Gender.* Berkeley: University of California Press, 1978.

———. *Feminism and Psychoanalytic Theory.* New Haven: Yale University Press, 1989.

Coole, Diana. "Beyond Equality and Difference: Julia Kristeva and the Politics of Negativity." In *Denken der Geschlechterdifferenz.* Ed. Herta Nagl-Docekal and Herlinde Pauer-Studer. Vienna: Wiener Frauenverlag, 1990.

Cornell, Drucilla, and Adam Thurschwell. "Feminism, Negativity and Intersubjectivity." In *Feminism as Critique: On the Politics of Gender.* Ed. Seyla Benhabib and Drucilla Cornell. Minneapolis: University of Minnesota Press, 1987.

de Beauvoir, Simone. *The Second Sex.* Trans. H.M. Parshley. Harmondsworth: Penguin Books, 1972.

Derrida, Jacques. "Différance." In *Margins of Philosophy.* Trans. Alan Bass. Chicago: University of Chicago Press, 1982.

———. *Positions.* Trans. Alan Bass. Chicago: University of Chicago Press, 1981.

———. *Writing and Difference.* Trans. Alan Bass. Chicago: University of Chicago Press, 1978.

Descombes, Vincent. *Modern French Philosophy.* Trans. L. Scott-Fox and J.M. Harding. Cambridge: Cambridge University Press, 1980.

Dews, Peter. *Logics of Disintegration: Post-Structuralist Thought and the Claims of Critical Theory.* London: Verso, 1987.

Eisenstein, Hester, and Alice Jardine, eds. *The Future of Difference.* New York: Barnard College Women's Center, 1980.

Elliot, Patricia. *From Mastery to Analysis: Theories of Gender in Psychoanalytic Feminism.* Ithaca: Cornell University Press, 1991.

Feldstein, Richard, and Judith Roof, eds. *Feminism and Psychoanalysis.* Ithaca: Cornell University Press, 1989.

Flanagan, Owen, and Kathryn Jackson. "Justice, Care, and Gender: The Kohlberg-Gilligan Debate Revisited." *Ethics* 97 (April, 1987), 622–37.

Flax, Jane. "Political Philosophy and the Patriarchal Unconscious: A Psychoanalytic Perspective on Epistemology and Metaphysics." In *Discovering Reality: Feminist Perspectives on Epistemology, Metaphysics, Methodology, and the Philosophy of Science.* Ed. Sandra Harding and Merrill B. Hintikka. Dordrecht: Reidel, 1983.

Fletcher, John, and Andrew Benjamin, eds. *Abjection, Melancholia and Love: The Work of Julia Kristeva.* London: Routledge, 1990.

Forst, Rainer. "How (Not) to Speak about Identity: The Concept of the Person in *A Theory of Justice.*" *Philosophy and Social Criticism* 18, 3/4 (1992).

Fraser, Nancy. *Unruly Practices: Power, Discourse and Gender in Contemporary Social Theory.* Minneapolis: University of Minnesota Press, 1989.

——. "The Uses and Abuses of French Discourse Theories for Feminist Politics." In *Revaluing French Feminism: Critical Essays on Difference, Agency and Culture.* Ed. Nancy Fraser and Sandra Lee Bartky. Bloomington: Indiana University Press, 1992.

Freud, Sigmund. *The Pelican Freud Library.* Trans. and ed. James Strachey. Harmondsworth: Penguin Books.

Frye, Marilyn. *The Politics of Reality.* Trumansburg, N.Y.: Crossing Press, 1983.

Fuss, Diana. *Essentially Speaking: Feminism, Nature and Difference.* New York: Routledge, 1989.

Gallop, Jane. *The Daughter's Seduction: Feminism and Psychoanalysis.* Ithaca: Cornell University Press, 1982.

Gilligan, Carol. *In a Different Voice: Psychological Theory and Women's Development.* Cambridge, Mass.: Harvard University Press, 1982.

——. "Remapping the Moral Domain: New Images of Self in Relationship." In *Mapping the Moral Domain: A Contribution of Women's Thinking to Psychological Theory and Education.* Ed. Carol Gilligan, Janie Victoria Ward, and Jill McLean Taylor, with Betty Bardige. Cambridge, Mass.: Harvard University Press, 1988.

Girard, René. *Violence and the Sacred.* Trans. Patrick Gregory. Baltimore: Johns Hopkins University Press, 1977.

Grimshaw, Jean. *Philosophy and Feminist Thinking.* Minneapolis: University of Minnesota Press, 1986.

Grosz, Elizabeth. *Sexual Subversions: Three French Feminists.* Sydney: Allen and Unwin, 1989.

Habermas, Jürgen. *Justification and Application: Remarks on Discourse Ethics.* Trans. Ciaran Cronin. Cambridge, Mass.: MIT Press, 1993.

——. "Moral Development and Ego Identity." In *Communication and the Evolution of Society.* Trans. Thomas McCarthy. Boston: Beacon Press, 1979.

——. "On Social Identity." *Telos* 19 (1974), 91–103.

——. *The Theory of Communicative Action.* Vol. 2. Trans. Thomas McCarthy. Boston: Beacon Press, 1987.

Hall, Lisa Kahaleole Chang. "Bitches in Solitude: Identity Politics and Lesbian Community." In *Sisters, Sexperts, Queers: Beyond the Lesbian Nation.* Ed. Arlene Stein. New York: Plume, 1993.

Harding, Sandra. "Is Gender a Variable in Conceptions of Rationality? A Survey of the Issues." *Dialectica* 36, 2–3 (1982).

Hartsock, Nancy. "The Feminist Standpoint: Developing the Ground for a Specifically Feminist Historical Materialism." In *Discovering Reality: Feminist Perspectives on Epistemology, Metaphysics, Methodology, and the Philosophy of Science.* Ed. Sandra Harding and Merrill B. Hintikka. Dordrecht: Reidel, 1983.

Hegel, G.W.F. *Early Theological Writings.* Trans. T.M. Knox. Chicago: University of Chicago Press, 1948.

———. *Phenomenology of Spirit*. Trans. A.V. Miller. Oxford: Oxford University Press, 1977.

———. *Philosophy of Right*. Trans. T.M. Knox. Oxford: Oxford University Press, 1967.

hooks, bell. *Feminist Theory: From Margin to Center*. Boston: South End Press, 1984.

Horkheimer, Max, and Theodor W. Adorno. *Dialectic of Enlightenment*. Trans. John Cumming. New York: Continuum, 1972.

Horowitz, Gad. *Repression: Basic and Surplus Repression in Psychoanalytic Theory*. Toronto: University of Toronto Press, 1977.

Irigaray, Luce. *Speculum of the Other Woman*. Trans. Gillian C. Gill. Ithaca: Cornell University Press, 1985.

———. *This Sex Which Is Not One*. Trans. Catherine Porter with Carolyn Burke. Ithaca: Cornell University Press, 1985.

Jaggar, Alison M. *Feminist Politics and Human Nature*. Totowa, N.J.: Rowman and Allenheld, 1983.

Keller, Evelyn Fox. *Reflections on Gender and Science*. New Haven: Yale University Press, 1985.

Kojève, Alexandre. *Introduction to the Reading of Hegel: Lectures on the Phenomenology of Spirit*. Trans. James H. Nichols, Jr. Ed. Allan Bloom. New York: Basic Books, 1969.

Kristeva, Julia. *Black Sun: Depression and Melancholia*. Trans. Leon S. Roudiez. New York: Columbia University Press, 1989.

———. *Desire in Language: A Semiotic Approach to Literature and Art*. Ed. Leon S. Roudiez. Trans. Thomas Gora, Alice Jardine, and Leon S. Roudiez. New York: Columbia University Press, 1980.

———. *The Kristeva Reader*. Ed. Toril Moi. Oxford: Basil Blackwell, 1986.

———. *Language: The Unknown: An Initiation into Linguistics*. Trans. Anne M. Menke. New York: Columbia University Press, 1989.

———. "The Pain of Sorrow in the Modern World: The Works of Marguerite Duras." Trans. Katharine A. Jensen. *PMLA* 102, 2 (March 1987), 139–52.

———. *Powers of Horror: An Essay on Abjection*. Trans. Leon S. Roudiez. New York: Columbia University Press, 1982.

———. *Revolution in Poetic Language*. Trans. Margaret Waller. New York: Columbia University Press, 1984.

———. *Tales of Love*. Trans. Leon S. Roudiez. New York: Columbia University Press, 1987.

———. "Women's Time." Trans. Alice Jardine and Harry Blake. *Signs* 7, 1 (1981), 13–35.

"Julia Kristeva in conversation with Rosalind Coward." In *Desire*. Ed. Lisa Appignanesi. London: ICA Documents, 1984.

Kuykendall, Eleanor H. "Questions for Julia Kristeva's Ethics of Linguistics." In *The Thinking Muse: Feminism and Modern French Philosophy*. Ed. Jeffner Allen and Iris Marion Young. Bloomington: Indiana University Press, 1989.

Lacan, Jacques. *Ecrits: A Selection*. Trans. Alan Sheridan. London: Tavistock, 1977.

———. *The Four Fundamental Concepts of Psycho-Analysis*. Ed. Jacques-Alain Miller. Trans. Alan Sheridan. New York: W.W. Norton, 1978.

Lloyd, Genevieve. *The Man of Reason: "Male" and "Female" in Western Philosophy*. Minneapolis: University of Minnesota Press, 1984.

Mead, G.H. *On Social Psychology*. Ed. Anselm Strauss. Chicago: University of Chicago Press, 1964.

McCarthy, Thomas. "Contra Relativism: A Thought-Experiment." In *Relativism: Interpretation and Confrontation*. Ed. Michael Krausz. Notre Dame: University of Notre Dame Press, 1989.

Meyers, Diana T. *Self, Society, and Personal Choice*. New York: Columbia University Press, 1989.

———. "The Subversion of Women's Agency in Psychoanalytic Feminism: Chodorow, Flax, Kristeva." In *Revaluing French Feminism: Critical Essays on Difference, Agency, and Culture*. Ed. Nancy Fraser and Sandra Lee Bartky. Bloomington: Indiana University Press, 1992.

Mitchell, Juliet. *Psychoanalysis and Feminism*. New York: Vintage Books, 1975.

——— and Jacqueline Rose, eds. *Feminine Sexuality: Jacques Lacan and the École Freudienne*. Trans. Jacqueline Rose. New York: W.W. Norton, 1982.

Moi, Toril. *Sexual/Textual Politics. Feminist Literary Theory*. London: Methuen, 1985.

Nicholson, Linda J. *Gender and History: The Limits of Social Theory in the Age of the Family*. New York: Columbia University Press, 1986.

———, ed. *Feminism and Postmodernism*. New York: Routledge, 1990.

Nietzsche, Friedrich. *The Genealogy of Morals*. Trans. Walter Kaufman. New York: Random House, 1967.

O'Brien, Mary. *The Politics of Reproduction*. London and Boston: Routledge & Kegan Paul, 1981.

Oliver, Kelly, ed. *Ethics, Politics, and Difference in Julia Kristeva's Writing*. New York: Routledge, 1993.

Petchesky, Rosalind. *Abortion and Woman's Choice: The State, Sexuality and Reproductive Freedom*. New York: Longman, 1984.

Radicalesbians. "The Woman-Identified Woman." In *Radical Feminism*. Ed. Anne Koedt, Ellen Levine, and Anita Rapone. New York: Times Books, 1973.

Rich, Adrienne. "Compulsory Heterosexuality and Lesbian Existence." *Signs* 5, 4 (1980), 631–90.

Rose, Jacqueline. "Introduction—II." In *Feminine Sexuality: Jacques Lacan and the École Freudienne*. Ed. Juliet Mitchell and Jacqueline Rose. Trans. Jacqueline Rose. New York: W.W. Norton, 1982.

——. *Sexuality in the Field of Vision*. London: Verso, 1986.

Silverman, Kaja. *The Acoustic Mirror: The Female Voice in Psychoanalysis and Cinema*. Bloomington: Indiana University Press, 1988.

Taylor, Charles. *Hegel*. Cambridge: Cambridge University Press, 1975.

——. *Human Agency and Language*. Cambridge: Cambridge University Press, 1985.

Warner, Marion. *Alone of All Her Sex: The Myth and Cult of the Virgin Mary*. New York: Knopf, 1976.

Weir, Allison. "Toward a Model of Self-Identity: Habermas and Kristeva." In *Feminists Read Habermas: Gendering the Subject of Discourse*. Ed. Johanna Meehan. New York: Routledge, 1995.

Wellmer, Albrecht. *The Persistence of Modernity*. Trans. David Midgley. Cambridge, Mass.: MIT Press, 1991.

Whitford, Margaret. "Rereading Irigaray." In *Between Feminism and Psychoanalysis*. Ed. Teresa Brennan. London: Routledge, 1989.

Young, Iris Marion. "Is Male Gender Identity the Cause of Male Domination?" In *Throwing Like a Girl and Other Essays in Feminist Philosophy and Social Theory*. Bloomington: Indiana University Press, 1990.

——. "The Ideal of Community and the Politics of Difference." In *Feminism/Postmodernism*. Ed. Linda J. Nicholson. New York: Routledge, 1990.

——. "The Ideal of Impartiality and the Civic Public." In *Justice and the Politics of Difference*. Princeton: Princeton University Press, 1990.

Index